THE PERFECT KILL

21 LAWS FOR ASSASSINS

ROBERT BAER

Weidenfeld & Nicolson

LONDON

First published in Great Britain in 2014
by Weidenfeld & Nicolson

10 9 8 7 6 5 4 3 2 1

A CIP catalogue record for this book is available from the British
Library.

ISBN (hardback): 978 0 297 86815 6
ISBN (trade paperback): 978 0 297 86816 3

Designed by Nicole Laroche
Printed in Great Britain

The Orion Publishing Group's policy is to use papers that are natural,
renewable and recyclable and made from wood grown in sustainable
forests. The logging and manufacturing processes are expected to
conform to environmental regulations of the country of origin.

Weidenfeld & Nicolson
The Orion Publishing Group Ltd
Orion House
5 Upper Saint Martin's Lane
London WC2H 9EA

An Hachette UK Company

www.orionbooks.co.uk

CONTENTS

PREFACE

When I started out working for the CIA I assumed, like a lot of people, that assassination would be an easy case to make. Assassinate Hitler, and we would have been spared a lot of death and destruction. Cut out a cancerous tumour and save the host. But the more immersed I became in political murder, the more that easy assumption started to lose ballast.

My conclusion that assassination doesn't work came at the end of a long, halting voyage – a failed attempt on Saddam Hussein, a failed attempt on a Hezbollah assassin, and, in a second life, as a Channel 4 documentary presenter looking into modern political violence. But any doubts I had about assassination were put to rest when I worked on an international investigation into the murder of a former Lebanese prime minister. It's as clear as these things get that his assassins got nothing for their pains, and in fact they pushed Lebanon to the brink of sectarian chaos. I recognize that enduring one's share of reality isn't a shortcut to the truth. But for me it's always been half the trip.

And it seems to me that modern European assassins have fared no better. It's now been thirty years since the IRA attempt on Margaret Thatcher at the Conservative conference in Brighton. One of her would-be assassins justified it by arguing that it destroyed the notion that Britain could contain violence in Northern Ireland. In other words, violence opened the door to the Good Friday agreement. Maybe, maybe not. But to truly justify an assassination there has to be a much cleaner line between cause and effect. Assassinate Caesar, and save the Republic. And, by the way, what did Pat Finucane's death produce other than a terrible, unnecessary tragedy?

What truly tipped the scales in my mind against assassination were drones. While I never had anything to do with them when I was in the CIA, I didn't need to be told that you don't kill militant Islam by killing its public face. Or take bin Laden's assassination. At the time of writing, it looks like we might have got something a lot worse in the Islamic State.

The case for tyrannicide is never going to go away. It's a foundation of natural law, Aquinas told us. Nor will the temptation for it. But from what I've seen it's best avoided: there is no shortcut in war and peace.

Robert Baer
September 2014

PROLOGUE

I never gave assassination a lot of thought until the morning two buttoned-down FBI agents flashed me their credentials, drily read me my rights, then even more drily informed me I was under investigation for the attempted murder of Saddam Hussein.

It was of apparent indifference to them that I was a duly sworn federal agent, that Saddam was this country's number-one enemy, that I'd been sent to Iraq to get rid of him. Which in my mind all added up to a blank check.

Things didn't lighten up any when halfway into my "interview" one of the FBI agents let it drop that the Department of Justice might consider further charging me with a capital crime. That one also went back to Iraq when a guerrilla force serving under me overran a couple of army positions, leading to the death of who knows how many of Saddam's soldiers.

I thought about asking the FBI agents to explain the difference between assassination and aiding a resistance movement organized to depose a sworn enemy. Aren't they both meant to end up in the same place, the death of the enemy? But I knew I wouldn't get an answer.

I also knew my employer wasn't going to be much help either. Before I left for Iraq, I'd asked my boss at the CIA for a definition of assassination. He paused a beat and said, "It's a bullet with a man's name on it." *What did that mean?* I asked myself.

It wasn't as if I hadn't been around political murder. The CIA had sent me to Beirut in the mid-eighties to track down the most notorious assassin of modern times. I stopped at pretty much nothing trying to put the man out of business, but only managed to get away with my own life. And then years later someone else took care of him, another bride who got away.

The FBI's heart was never really in the Saddam investigation, and they dropped it. Life returned to normal, but I never did stop thinking about assassination. Two misses don't make me an expert, but I'm a firm believer that engagement is the easiest path to understanding.

And there's this that's been on my mind for a long time: Dostoyevsky said we can know everything we need to know about a society by taking a look inside its prisons. But it seems to me who and how we murder for political ends tell us a lot more.

INTRODUCTION

Buttonwillow, California, Fourth of July weekend, 2011: It's not even eleven a.m., and already it's more than a hundred degrees. There's some pewter crap in the air draped over the Central Valley like a dirty sheet. With a lane of the I-5 closed for construction, traffic's moving at an infuriating crawl. To relieve the monotony, we pull off for coffee.

While my wife and daughter order at Starbucks, I drive across the street to the Valero station. Waiting for a pump to free up, I check my cell phone to find a text message from a British journalist in Lebanon: "Congrats. U just featured on Al-Manar during Nasrallah's speech defending the indictments."

I stare at my phone as if somehow the words are going to rearrange themselves so I don't figure into them. Getting mentioned in any context on Hezbollah's TV station is never a good thing. But "featured" on it can only spell some special doom.

Until al-Qaeda, Hezbollah had more American blood on its hands than anyone outside traditional war. In the eighties, Hezbollah blew up two of our embassies in Beirut; murdered the CIA chief there; and truck-bombed the Marine barracks near the airport, killing 241. They spread mayhem around the rest of the world, from Bangkok to Buenos Aires, from Paris to Berlin. As for "Nasrallah," he's Hassan Nasrallah, the fierce, black-robed cleric who heads Hezbollah. He's a man as steeped in blood as any of his underlings.

The "indictments" are no mystery either. They refer to news leaks that the special tribunal for Lebanon is about to name four Hezbollah members in the assassination of Rafic Hariri, the billionaire and former Lebanese prime minister. His end came on Valentine's Day 2005, when a suicide bomber rammed an explosives-filled van into his convoy as it traveled through central Beirut, incinerating Hariri and twenty-one others. The business tycoon was a darling of the White House and Riyadh's royal palaces, and his murder rattled a lot of powerful people.

Since then, Hezbollah has tried everything to erase its fingerprints from Hariri's assassination, from murdering key investigators to putting forward a patsy to falsely claim responsibility. So forget what the journalist just texted me: Nasrallah was damning those indictments, not "defending" them. It's a difference of only a few letters, but one with potentially lethal consequences.

It's too late now, but the truth is I walked into this shitstorm on my own two feet and with eyes wide open. It was two years ago when The Hague called me out of the blue to pick my brain on Hariri's assassins. Finding I had a couple of ideas, they hired me as a consultant. They didn't seem to mind I was an ex–CIA operative with a murky past. But idiot me failed to foresee Hezbollah would find out and squeeze it for all it was worth.

I call the British journalist in Lebanon, who gets right to it: Nasrallah railed against The Hague and everyone connected to it. He denied having anything to do with Hariri's murder, reassuring the flock that Hezbollah is the victim of a frame-up.

I picture Nasrallah unloading on The Hague in all of his righteous fury and outrage, not to mention with the awesome authority of a descendant of the Prophet, which Nasrallah believes he is. He's a mousy man with a fat salt-and-pepper beard and fish-cold eyes swimming behind clunky glasses, but the faithful pay rapt attention when he speaks.

The journalist says that halfway through the piece I make my appearance in the guise of a two-year-old TV clip. A voice-over narrator then comes on to accuse me of conspiring with The Hague to frame Hezbollah for Hariri. The motivation? We're both in it for Israel, the narrator says. Zionist lackeys.

The Brit: "Listen to this."

To make certain Al-Manar's viewers know that I'm not just any bastard CIA operative, the narrator "reveals for the first time" that I was behind an old CIA attempt on Lebanon's only ayatollah. Lest anyone forget that infamous moment, they run an archival clip of a neighborhood in flames, burning cars and bodies scattered everywhere. The car bomb missed the ayatollah but killed more than eighty people, women and children too.

The ayatollah, in fact, died of natural causes just a couple of years ago, but even today he possesses a vast, devout following, including hundreds of thousands here in the United States. (For some bizarre reason, many of them supposedly work in the used-car business.)

I'm about to plead that I had nothing to do with trying to murder the ayatollah, but now I consider the possibility some sort of jihad might have been declared on me. If so, the faithful won't slow down long enough to consider it might be me who's being framed in order for Hezbollah to divert attention from its own bloodletting.

I swat away my rising paranoia by comforting myself with the thought that the Lebanese have a venerable history of smoothing over political violence by blaming it on hapless scapegoats, especially foreigners. But would they really bother with a doughy, has-been CIA agent driving to his in-laws' for the Fourth of July? As I'm about to point this out, the Brit chimes back in.

"It gets worse."

Accompanied by some bizarre mix of timpani and a seriously warped version of Tchaikovsky's *1812 Overture*, the narrator's voice starts to quaver as he steadies himself to let viewers know that I once planned a crime even more heinous than the attempt on Lebanon's only ayatollah—assassinating Hezbollah's revered bang man.

He was at the center of all of Hezbollah's mayhem-sowing: the Beirut embassy bombings, the Marines, the attacks in Buenos Aires and Bangkok. He captained the most ruthless guerrilla campaigns in modern history, obliging Israel to vacate Lebanon; it was the first time in that country's history that it gave up ground under fire. And by the way, in a fitting end, the man was assassinated in Damascus in 2008.

It was a biblical setback for Hezbollah, sort of as if the Jews had lost Moses crossing the Red Sea. Which makes him Hezbollah's greatest "living martyr." Today his picture's up on giant placards all around Lebanon, his gravesite a shrine. They even built a museum dedicated to him. No one seemed to mind he was up to his lashes in blood, including Hariri's. The way these people look at him, he's their George Washington and Saint Francis all rolled into one, and that's damn well it.

It takes me a beat, but it starts to dawn on me just how deeply I've waded into it now. I, indeed, had made a half-baked attempt on the man; I'd even alluded to it in one of my books. But come on, it was a lifetime ago, it failed miserably, and not a hair on the man's head got touched. Why would they resurrect it now?

My thoughts by now are flapping around like trapped birds. Are they trying to pin his assassination on me? I sweep the Valero station, stupidly expecting to catch some Hezbollah cutthroat creeping up to righteously slit the throat of the evil CIA operative.

I'm about to tell the Brit I had nothing to do with murdering the man, but the connection's gone scratchy. I want to reach down the line and grab him by the throat to get his attention, but I settle for yelling at my cell phone.

"Nasrallah should think about it the next time he goes around murdering people. He's the assassin, not me."

Out of the corner of my eye, I catch a bug-eyed man on the other side of the pump in a strawberry baseball cap and khaki shorts. He's stopped licking his ice cream cone to stare at me.

The line's gone dead, but rather than call back, I finish filling up and drive back across the street to pick up my wife, my daughter, and my Frappuccino.

A s we pull back into traffic on the I-5, a trickle of sangfroid starts back through my veins, enough, at least, to think about assassination in generic terms. My old promise to myself to take a look into its dos and don'ts isn't going to let me be. By the way, it's the way things usually work with me, pestering me until I finally do something about it.

I've been around enough political murder to know that with The Hague's Hariri probe I've been sucked down into a poisonous swamp. Operating off dark rules and a pitiless logic all its own, it's a place where the capable assassin does win with one swift, precise, and violent act. One scalp's enough to end any discussion. I could take a couple pages to list the political blank spots on the map where the rules still hold. But I wonder if it's not more instructive to take a run at answering my old question of why it is that most assassinations add up to nothing.

Normally, I'd go home and dust off the standard references—some Clausewitz of assassination, say. But there isn't one. Nor are the historians much help either. They're more than happy to serve up long laundry lists of political murder, but they are too timid to include even the most deeply buried footnote about a set of possible tactics for assassination. Is it because assassination is still taboo? Then again, I suppose it's only the fool who puts on paper that there might be a science to culling out the bad apples.

What I know for certain is that I'll have to hack assassination down to manageable proportions. Ignoring the legality or formal justification for the act is the easiest decision. Did Hariri's assassin care? Does any assassin care? Anyhow, that's someone else's book. The same holds for what Hunter S. Thompson called "celebrity assassinations"—a psychotic lone wolf with a gun. "Squeaky" Fromme's taking a potshot at Gerald Ford tells us nothing about political murder. Finally, assassinations tied up in armed mutinies, palace intrigue, dynastic struggles, and racial hatred aren't of much interest either. They're more about prejudice, greed, and personal ambition than genuine politics.

What intrigues me more are political murders that truly alter history, for better or worse. For instance, Israeli prime minister Yitzhak Rabin's. Two bullets put an end to the best chance of a Middle East peace we'll have for who knows how long. But what makes his any different from the rivers of blood that have drowned the Middle East all these centuries?

Long ago, the ancients decided that the most efficient way to put an end to an intolerable tyranny is tyrannicide. It beats war and civil war hands down. No one since has seriously argued against it. Which makes me wonder why I can't borrow the same measuring stick for modern political murder. If a murder reduces violence or moves history in the right direction, it's an acceptable social bargain. If it doesn't, it isn't. Going by this standard, very few assassinations would make the cut. But of those that do, surely there have to be lessons attached.

Since assassination, even pared down, is a big, unwieldy subject, I've decided to take as a guide someone who followed the rules and made it work. Namely, Hariri's assassin. In one flick of a switch he decapitated his main enemy (Lebanon's Sunni Muslims), leaving them fragmented and rudderless. With Hariri out of the picture, he and his side (Hezbollah) inexorably tightened its grip on Lebanon, and in the bargain brought a sort of peace to that troubled nation. If it hadn't been for the Arab Spring, Hezbollah's authority until this day would be effectively uncontested. (I'll get serious pushback on this, but let me develop the argument as I go.)

And Hariri wasn't a one-off either. I was pretty much there at his assassin's coming-out—Lebanon in the early eighties. I watched as he rose from its smoldering civil war like Venus from the half shell, fluently conversant in the fine and shifting relationship between violence and power. He instinctively understood how symbolic murder and blind slaughter get the assassin nothing. How with each bloodletting, the assassin needs to measurably augment his power. How assassination is a conservative force designed to preserve force and postpone war. How, at bottom, it's a detour around war and civil war.

Like the young Buddha, Hariri's assassin learned the plumbing at an early age—his bombs always went off, he never killed the wrong person, he didn't get caught (or, at least, until Hariri). When you put him down on the examining table with other modern assassins, with all of the dumb blood they've splattered the world with, he was the Leonardo da Vinci of political murder. Even his most implacable enemies conceded him that honor. Or as Hariri's assassin would tell us if he were still alive, either get the basics right or don't touch it.

I understand that borrowing the eyes of a dead, cold-blooded murderer to examine anything isn't everyone's idea of stretching out on a hammock for a pleasant summer's read. (Nor will it be a particular recommendation that the author once plotted his protagonist's murder.) But it's drone strikes, not me, that have turned political murder into a fixed instrument of statecraft. In the primal ooze, as anyone who's been there will tell you, one takes one's lessons where one finds them. And there was never anyone better at it than the man we knew best as Hajj Radwan, roughly the "Delightful One," a nickname not without a little irony.

I spent my best years on the bastard's trail, and although I never laid eyes on him, we were the most intimate of enemies. His rules, as I understand them, follow. So does his life, because he lived the rules. So does mine, because for so long I lived in a world of his invention.

THE ASSASSIN'S CATECHISM

Assassination is an act of war and must be approached as such.

Assassination is a quick release from intolerable fate, an act of sunny optimism that one man's end will alter the flow of events in society's favor.

Assassination is a state of mind, a checkmate. Your opponent may still have pieces on the board, but with his king gone, he's lost the game.

Assassination is an efficient and merciful act. Rather than killing everyone in the room, the assassin shoots the one person he needs to.

Assassination is the highest form of triage, its ultimate ratio being to save society rather than destroy it.

Assassination is a conservative force, the paring down of war to its absolute minimum. One murder in excess is mere murder.

Assassination is a fantastically leveraged act, a David and Goliath contest where cunning and surprise overcome brute force.

THE BASTARD HAS TO DESERVE IT

The victim must be a dire threat to your existence, in effect giving you license to murder him. The act can never be about revenge, personal grievance, ownership, or status.

So the assassin—the genuine assassin, not the murderous lunatic—is, as it were, that particularly sensitive cell of the social body which reacts first and most quickly to preserve the social body.

—EDWARD HYAMS

Beirut, September 1986: Of the five of us who decided to assassinate Hajj Radwan that morning, I'm the sole survivor. The ambassador died of leukemia a few years ago. My boss died in his sleep. His deputy blew his brains out in the parking lot of a northern Virginia hospital. Chuck, my friend, died on Pan Am 103, which was blown up over Lockerbie, Scotland, on December 21, 1988. (The operative who would take over my cases also went down on Pan Am 103.)

Don't get me wrong: I'm not saying Hajj Radwan was the author of their deaths. It's just that when it comes to longevity he didn't fare too badly. As a point of fact, Hajj Radwan's passage through political murder lasted a very long and bloody quarter century, a lot longer than even his friends had predicted.

The idea of assassinating Hajj Radwan came up casually, almost as a conversation filler. The ambassador had called us up to his office in the embassy to talk about something I now can't remember. I also can't remember how it was we came around to talking about Hajj Radwan.

The Department of Justice had issued a sealed arrest warrant on him for the 1985 hijacking of an American airliner to Beirut and the murder of a passenger, a Navy diver. But there was nothing in the small print about how it wanted the warrant executed. And of course, there was nothing about taking a shortcut like murder.

The conversation started out as one of those what-ifs. What if we did manage to run Hajj Radwan to ground? What if we did find someone to do something about it?

Chuck shot me a conspiratorial smile. There was no doubt in his mind what he'd do. An Army Ranger detailed to the CIA, he badly wanted in on the action, never leaving the office without his assault rifle and a satchel of hand grenades.

My boss, a Vietnam vet and former rodeo rider, didn't waste any time throwing cold water on the party, thinly noting that we didn't even know where to start looking for Hajj Radwan, let alone have a way to grab him.

The deputy, who looked at Lebanon as a madhouse best treated with black humor, said something about knocking on Hajj Radwan's door with a 155mm artillery round traveling at five hundred miles per hour.

The ambassador didn't let him finish. "Gentlemen," he said, looking over the top of his reading glasses, "I have a call to make."

But as we started to file silently out the door, the ambassador called after us: "Find the man, and then we'll decide how much force will be needed."

My boss: "Sir, you know he'll never be taken alive."

"Keep me posted," the ambassador said as he picked up the phone.

Out in the hall, Chuck stopped me while the others walked ahead. "I didn't hear a no."

I knew he was talking about assassinating Hajj Radwan. It's something we'd been batting around for the last couple of months, with roughly the seriousness of adolescent boys threatening to join the French Foreign Legion. But Chuck was right. The ambassador had left the barn door wide open. Okay, it wasn't exactly a *Murder in the Cathedral* moment—Henry II shouting at his knights, "Who will rid me of this meddlesome priest?"—but it was enough to look into the possibilities.

Chuck was a huge man, about six-foot-four, and had the manners of a surly bear. Like me, he took Hajj Radwan deadly serious. For the last couple of months, he'd been telling me how he was convinced that Hajj Radwan knew who he was and intended to kill him. After Chuck died on Pan Am 103, a couple of security people went to his apartment to clean it out. They found wires leading from the door to the overhead air-conditioning vents in the vestibule. The wires were attached to Claymore mines tilted toward the front door. Hajj Radwan's little surprise? Fortunately, Chuck had disarmed them before he left Beirut.

I turned away to keep walking, but Chuck stopped me again. "I'm in if you are."

I laughed. *Fat chance we'd ever succeed,* I thought. *But what the hell?* I shook Chuck's hand to cement the deal.

As whimsical as it sounds, it was pretty much from that point forward I started to look at Hajj Radwan through the prism of assassination. I knew even then it was a stunted way of looking at anyone. But wasn't it the way Hajj Radwan looked at us?

Chuck had every reason in the world to be paranoid about Hajj Radwan. Like I said, the assassin had truly mastered that eternal intimate dance between politics and murder, never missing or wasting a bullet. Hajj Radwan was the real-life Jackal (as in the Frederick Forsyth novel *The Day of the Jackal*). And it was the rare person who was beyond his reach. What I'm trying to say is that if one day Hajj Radwan decided to kill Chuck a crate of Claymores couldn't have stopped him.

It took a while, but all too soon we came to recognize Hajj Radwan as a tactician on par with history's best. By turning the common automobile, a ton of explosives, and a suicide bomber into a guided missile, he'd beaten the Israelis on the field of battle and did it virtually cost-free. He'd driven the West out of Lebanon the same way. The fact that he'd been able to inflict the largest single-day loss of life on the Marines since World War II forced us to adjust the way we fight war.

And, in a troubling twist, Hajj Radwan, like Caesar in Gaul, had taught himself to narrowly channel violence to more efficiently obtain well-defined and valid military objectives. Combining the meticulous application of surprise, speed, and precision, he threw his enemies into disarray and retreat. When offered the occasion, he preferred to limit violence to a single man. He intuitively grasped that the unexpected apparition of precise and efficient violence touches a raw nerve in man. It's some primeval fear that trumps all other violence.

When Hajj Radwan hijacked the TWA airliner to Beirut in 1985—the same hijacking that earned him a sealed arrest warrant—he murdered only one passenger, the Navy diver. He ignored the other Americans on the plane. In an earlier hijacking to Tehran, in 1984, he murdered two American diplomats rather than the other Americans on the plane. Was it a message that his war was against the American government rather than the American people? I expect so, but the point is that these two hijackings, added to the attacks on the Marines and two of our embassies in Beirut, came with such disciplined and focused violence that it left Washington in a state of dumb dread: Who was this fucking barbarian so meticulous in the application of violence?

When, twenty years later, he came to the aid of his fellow Shiites in the 2003 Iraq war, it was evident Hajj Radwan was only getting better. One of his people was caught with a laptop oscilloscope capable of reading jammer frequencies. (Jammers counter radio-detonated roadside bombs.) It demonstrated he could beat us at our own game, steal our technological fire. But it wasn't as if he'd let his tactics go.

At a little before six on the evening of January 20, 2007, up to a dozen sport-utility vehicles came racing up to the joint American-Iraqi provincial headquarters in Karbala. They contained about a dozen men, all dressed in American combat fatigues and armed with American weapons. They had American badges around their necks. At least one of them spoke English. One had blond hair.

As soon as they pulled up in front, they jumped out and began their assault on the compound. Their intelligence impeccable, they knew exactly where to find the two top American officers. They also knew where to put up a blocking force to keep anyone from coming to the officers' rescue. One American soldier was killed in the attack, and another four, including the two officers, were captured and taken out into the desert and executed. But was murdering five men symbolic of something or just a coincidence?

Nine days before Karbala, American forces had arrested five Iranian intelligence officers in the northern Iraqi town of Irbil. No one officially drew the connection between the Karbala murders and their arrests, but my hunch is that the attackers murdered five American soldiers in response to the five Iranians taken in Irbil. A gruesome warning from Iran not to touch its people. (The Iranians were released in 2009.)

When I heard that one of Hajj Radwan's lieutenants had been involved, I remembered another time when Hajj Radwan matched numbers. In the eighties, there was a small college on the Muslim side of Beirut that was anxious about the safety of its foreign staff, its American professors in particular. The Americans weren't let off campus without an armed escort. Things went fine until one morning a contingent of police officers showed up announcing they needed to brief the Americans on a new security threat. As soon as the Americans were assembled, the faux policemen spirited them off for a long and unpleasant captivity.

The stolen uniforms, faultless intelligence, and lightning speed were Hajj Radwan's hallmark, as was the application of proportional violence. The kidnappers had taken the four American professors because a Christian militia allied with the United States had kidnapped (and murdered) four of Hajj Radwan's allies, three Iranian diplomats and a fellow Lebanese Shiite. Five for five at Karbala, four for four in Beirut.

I realize that when your life amounts to waiting around for a very talented and successful assassin to come cut your throat, you tend to assign him godlike powers. Did Chuck and I overestimate Hajj Radwan? Maybe. But again, it does help explain why Chuck and I came to the decision we did.

THROWING THE DOGS OFF YOUR SCENT

Finding Hajj Radwan wasn't our only problem. For a start, the full and weighty canon of American law didn't exactly stand foursquare behind us. In fact, assassination had been declared outright illegal in 1981 by President Reagan when he issued Executive Order 12333 banning the act.

> No person employed by or acting on behalf of the United States Government shall engage in, or conspire to engage in, assassination.

But at this point in my career I knew the world well enough to know the trick is never to call anything touchy by its real name, and definitely not to use the word "assassination." Take, for example, the SEALs' order to "arrest" bin Laden at his Abbottabad compound in 2012. No one with any common sense expected the man to walk out on his own two feet. Or take drone attacks. Not too long ago, I was privately asked if, in my media appearances, I'd kindly stop referring to drone assassinations as assassinations. It would be more judicious to call them "counterterrorism actions against high-value targets." Anyhow, what I'm getting at is that our first order of business was to assassinate the English language. I.e., if Chuck and I did miraculously find a way to drop Hajj Radwan into the void, we'd have to make it look like an arrest gone wrong.

The other thing I had to come to terms with was that I'd be pretty much singing this baby a cappella. While Chuck and a couple of other like-minded conspirators were ready to lend me a hand, I was the one who happened to have a couple of well-placed sources on the Muslim side of Beirut where Hajj Radwan lived. I also had a good line to a couple of professional killers. And it would be me—God help us—interpreting American law for them.

Finally, by happenstance, I knew more about Hajj Radwan than most people did. I can even mark the day I was anointed an expert. I was sitting in my pod at the CIA counterterrorism center browsing the morning traffic when I noticed my boss, Duane Clarridge, hovering behind me. Standing next to him was a neatly groomed, compact man in an expensive suit.

I stood up and Clarridge introduced me to Oliver North, then the White House's front man on terrorism. Never one to waste an opportunity, Clarridge told North (not quite accurately) that I knew everything there was worth knowing about Hajj Radwan. He added that I'd even created a sort of Venn diagram to help explain the man.

At Clarridge's invitation, I went over to a chalkboard and produced a spaghetti chart of Hajj Radwan's ties as I understood them—how he'd started out as a foot soldier fighting for the Palestinians but on the side did a couple of jobs for militant Islamic groups. He only later offered his services to Iran and Hezbollah.

As soon as I started getting into the grass of it, I could see North didn't give a shit. So I decided to throw him a piece of red meat: "We may have traced parts of his family to West Africa."

"You know where they live?" North asked, now clearly interested.

I nodded.

"So what do we do about it?"

It was at that point I wandered onto unfamiliar and forbidden ground. Clearly, the answer should have been "Sir, I don't know." Instead, I impulsively and stupidly suggested we grab a couple of them and hold them in some secret dungeon until Hajj Radwan saw the light and stopped killing and kidnapping Americans. Blackmail him.

Before it was even out of my mouth, I recognized the idiocy of it. Hajj Radwan had a soul of blue ice. His own mother eviscerated before his eyes wouldn't have moved him. As we were coming to realize to our mounting anxiety, the only thing the man cared about was raw, uncompromising power.

But North took the bait, confiding in me it's exactly what he'd recommend to President Reagan. As North was about ready to leave, he put a hand on my shoulder, telling me that I was now 1600 Pennsylvania's point man on Hajj Radwan. North added that if I was ever to locate Hajj Radwan he'd find me all the "firepower" I needed to "get" my man.

Trust me, I took North seriously. I'd just heard that he'd authorized Delta Force to randomly hijack an innocent and unsuspecting freighter plying the Mediterranean, hold the crew hostage, and under the guise of noble commerce, sail into the middle of whatever crisis du jour there was. By the time the world had figured out the United States had stooped to piracy, the hostage rescue or whatever mission Delta had been charged with would be done and over. As far as I know, Delta never did commandeer a ship, but what it told me was that North was game for the bold and audacious—just the sort of boss you need when you're out there where the fires burn brightly.

From that day forward, I started to scour every official file and public record I could think of for little gems related to Hajj Radwan. I spent weeks in the Library of Congress, reading archived Lebanese newspapers, thick references on Lebanese families, and every book there was on the Lebanese civil war. I enlisted the National Security Agency to do a run through its "chatter"—intercepted telephone and walkie-talkie conversations—connected to Hajj Radwan. I studied high-resolution satellite images of his Beirut neighborhood and village.

A year of this, and I'd produced a not-bad family tree for the man, tracing his ties by blood and marriage. I also came up with a fairly comprehensive list of his friends and schoolmates and, of course, the gunmen who worked for him. We dubbed them the "Ayn al-Dilbah Gang" because most traced their origins to a Beirut slum of the same name.

As nice as all the trivia was, I was convinced it would be the chatter that would put me in the game. The Lebanese may be a dear and generous people, but their political currency is rumor and conspiracy mongering rather than hard fact. A conversation grabbed out of the air would be my best chance of fixing Hajj Radwan. And with the right combination of lady luck and a little Kentucky windage, I'd get a nice, clean shot.

After our meeting with the ambassador, I went back to my office, which was as dark and rank as the bottom of an elevator shaft. I didn't need to flip the switch up and down to know it was thanks to a city-wide electricity cut. I would have pulled back the curtains, but I knew on the other side was a foot-thick steel blast wall and a hermetic outer cocoon of antimortar screens and razor wire blocking out the rest of the natural light. If I wanted to see, I could go find a flashlight.

As I sat there in the dark alone with my thoughts, there was no avoiding the cold truth that I was forced to exist in this shithole of a modern-day Crusader's castle thanks to Hajj Radwan. Since he'd blown up two of our embassies and the Marine barracks, we could only assume he'd try again.

The more I thought about it, the more I realized that the chances of finding and murdering Hajj Radwan were about even with those of the Bolshoi Ballet's calling me out of the blue for a tryout. I just couldn't see my way around the fact that while I was obliged to cower in an iron-and-concrete womb, Hajj Radwan was out there somewhere as invisible as a wish and with all the time and opportunity in the world to experiment with his endless ingenuity for murder. And indeed, even to this day, I wonder just how many of us Hajj Radwan did manage to kill.

It was almost as if Hajj Radwan had been there at the meeting that morning in the ambassador's office, a ghost standing in the corner, his arms crossed, coldly taking our measure for death as we joked about ramming a hot 155mm artillery round up his ass. I know it's not the officially sanctioned view, nor do I have anything like irrefutable proof to offer the reader in support of it. The Department of Justice would dismiss it as worthless hearsay.

Here's what I believe to be fact: The American ambassador to Lebanon was booked on Pan Am for its December 21, 1988, flight from London's Heathrow to New York's JFK, but the reservation was canceled that same morning. It's a small detail generally overlooked, thanks to the fact that the embassy administrative officer had made the reservation in a name not the ambassador's. Not even Pan Am management knew it would be carrying the ambassador on its Flight 103 that fateful night.

It's also generally not well-known that the State Department was in the middle of an investigation into whether Hajj Radwan was running a mole in our Beirut embassy, a local-hire Lebanese guard. By the time Pan Am 103 exploded, the investigators had narrowed it down that the mole was very likely in the ambassador's security detail. From that perch he would have been aware of the ambassador's every movement, including plans to travel overseas.

None of this went beyond a working hypothesis, but several investigators wondered whether Pan Am hadn't been an attempt on the ambassador . . . with Hajj Radwan at the center of it. It was all the eerier because one of the investigators looking into the mole also went down on Pan Am 103.

When I first heard this theory, I dismissed it as conspiratorial hogwash. A Libyan intelligence official was indicted, tried, and found guilty of the bombing. One of the lead FBI Pan Am investigators told me—categorically, I might add—that I was flat-out wrong about the Hajj Radwan angle, as well as the Iranian role. Case closed.

I never thought about it again until it came out in the Hariri investigation more than twenty years later that Hajj Radwan's people had been making multiple calls to the embassy, most likely to a local Lebanese employee. To the same mole? Maybe. Or just as likely, with retirements and all, a replacement. Anyhow, you get the point that I still have my suspicions that Pan Am 103 was bigger than one Libyan intelligence officer.

There is, of course, no way for me to prove that the calls from Hajj Radwan's people to the embassy had any connection to Pan Am 103. I also can't tell you for certain whether the downing of Pan Am 103 had anything to do with an attempt on the American ambassador to Lebanon. Easy to believe, impossible to prove.

I only dredge up this old history to show the kind of grip Hajj Radwan had on us in Beirut—and why we thought he deserved it. I also should add this wasn't some random epiphany. In a fashion, I'd crossed paths with Hajj Radwan years before.

NOTE TO ASSASSINS: Murder, like treachery, works best when it's deserved.

MAKE IT COUNT

Power is the usurpation of power, and assassination its ultimate usurpation. The act is designed to alter the calculus of power in your favor. If it won't, don't do it.

THE PARADOX OF THE MORAL ASSASSIN

Sam Thong, Laos, early 1970s: It was with a profession in mind that Joseph Westermeyer decided to go to medical school. But his other love was anthropology, that abiding curiosity about how different people go about their lives. While still studying medicine at the University of Minnesota, Westermeyer carved out the time to start taking anthropology courses. He would go on to get a master's in it. It then didn't take much for one of his professors to convince him he needed to do some original fieldwork. Having cut his teeth on the Cheyenne Indians, his teacher advised Westermeyer to pick a people as different from average Americans as he could find.

Mrs. Westermeyer wasn't exactly thrilled to move to hot, dirty Vientiane, Laos. On top of it, the country was in the grip of civil war. Large parts of it were off-limits to foreigners, especially to Americans, whose country had taken sides. But it didn't keep Dr. Westermeyer from help-

ing out at a remote up-country clinic, in a place called Sam Thong—
Three Jars. His wife and small son stayed in Vientiane.

Westermeyer's work at the clinic involved tending to casualties of the
war, both soldiers and civilians. But during the monsoon season, when
the fighting abated, he had occasion to travel to even more isolated parts
of Laos. It wasn't long before he started to come across odd cases of political murder. They were particularly intriguing because they didn't fit
the character of the Laotians, some of the least violent people in the
world.

Although there was nothing like an official account, Westermeyer
was able to piece together that in each case the local community had
come to a consensus that the man or woman to be murdered represented
a grave threat to its existence. Whether the crimes were imagined or
real, it was believed that if they didn't act, the community would suffer
terrible harm or even extinction.

Westermeyer told me that in one case the victim was selected because
he had started burning grain stocks, which resulted in shortages and
price spikes. The way the local community saw it, they could either murder him or starve.

Since none of the victims was elected, there was no voting them out
of office. And since the central government's writ didn't reach these remote communities, there was no appeal to higher authority. Attempts at
mediation failed. In other words, assassination was the first and only
recourse to justice.

After the act, none of the Laotian assassins was arrested or punished,
and all returned to their normal lives. There were no revenge murders or
reprisals. No blood money was ever paid. In fact, the assassins were quietly celebrated as heroes.

Westermeyer came across no evidence the assassins suffered from
psychopathic illness or murderous ambition for political office. Nor was
there evidence of spontaneous rage—no mob violence or lynchings. The

wrong person was never killed, and no assassin missed. "Cool decisiveness" weighed in all cases, Westermeyer wrote in a monograph on the subject.

At the time, Westermeyer couldn't help but compare the Lao assassinations to contemporaneous ones in the United States—John F. Kennedy, Robert Kennedy, Malcolm X. While the American assassins were mostly loners, the Laotian assassins were anything but. All well integrated into their communities, they conducted the murders from an unshakable conviction that the murders served their communities. Again, personal grievance or revenge played no part in any of it.

"After each assassination, there was this big sigh of communal relief," Westermeyer said. "They were, I guess you might say, family affairs—the face-to-face settlings of scores. But hasn't murder of this sort been around for eons?"

He paused a moment before adding, "But I suppose what the Lao assassinations really come down to is conflict resolution, albeit the extreme form. The sacrifice of one man to save society."

Kill or perish.

The first condition of understanding a foreign country is to smell it.

—RUDYARD KIPLING

Beirut, December 1982: It's the rare moment when some earth-shattering event comes barreling down on you like a freight train with its brakes burned out . . . and you're too blind and deaf to jump out of the way. I got my opportunity when I decided to make a short personal trip to Lebanon. Like most things in my life, it took me a long time to put it in perspective.

When I cabled the chief in Beirut to ask permission to make a visit, I detected in its terse reply a sotto voce bitching. Did I really need to take a vacation to Beirut less than six months after the Israeli invasion? In my favor, though, the chief wasn't exactly in a position to say no. For some months now, the Reagan administration had been billing Lebanon as this phoenix miraculously risen from the ashes. It was as safe as a Sunday-afternoon stroll down Fifth Avenue.

As the plane started to circle Beirut on approach, I fell in love with the country at first sight. The snowcapped mountains spilling out into the sea were a thing of great beauty. My enthusiasm wasn't in the least dampened by Beirut's shot-up, rocketed terminal leaking rain by the bucketfuls. I'm not sure what it was that attracted me to the Lebanese. Their effervescence, their polyglot chattering, all the pandemonium they made tempered by a Mediterranean lightheartedness? Okay, even at the time I knew it was the sort of love only an outsider could feel. If I'd been through the shit the Lebanese had, my take would have been a bit more jaundiced.

Here in a nutshell is Lebanon's recent history: Israel invaded Lebanon on June 6, 1982, thanks to a Palestinian attempt on Israel's ambassador to London on June 3. It was a massive display of force meant to teach the Palestinians a lesson they'd never forget. But three months later, Lebanon's pick for president was assassinated before he could assume office, which caused things to really fall apart. President Reagan sent the Marines in as peacekeepers, but they were soon sucked into a hopeless quagmire that included the October 23, 1983, bombing of the Marine barracks at the airport. Reagan wisely threw in the towel, pulling out the Marines. The tally: One assassination attempt, one assassination, and one suicide bomber forced the United States to abandon its old dream of turning Lebanon back into the Switzerland of the Middle East. But I've gotten ahead of myself. The unraveling wouldn't start until two months after I left Beirut.

I also owe it to you to let you know that as I walked out of the terminal I didn't have the faintest premonition of the coming storm. In fact, when I caught sight of a jeep with three Marines chatting with a couple of Lebanese kids, the Stars and Stripes snapping in the wind, I fell for the phoenix myth hook, line, and sinker: America, indeed, was about to succeed in Lebanon where so many had failed.

Leave it to me to find the worst taxi driver in Lebanon. On the ten-mile-or-so run into town, the lunatic weaved through traffic like he was at the wheel of a penny-arcade race car, deliberately aiming for the cars in front of him, only peeling off with an inch to spare. Another challenge to his virility seemed to be the craters in the road. He'd laugh evilly every time one of them would catapult me into the ceiling. Never for a moment did he take his hand off the horn of his ancient piece-of-shit Mercedes, which, by the way, had three bullet holes through the front window at head level. The icing on the cake was when he'd yell back at me: "Welcome to Lebanon! I love America! Give me visa!"

I noticed that the airport road ran right through a miserable slum. But like most foreigners, I ignored it, sort of like how people ignore Jamaica as they drive into Manhattan from JFK. Beirut's glitter is what I came to see, not its ugly poor.

As soon as he pulled up in front of the Palm Beach, I grabbed my backpack, dropped a twenty-dollar bill into the front seat, flung open the door, and ran into the hotel before the maniac could stop me. I didn't care that what I'd left him was probably ten times more than the going rate, just as long as I didn't have to argue about the visa.

While the outside of the Palm Beach was scalloped with bullet holes and shrapnel and its shot-out windows were covered with plastic sheeting, the inside was a sea of tranquillity. The manager himself—white linen shirt, a heavy gold watch, cashmere blazer—showed me to my room. He opened the curtain to a luminous topaz sea.

He stood behind me and pointed at an abandoned, fire-scarred Venetian-style pink building a little ways up the Corniche: "The St-Georges."

If you had to pick one center of French colonial gravity in this city, it would be the venerable and celebrated St-Georges hotel. British secret agent turned KGB mole turned defector Kim Philby started to drink himself to death here. It was supposedly Elizabeth Taylor and Richard Burton's favorite hotel in Beirut. At the beginning of the civil war, the hotel's last guests famously fled in armored limousines, leaving the hotel to be looted and burned.

"They're going to refurbish it," the manager said. I thought about telling him it was "restore" it, but I didn't; his English was better than my French and Arabic would ever be.

Right next to the St-Georges sat a row of one-story shops with sunfaded touristy crap in the windows. In one window, though, there was on display what looked like Greek and Roman antiquities. Could they be genuine?

Going out for a walk that night along the Corniche, I didn't see any lights on in the hotel other than my own. Was I the Palm Beach's only guest? There was always a lot of banging and yelling in the kitchen, but I never ran across any other diners. No wonder the manager had so much time for me.

Every morning when I came down, he'd be at breakfast. "Our establishment has everything one could ask for," he'd say, pulling back my chair. "Bacon and eggs, French toast, Cheerios." His smile couldn't hide his disappointment when I would stick with a croissant and a coffee.

One night a violent thunderstorm knocked out the electricity. It wasn't ten minutes later that there was a knock on my door. The manager was outside holding a candle cupped in his hand as if he were a monk. He came in and set it on my side table. He asked if I needed anything. When I said no, he said he would be downstairs. I decided he must live in the hotel.

I spent my days walking around Beirut. I'd start off heading due east in the direction of Martyrs' Square and the old gold market. The fighting had reduced this part of town to great mounds of rubble crowned by weeds and saplings. The old Ottoman buildings still standing looked like sandcastles hit by a wave, some with their top floors completely blasted off. When I'd seen enough of this, I'd usually make my way to the old Christian neighborhood of Ashrafiyah, which the fighting had barely touched.

Afternoons, I'd usually end up in Hamra, the old business district. There were a couple of first-class bookstores there where you could find just about anything decent written on the Middle East. I'd buy as many books as I could carry and head back to the Palm Beach. Invariably, I'd stop at the Café de Paris and start leafing through them, sitting among the old men in their elegant suits drinking coffee and reading newspapers.

I'd been living in the Middle East almost a year now, but I was still in the first inning of a furious catch-up game, trying to make sense of the place. The unfamiliar names, the important dates, the sharp, unexplained turns in history were an endless source of confusion. For instance, how was it that Egypt and Syria, two countries that don't share a border, managed to unite as one country for a couple of years? It was nuts.

What I did figure out early on was that I'd better understand the logic of the violence that was so endemic to the Middle East. If the locals have a nuanced sense of it, I'd better have one too.

When I was in the middle of studying Arabic in Washington, D.C., I'll never forget watching on television the 1981 assassination of Anwar al-Sadat. I kept asking myself what kind of people these were, the Egyptian president's own soldiers, approaching the reviewing stand in a half crouch and emptying their Kalashnikov rifles into him. What induced them to take a life in such a disciplined way, not to mention trade their own lives to destroy someone they didn't know? More important, I wanted to know how it was that Sadat's assassination failed to change anything in Egypt. Because the fact is the Egyptian military came out of it all the stronger.

The 1982 assassination of the Lebanese president-elect seemed to me to be of a different order altogether. It set in motion hidden forces that sharply altered the course of events, becoming a shot to the head of the Lebanese phoenix. Why then did Sadat's assassination fail to move history but the Lebanese president-elect's did?

One obvious answer is that a junta runs Egypt, meaning the generals are pretty much interchangeable and easily replaced. While on the other hand, Lebanon is a continuously negotiated compromise between squabbling tribes. When France gave Lebanon its independence in 1943, the pro-French Maronite Christians were left in charge, controlling both the presidency and the army. But as the demographics shifted against the Maronites in favor of the Muslims, the consensus naturally started to fray. It didn't help that the last census was conducted in 1932, leaving a lot of people to simmer about usurped power. It was made all the worse after a large influx of Palestinian refugees arrived in the seventies and started to arm themselves. Couple that with the fact there are eighteen officially recognized religious sects in Lebanon and the country became the perfect laboratory for me to study political violence.

My way of imposing order on chaos was to write down important facts and dates on three-by-five cards and arrange them in various orders. For instance, I noted down the name of the young man who had loaned out the apartment used to blow up the hall where the Lebanese president-elect was giving a speech. He was a secret member of an obscure Christian political party called the Syrian Social Nationalist Party. The party had a long history of violence, but naïf that I was, I couldn't fully grasp its motivations for murdering the president-elect. It was something I promised myself to look into one day, adding new cards to my stacks.

As I wrote this book after all of these years, my five broken-down boxes of three-by-fives were indispensable in reconstructing Hajj Radwan's story. The grainy detail I jotted down on them you won't find on Google or anywhere else on the Internet. Okay, I understand they at best amount to a partial truth, and are certainly not material that scholars could ever put any stock in. But without them, I'd have to depend on that notorious liar, my memory.

The other thing worth noting is that when I first visited Lebanon in 1982, I knew violence only from a distance—I knew the Vietnam War from protests and watching Walter Cronkite on TV. And to be sure, I never had to face the decision the Lao assassins had to, that binary choice whether to kill or not. And when the CIA did have the occasion to issue me a gun, the only advice offered me was to avoid gunfights at all costs, and of course to never even think of provoking one. In other words, I didn't have a clue under what conditions murder could be a moral or legitimizing force. Things like self-defense and tyrannicide were too abstract for me to do anything with.

Which brings me to this: To paraphrase Stendhal, the "I" in this book isn't so much about ego as it is a shortcut to telling a story. I've written about my hunt for Hajj Radwan in other books, as I have my Iraq story. While I would have preferred to avoid the self-plagiarizing, I can't be-cause my understanding of political violence depends on those events. And anyhow, the way I look at it, I needed to sit through Act III—Hajj Radwan's assassination—before I could complete my journey through political murder. This will sound pathologically callous, but it's a fact that you have to watch something die before you can truly understand it.

Finally, you need to know that there was no getting around my CIA censors, which in practical terms meant that I've unfortunately been uable to write about the true set-piece plot against Hajj Radwan. It left me with writing about a couple of sideshows. It's for this same reason I've had to alter the names of sources, change personal details, and adjust time frames. And for reasons too obscure to bother with here, I can't get into all the details of my CIA career. What I can say is that I was assigned to Beirut from 1986 to 1988, and then spent three years in Paris—the main years of the Hajj Radwan story. I understand that leaving out the key event is akin to Homer writing the Odyssey but omitting the scene where Odysseus returns to Ithaca. But there's nothing to be done about it. In the end, though, does any of this really matter? It's a rulebook rather than history I'm trying to write.

I don't intend to give away the ending here, but what I will do is state the obvious: The utility of political murder can only be judged in context and time. Assassination may have worked for the Laotians at a certain point in their history, but that doesn't mean it's a universal instrument of justice. Like pornography, you know a good kill when you see it.

O ne night after dark I walked up Hamra Street. It was dry when I started, but the air was heavy and fresh: A storm was on the way. When it did start to rain, I ducked into the first shelter I came across, a below-street-level movie theater. *Blade Runner* was showing. Since the movie had just come out in theaters in the United States, I expected a crappy pirated copy. But it was the real thing.

Afterward, it was sheeting rain outside. Just like in the movie, broken lights sparked, coils of steam coming off them. It wasn't keeping people inside, though. Couples leaning into each other under umbrellas ran along the sidewalks. I watched as one disappeared down into an underground nightclub. A French armored personnel carrier passed by, a tricolor at the top of its whip antenna and a soldier in a poncho and beret in the hatch. From under a store marquee, three giggling, sleek Lebanese girls in tight jeans and leather jackets waved at him. He waved back. It was at that moment I decided to ask for a transfer here, to join whatever party this was at the edge of the apocalypse.

The next morning I made a courtesy call on my contact in the embassy. The view from his office made me feel like I was standing on the bow of a ship cutting through an emerald sea. He pointed at a chair for me to sit down.

"I've only got five minutes," he said. "So, what's up?"

He was a slight, nervous man, someone I couldn't imagine ever at rest. His tie was loose at the neck, his shirtsleeves rolled up, a pencil behind his ear. I'd met his wife earlier, a charming young woman who also worked in the embassy. I got the impression neither of them was happy about being here.

The phone rang. His French was curt and halting. He said something about pushing back lunch. His secretary stuck her head into the office, walked over to his desk, and left a piece of paper. He picked it up, glanced at it, and dropped it into his out-box with a sigh. When he looked back up at me, it was with an expression that made me wonder if he'd forgotten who I was.

I got to it before he was interrupted again: "Do you think they could use another Arabic speaker here?"

I was about to add that I'd be more than happy to break my next assignment for Beirut, but the phone rang again. He listened for a moment before pointing at the door to let me know he'd need to continue the call in private. I never did get an answer to my question.

For dinner that night I stopped by a bakery and bought a sort of pizza topped with olive oil and thyme. The Lebanese call it *manaeesh*. When I made it back to Beirut four years later, it pretty much became my staple. Chuck and I would take turns buying a stack of them in the morning, warm out of the oven and wrapped up in waxed paper. When it came Chuck's turn, he'd come in and drop them on whatever file I was reading, usually Hajj Radwan's. If the file hadn't later been burned during a particularly bad round of fighting, I'm sure it would still smell of thyme. If there's a smell for the world's most accomplished murderer, in my mind it's thyme.

Thyme *manaeesh* is usually meant for breakfast, but right now, as I stood in the window of my room watching the sea, I couldn't imagine a better dinner. I opened the window to get a better look at the St-Georges' black hulk, imagining what it must have been like for the last guests leaving in their bulletproof limousines. Did they know it was the end of the Lebanon they'd fallen so hard for?

The traffic along the Corniche was thinning out now, the honking dying away to the occasional beep of a taxi looking for the last fare of the night. I noticed in front of the faux-antiquities store a parked car, two men standing by it smoking cigarettes. The tremulous streetlight played over their clean-shaven faces. Were they waiting for someone?

One of them looked up at my window, saw me, and said something to the other one. They flicked their cigarettes in the middle of the road, got into their car, and drove away. There's no way to know whether or not they had any connection to what was to follow less than four months later. It's unlikely, but it doesn't keep me from associating the two events in my mind.

On April 18, 1983, at about a quarter to one, a young man sat behind the wheel of a late-model GMC pickup parked along the Corniche in almost the same spot where the two men had been standing smoking. The truck's engine was running. According to witnesses, the pickup was sagging on its springs, something heavy under the tarp-covered bed. No one would remember the driver other than he was young, like the tens of thousands of men who'd flocked to Beirut to help with the back-breaking job of rebuilding it after nearly ten years of civil war.

Other witnesses said they saw an old green Mercedes race up the Corniche, weaving through traffic and honking. There were three men in it. When it came abreast of the GMC, the driver of the Mercedes stuck his head out the window and motioned to the GMC's driver to get going. The GMC's driver put the pickup in gear and slowly started down the Corniche in the opposite direction the Mercedes had come from.

With lunchtime traffic, it took the GMC about fifteen minutes to reach the American embassy. When the pickup finally came parallel with the embassy's covered portico, it abruptly dove through a gap in the oncoming traffic and headed up the embassy's semicircular drive-way. When it came to a short flight of stairs leading to the front en-trance, it exploded. The embassy's center collapsed like a failed wedding cake. Among the dead was my embassy contact, as well as sixty-three others. My contact's charming wife wasn't in the embassy and survived.

MAKE IT SHARP, DISCRETE, AND FINAL

The April 1983 Beirut embassy bombing brought to an end the long love affair between Lebanon and the United States. But the main reason I retell this story is that it's likely the bomber's intent was to assassinate President Reagan's envoy to the Middle East, Ambassador Philip Habib. The evidence for it is circumstantial but, taken in context, convincing.

Within days of the bombing, a local embassy guard confessed under interrogation that the three men in the green Mercedes had stopped by the embassy shortly beforehand to ask him one thing: Is Ambassador Habib in the building? The guard told them he was, and without another word, the Mercedes roared off, heading up the Corniche—in the direction of the idling GMC.

The guard said he immediately regretted not having told the three that he hadn't actually seen Habib; he'd just heard someone say something about Habib's having returned to the embassy. (Habib, in fact, was in a meeting across town, and as a consequence, survived the attempt on him.)

It's no surprise at all that there were Lebanese who wanted Habib dead. He was Reagan's point man in the attempt to broker a peace treaty between Lebanon and Israel. With the deal set only in diplomatic aspic, it's likely they calculated that with Habib gone Reagan would pull out of the negotiations and the treaty talks would collapse. There, of course, was the symbolism of destroying an American embassy, but if the guard was telling the truth—from my reading of the transcripts, I believe he was—the April 1983 embassy bombing was a clear case of a bullet with a man's name on it.

I'll go farther out on a speculative limb and say it's almost certain

Habib's would-be assassins framed the act in their minds as one of survival. The way they looked at it, a peace treaty between Israel and Lebanon would lead to a strong central government and ultimately to their destruction. So, à la Laos, it was a case of kill or perish.

Hajj Radwan's name would eventually be attached to the embassy bombing. But he would only have been twenty-one at the time. Was it possible for a man so young to carry out a complicated attack like this? Based on circumstantial evidence, I believe so. And if I'm right, it meant that at an early age Hajj Radwan recognized the tactical advantages of narrowly channeling violence to obtain a precise objective. It certainly wouldn't be the first or the last time he'd take or try to take a scalp to end an argument.

A little more than twenty-two years after my first visit to Beirut, a suicide bomber would drive by the Palm Beach on his way to assassinate Hariri. His van would blow up in front of the St-Georges, destroying what was left of it. The St-Georges and the Palm Beach, of course, would only be mute witnesses to history, collateral in what otherwise was a fairly precise attack.

I'll get more into it later, but Hariri was murdered because the assassins, one, believed he was a threat to their survival, and two, believed he couldn't be replaced. Like the Lao assassins, they believed they had no choice in the matter. To be sure, not everyone will share this view, but the point is that it's what Hariri's assassins believed.

> **NOTE TO ASSASSINS:** The assassin can't afford to entertain abstract notions such as determinism and cowardly fatalism. Nor does he think people are of equal value. He must grasp how it's possible to adjust history (in his favor) by the destruction of one man.

PLACATE THE EDIFICE UNTIL IT'S TIME TO BLOW IT UP

Owe and own nothing to push back against. Never wear your beliefs on your sleeve. In assuming an impermeable façade of ignorance, poverty, and banality, you blind the enemy to your true strength and intentions.

KILL 'EM ALL

Beirut, October 1986: The apartment they assigned me came with cheap, scuffed-up, imitation Ethan Allen furniture. Passed on from one tenant to the next, it was the kind of crap people back home put out on the sidewalk in the dead of night. But what more than made up for the furniture was the view—the glorious, shimmering, opalescent Mediterranean at my feet. It was better than the Palm Beach's.

I'd never tire of sitting on my balcony with my first cup of coffee in the morning, wondering if there was a scrubbier patch of earth more courted, inveigled, meddled with, and invaded than Lebanon. The Persians, Alexander the Great, the Ottomans, and just about everyone else with imperial ambitions had felt obliged to trample across it on the way to someplace else. The Israelis invaded with a predictable rhythm, sometimes it seemed only for practice. But what intrigued me was how the Lebanese all of a sudden had learned to say enough is enough and actually got good at driving off invaders.

Just north of me was an ancient Phoenician port called Jounieh. With its red sandstone Ottoman-era buildings, limestone quays, hip boutiques, French restaurants, and nightclubs, it was one of those cosmopolitan entrepôts where the Orient happily consorts with the Occident. But the truth is, Jounieh—which is almost all Christian—fully and cheerfully tilted West.

The nightclubs were always packed, thrumming into the early morning with the latest Western music. Outside, you'd always find rows of new BMWs, Range Rovers, and Mercedes, their owners snorting coke in the backseat. It wouldn't be until first light that the clubbers would pour out into the street in search of an espresso and a shot of brandy. They'd be out again for lunch, the kind that lasts into the late afternoon. I couldn't figure out when these people slept.

I couldn't see it from my balcony, but one peninsula over from Jounieh was a posh yacht club, where the criminally rich and gorgeous girls in bikinis lounged on the decks of world-class yachts. Supposedly the club never closed, no matter how bad the civil war got. When the wind was right, you could hear the fighting in downtown Beirut. But people didn't pay attention, or they just turned up the music.

There was nothing you couldn't buy in the Christian enclave, from new Porsches to the latest Patek Philippe watches, from fresh truffles to long-stem roses. It didn't matter that the high-end stuff had been hijacked at sea. My Lebanese friends would shrug their shoulders: In war, you make do the best you can.

It's a gross and unfair generalization, but Lebanon's Christians didn't have the slightest doubt about what they wanted from life: a comfortable apartment with comfortable furniture, a nice car, regular trips to Paris or London, an education for their children to brighten their future prospects. But what they absolutely had to have was a fat nest egg for when things got really bad and they needed to run for it. And the higher-end the bolt-hole the better, luxurious places such as Geneva and Beverly Hills. But in fact, it didn't matter where, just as long as the chances of meeting a violent death were removed.

Like the wealthy anywhere, the Lebanese Christians were reluctant warriors. They relished power as much as the next Lebanese, but it was always more about position and money than some abstract higher good. When the civil war forced them to take up arms, they had no idea what to do with them. They'd resort to indiscriminately firing artillery barrages into Muslim Beirut, setting off car bombs in densely populated neighborhoods, or unremittingly machine-gunning a suspected enemy position. The object was to kill anything that moved.

The Christians' unexamined premise was that overwhelming force— a deluge of firepower, bigger and better guns, fancy technology, and lots of money—was what would keep the barbarians at bay. It wasn't all that different from Americans using their expensive fancy weapons to rack up body counts in Vietnam, or lately in Afghanistan and Iraq.

Another thing about the Christians is that they didn't care to consider that on the other side of the Green Line there were people who devoted their waking lives to efficient murder. While the Christians were happy to pelt their enemies with everything they owned, these people preferred murder with a more personal touch—a bullet with a man's name on it rather than a 155mm artillery round.

It's tempting to blame the Christians for willful blindness. But it's also true that those same people living on the other side of the Green Line were particularly good at making themselves invisible. They saw no point in the Christians' show and pomp, it never being far from their minds that you can't kill what you can't see.

AS DEEP AS HELL IS HOT AND DARK

Sidon, Lebanon, 2008: A couple of months after Hajj Radwan is assassinated, I'm in the Middle East filming a documentary on car bombs for a British television station. One of our not-to-miss stops is a miserable Palestinian refugee camp called Ayn al-Hilweh—"the sweet-water spring." It sits in the hills just east of Sidon.

Since the Lebanese state's writ has never reached into Ayn al-Hilweh, the camp's inhabitants have been at liberty to arm themselves to the teeth and turn their camp into an impregnable fortress. By the mid-eighties Ayn al-Hilweh had won itself a well-deserved reputation as the main rear base for the "Islamic resistance"—the Hezbollah guerrilla force that would drive Israel out of Lebanon in 2000. Although the Israelis would have dearly loved to, they didn't dare send in a commando team on any mission. They would have been cut down in minutes. Nor could they bomb it from the air without killing hundreds of people and provoking an international outrage.

Getting Lebanese permission to enter Ayn al-Hilweh takes some doing. Not too long before our visit, a Lebanese military intelligence officer in mufti snuck into the camp to check on something, but he was quickly recognized and shot dead. The Lebanese soldier at the checkpoint to the camp's entry makes a point of telling us we could very well meet the same fate. We brush it off, though, convinced we'll be fine sailing under the banner of a free press.

As arranged, two fierce-looking Palestinian gunmen meet us just inside the camp's confines. Both have Kalashnikovs slung over their shoulders. One man is about five-foot-two, the other six-foot-something. Mutt and Jeff.

We follow the two in silence as they disappear down a crooked, cramped, foul-smelling alley. Rickety overhanging additions, tangles of wire, and laundry turn day into night. The roar of generators beats the air, producing a layer of smoke as thick as Shanghai smog. An open ditch along one side serves as a sewer. Eyes follow us from darkened doorways.

As we head down an even narrower alley, I try to strike up a conversation with our escorts. Mutt pretends not to hear me, and Jeff only grunts. It isn't long before I lose all sense of direction. I now completely get why the Israelis and the Lebanese avoid this place as if it were a viper pit.

We emerge from the dark into a trapezium of jagged sunlight, the camp's version of a main street. We turn left and walk about ten feet until we come to what amounts to a covered grease pit. "Here's your garage," Mutt says.

Warped fiberboard screwed and nailed together by large flattened tin cans stands in for a roof. Carelessly stacked cinder blocks serve as walls. If tools come with the place, they aren't on display.

A skinny teenager emerges from somewhere only to be disappointed that we aren't here to get our car fixed. His disappointment turns to bewilderment when we tell him we want to film his "garage." (We've already decided it would be impolitic to tell him his establishment is our stand-in for the kind of place we imagine car bombs are made.)

Our visit to Ayn al-Hilweh would amount to more terrorism-gawking if it were not for our making a courtesy call on the camp commander on our way out. I don't say anything to the crew, but I know from chatter that the commander was close to Hajj Radwan.

As we are milling outside his office, one of his aides sidles up to me for a chat. I now can't remember how Hajj Radwan's assassination comes up, but it does.

"He was here a couple months before," the aide says. He points to a pile of broken masonry and trash not ten feet from us: "He was standing right by there."

"He was here in Ayn al-Hilweh?" I say, thinking, So much for my theory that Hajj Radwan fled to Syria after murdering Hariri.

"That's what I'm saying."

I couldn't help myself. "But why?"

"How should I know?" the aide says as he walks away to join another conversation.

For a split second I consider running after him to remind him that the fucker's dead and buried. So what's the big deal about telling me what he was doing here? But I know it's pointless. Whatever unnatural aura that follows Hajj Radwan's memory around would trump whatever pleading I can bring to the table.

As we head out of the camp, following Mutt and Jeff, I can't help but consider the very real possibility that it was here, in a makeshift garage not unlike the one we've just filmed, that Hajj Radwan prepared the truck bombs destined for the two U.S. embassies and the Marine barracks. It runs counter to the press's reporting that those bombs were assembled in the Bekaa Valley and driven down to Beirut. But as I know, those reports are as flimsy as my speculation that the bombs might have been made here.

As hard as I try not to let it, my favorite idée fixe, Pan Am 103, pops into my head. What we know for certain is that in July 1988 a meeting of Hajj Radwan's associates took place in a Palestinian camp very much like Ayn al-Hilweh, this one just south of Beirut. The meeting had been convened to plan the blowing up of five civilian airliners in midflight.

The venue was a shabby, nondescript travel agency—cheap plastic furniture, dirty terrazzo floor, crowded, stifling hot. It wasn't in the report, but I imagine the plotters stood in a corner whispering to one another, their voices masked by the general din. But who knows, maybe the owners were in on the plot. It was only thanks to dumb luck we even found out about the meeting.

It wasn't as if that camp wasn't on our radar. We knew Hajj Radwan borrowed it as an ad hoc sanctuary, just like he did with Ayn al-Hilweh. He'd arrive without fanfare, do his business, and then take off without a word. Once, a couple of days after we had picked up chatter that Hajj Radwan had been there for a meeting, Chuck and I drove up into the hills above it to take a look.

The camp's narrow streets were packed, people going about their innocent quotidian business. Granted, we were at a good distance, but it all looked benign enough to me. Even after Pan Am 103 went down, and I'd read about the meeting at the travel agency, it was hard to think of this camp as somewhere someone would plan mass murder.

"You give me the plates of the fucker's car and enough time to set up," Chuck said, "and by God, I'll reach out and touch him."

Chuck went back to our car and grabbed a foreshortened Kalashnikov equipped with a laser sight. He picked out at random a parked car, put the rifle to his shoulder, and held it steady, looking in his scope. He lowered so he could read the ballistic performance tables taped to the stock. He put it back to his shoulder, locking on to the car again. "Yep. A no-misser."

I started to get nervous. Two weeks before, Chuck and one of our techs were close to here when they were arrested by one of the local Christian militias. They were held until someone up the chain of command passed down the order to let them go. Now I was afraid of a repeat. Since Langley was already nervous about what we were up to, we couldn't afford to give them an excuse to pull us out.

"We're out of here," I finally said. Chuck lowered his rifle and took it back to the car.

Even to this day, I wonder if at that very moment Chuck's murderers weren't down there in that camp designing his murder—I don't know—perfecting the bomb that would blow a hole in the skin of Pan Am 103. The assembling and testing of it would have been too risky in places like Malta, Frankfurt, London, or wherever the Pan Am device was checked in.

I'd come to look at Palestinian refugee camps as underground rivers. You vaguely know they're there, but you don't know much else. Without the landmarks we're accustomed to—fixed addresses, fixed telephone lines, and censuses—it's impossible for us to get our bearings. Which, in turn, means it's impossible to conduct a proper police investigation, or for that matter an assassination.

Hezbollah sprouted out of the same soil as the Palestinian camps—Beirut's anonymous and insular slums. Although it was secretly formed in August 1982, it didn't go public until 1985. And even after that, Hezbollah's military command was unknown. Shuttling between tenements in the southern suburbs and poor villages in the south, the key military commanders aren't known to even Hezbollah's rank and file. It's as if General Motors were managed by a mail clerk somewhere in the basement, but no one knows his name or how to find him.

THE OTHER SIDE OF MANHOOD'S TRACKS

Beirut, October 1986: From my balcony, I could see a good slice of Muslim Beirut. It was like looking down into the Ninth Circle of Hell. Not only did Hajj Radwan operate somewhere over there; so did a lot of other political psychopaths, from the Japanese Red Army to the German Red Army Faction. They were all people who'd have dearly loved to get their hands on a CIA operative. If I ever made the mistake of crossing over, even for a short visit, my life wouldn't have been worth an hour's purchase.

The upshot of it was that the CIA lived by the ironclad diktat of never crossing over. No more hanging out at the Palm Beach for me or going to movies in Hamra. The American ambassador occasionally did go over, but it was always for an unannounced visit, and for only a couple of hours. And he was escorted by what amounted to a reinforced company. (The American embassy possessed what amounted to the fourth-largest militia in Lebanon.)

But it wasn't as if I entertained any illusion that holing up in the Christian enclave kept me a hundred percent safe. Directly down the hill from me was the bombed-out American embassy annex, now a forlorn carcass. With its siding completely stripped off, it looked like an abandoned parking structure. I often thought of it as an architectural statement that Hajj Radwan could come get us any damn time he pleased. It's pretty much what he was doing to the French.

About the time I arrived in Beirut, Hajj Radwan was in the middle of a bloody campaign against France, hijacking French airliners and setting off bombs in Paris. Along with it, he'd taken to picking off French officials in Beirut, one after the other. In the course of a year, he assassinated one military attaché, one intelligence operative, and three gendarmes. The gendarmes were killed less than a mile from my apartment. Who knows exactly how he managed it, but Hajj Radwan clearly had free run of the Christian enclave. He reminded me of a shark that keeps to the depths and only breaks surface to strike; he knew our world, but we didn't know his.

What certainly helped, as I'll keep pointing out, is that Hajj Radwan didn't care about the personal trappings of power and money. He never felt he needed to ape the ways of Lebanon's warlords, racing around town in their Range Rovers and firing Kalashnikovs out the window into the air. He didn't keep bowing and scraping aides around him. And there was no tossing gold coins from his purse or beating his chest to remind people of who he was. For instance, although it was a spectacular, history-altering attack, he never did claim responsibility for the Marine barracks bombing. In fact, his name can only be attached to it by the flimsiest of hearsay.

Hajj Radwan lived a monk's life, or at least he did in the early days. He preferred a shared taxi to his own car and lived in small, cramped apartments without air-conditioning or central heating. By shunning Beirut's flashy restaurants and nightclubs, places where people go to be seen, and all the other status symbols of Beirut's villains and plutocrats, he freed himself up for the business at hand—murdering his enemies.

Hajj Radwan wouldn't even allow his name to appear on Hezbollah's internal organizational charts. On the rare occasion he needed to visit an official Hezbollah facility, he arranged in advance for an escort to walk him past the guards. No questions asked or answers proffered. It was as if he were just a guy who'd wandered in off the street.

Hajj Radwan didn't carry a gun. He knew that wannabes strap on a Glock to let people know they're not to be fucked with. Guns may be an indispensable credential for the insecure, but they're one more marker to avoid.

The same standard held for the rest of Hajj Radwan's people. They lived life as nonentities, often in apparent poverty, below remark or notice. When they needed to, they adopted the protective coloration of the law-abiding bourgeoisie. From examining telephone records, it was determined the on-the-ground coordinator of Hariri's murder—Hajj Radwan's brother-in-law—had posed as a nouveau riche Armenian jeweler living in a Christian neighborhood. Although there wasn't a drop of Christian blood in him, the gold cross around his neck and a self-taught Christian accent were enough to fool even the wary. He threw more dust in people's eyes by owning a large pleasure yacht, keeping the company of beautiful women, and spending his nights at the Casino du Liban. (On the basis of the telephone analysis, he coordinated Hariri's assassination from the casino.)

To reduce his footprint to nothing, Hajj Radwan cut off contact with even his family. It meant no Sunday barbecues, no weddings, no funerals, ever. He never set foot in his home village because he had to anticipate that the Israelis would have placed a mole there whose sole task was to alert them to his visits.

It wasn't for a lack of trying that the CIA couldn't get a fix on Hajj

Radwan. Over the years, it canvassed every tough, greedy profession in its hunt for Hajj Radwan, from heroin peddling to arms dealing. But no matter what amount of money was put on the table, the CIA always came up empty-handed—not even the thinnest lead, let alone one that would allow it to grab him.

For the longest time, rumor had it that Hajj Radwan had undergone plastic surgery in order to assume an entirely fresh identity. But after his death, when pictures of him were put up around Beirut, it was obvious this wasn't true. It was rather a case of Hajj Radwan's having truly mastered the art of invisibility.

What it all comes back to is that he knew our world, but there was no way for us to know his.

Calculate like a hungry man.

—SUN TZU

AUTHOR — THE ART of WAR

Hajj Radwan didn't grow up in a Palestinian refugee camp, but his Beirut slum might as well have been one. It was a world of crushing poverty—sewers running out onto dirt streets, piles of burning trash, the din of despair and lost lives. Electricity and water were sporadic, often out for days at a time. I never saw Hajj Radwan's house, but I didn't need to, to know it was a cold freeze in the winter, a bagel oven in the summer.

Insular and forced in on itself, Hajj Radwan's slum was as deep and black a hole as Ayn al-Hilweh. Any outsider who made the mistake of wandering in would be immediately confronted and interrogated. As for an American like me, he'd be ipso facto taken as a spy, arrested, and hauled off to a Hezbollah prison.

It was easier for me to see Hajj Radwan by seeing what he wasn't. Escaping poverty was all but impossible for poor Shiites. When the war got bad, there wasn't the money to pick up and flee to London or Paris as the rich Christians did. Lebanese colonies in Africa were an escape for some. But in a place like Kano, Nigeria, life was no less precarious than it was in Lebanon. The better alternative was to stay put and defend the little you did possess, even at the risk of violent death.

In Hajj Radwan's world there was no time for our preciosity and abstract political fancies, things like the Clash of Civilizations, Progress, and Universal Justice. People didn't have the time to read *The New York Review of Books* or talk about the Academy Awards, write blogs about their inner turmoil, or take off a year to find themselves.

Call it a natural advantage or a curse, but for poor Shiites in Hajj Radwan's slum, reality let them know exactly what they were worth. Without crutches such as trust funds for the wealthy or social safety nets for the poor, profligacy wasn't an option. With few chances coming along in life, you knew you absolutely had to take the ones that did. While we in the West go to sleep thinking about what we've lost, Lebanon's poor Shiites stay awake dreaming about what's to be gained.

Straight-up politics wasn't a salvation either. The Shiites knew from hard experience that elections are rigged or bought, justice is a luxury for the rich, and the rule of law is a deceit perpetuated to keep down the weak. The few Shiites lucky enough to make it to the top immediately forgot their roots and started to sing the elite's tune and devote themselves to their comforts and entertainment.

What the Shiites had left was the extended family, clan, and tribe. As in Homeric Greece, all satisfaction came from blood ties—livelihood, work, duty, social ties, and even relations with God. In Arabic, there's a word for it—*asabiyyah*. Tribal solidarity. A sort of esprit de corps, I guess you could call it. The Sicilians have something like it, *sangu du me sangu*. Blood of my blood.

With tribal solidarity comes the notion that there can be only one undisputed chief, the tribe's shepherd. Invested in him is every important decision related to the tribe's welfare and security, especially decisions related to war and peace. His decisions are personal and binding; he's prosecutor, jury, and judge. Something like homicide isn't a crime in the public sense, but rather a personal matter for the chief to decide—name the transgression and then decide the appropriate penalty.

It's a world where power is never ambiguous, words are meaningless, and the act alone counts. There are no second-place finishes, no also-rans, no consolation prizes, no satisfaction from straddling the top of the bell curve. The only thing that matters is authentic, unadulterated power—holding on to what you have and usurping more given the opportunity. Those who can't adapt to the world as it is are doomed to misery and early death.

Guesses will always be guesses, but I believe it's in this context that we need to view Hajj Radwan's attempt on Ambassador Phil Habib. It goes some of the way in answering the question why Hajj Radwan didn't murder the first American he came across in Beirut. There were hundreds of them wandering around, all blissfully unaware of Hajj Radwan's existence, let alone knowing that he might have an interest in killing them. If he'd taken this route, he would have racked up a much higher body count.

There was the obvious symbolism of destroying a building belonging to the American government, but I suspect it's more complex than that. In his attempt on Habib, Hajj Radwan almost surely hoped that by making it personal—decapitate the invading enemy—his act would be a stronger incentive for the Americans to decamp and go home. Killing a second secretary from the American embassy or a spook like me lacked the act's full import. In Hajj Radwan's world, you kill the owner, not his dog.

Theory aside, what's for certain is that Hajj Radwan didn't learn

THE PERFECT KILL 39

about the instrumentalities of murder at the polo club. He arose out of a world whose insides are blackened by murder and poverty, where beautiful theories are burned to a crisp, and easy-to-come-by morality is slain by brute fact. It's a world where people survive solely thanks to their reptilian instincts, and by sticking to the essential . . . and definitely not by throwing money at a problem.

A NOTE ON COLD EMPATHY

The day Chuck and I decided to murder Hajj Radwan, we knew we had to find a way to inhabit his world. Unfortunately, this meant entertaining something like empathy for his point of view, including his politics. When you caricature and vilify people, it makes them hard to see, and even harder to get a clean shot at.

Long ago I realized that holing up in some cloistered office, watching CNN, reading regurgitated analysis, and attending vapid meetings in Washington were not going to put me in Hajj Radwan's world. No, getting a feel for a strange tribe is really hard work. You have to eat their food, pray in their mosques, and consort with their women. *Shum al-hawah,* as the Lebanese say. Breathe the air. You need to get to a point where nothing an enemy can say or do will ever come as a surprise to you.

I never flattered myself that I could go completely native, crawl into the skin of a tribe like Hajj Radwan's, and arrive at the undiluted truth. Lawrence of Arabia got a lot deeper into the Arab mind than I ever would, but he never did truly come to understand the Arabs. I consoled myself with the thought that it wasn't a deal breaker. I'm no anthropologist, and like I said, all I really needed to do was understand Hajj Radwan well enough to figure out his next destination and get there before he did.

One thing it meant was I had to erase every prejudice I had, such as when America murders abroad, it's benevolent, but when the locals do it, it's terror. I had to treat Hajj Radwan as a rational human capable of accurately calculating his own interests and then finding the most efficient means of furthering them.

Hajj Radwan didn't murder Americans because he hated their culture or their freedoms. He didn't have the time or inclination to murder for "values." He didn't give a damn about American women wearing skimpy bikinis to the beach. (Lebanese women wear a lot skimpier ones, and he never said a word about it.) He didn't kill Israelis because he hated Jews, but because they were an occupying power.

Hajj Radwan possessed a neat, clean hatred, which translated into driving the odious foreign invader from his land. It was a straight-line calculation, which, like I said, very much accorded with the Lao assassins' point of view. Again, he made an attempt on Ambassador Habib because he believed it was the shortest and most expeditious means to persuade the Americans to leave. He kidnapped the CIA chief because he thought it would shut down the CIA in Lebanon, or at least force it back behind high walls and, in the bargain, blind it. (By the way, it worked.)

Power alone mattered to Hajj Radwan, usurping and preserving it. It's why he never picked fights over personal slights, historical wrongs, or whims. When the Israelis murdered his brother, he didn't retaliate. By both necessity and design, he tailored assassination to obtain well-defined and tangible objectives—seize a strategic position, assassinate a particularly effective captain to demoralize the enemy's troops, hit at an enemy's most vulnerable point to disrupt its ranks.

Who knows whether Hajj Radwan read Machiavelli, but it's clear that he shared the belief that power is the ability to hurt others. And the more discerning you are about it, the more power you win. Hajj Radwan didn't assassinate the Swedish ambassador because Sweden possesses no power anyone would want to usurp. But more to the point, Sweden wasn't foolish enough to invade Lebanon.

The point of it all is, if Chuck and I had any chance of pulling this off, we'd have to infiltrate the enemy's camp. Conceptually, that is.

> NOTE TO ASSASSINS: The assassin is an iconoclast cruelly devoted to the truth.

EVERY ACT A
BULLET OR
A SHIELD

It's an efficient act—cheap, fast, scalable. Only take on baggage as needed. Throw money at it and you're guaranteed to screw it up.

AS FAST AND EASY AS INFIDELITY

I'd guess I'm not the only sad bastard on earth who has suffered through a baleful Christmas en famille. In my family, at least, there was always some poor soul who seemed to catch a couple of well-grouped shots (metaphorically speaking). And by the way, it didn't always occur around the family hearth.

I'll never forget one Christmas when Mother took down a big-name Broadway producer. We were spending Christmas in Klosters, Switzerland, at the staid old Chesa Grischuna. I was ten. As was Mother's wont, she introduced herself around and soon became friendly with the Broadway producer and his wife. Right away Mother had her suspicions about the man, how at night he'd disappear after dinner on mysterious errands.

With her unerring smell for philanderers, she finagled it out of the assistant manager that the husband paid him fifty francs to leave a window open at night so he could sneak in after the hotel's front door was locked. Mother outbid the producer with a crisp new hundred-franc note, persuading the assistant manager to lock the window instead of leaving it open. The next day the producer and his wife abruptly checked out.

I won't even get into whether he deserved it or not; I suspect the couple were already having their problems. But the point is, a fifty-franc prime was enough to do the trick. (In those days it wasn't much more than ten dollars.)

What I'm trying to get at is that life is a lot more fragile than we care to admit. Let me go back to real murder. An ice pick through the medulla oblongata is a hundred percent fatal, for instance. Or jabbing the femoral artery with a penknife. And if you don't want to get caught, an injection of the nucleoside adenosine into the nictitating membrane on the inside of the eye will do it. If you use a tiny .50-gauge needle, no coroner will ever spot it.

For the assassin, what it means is that it's not the taking of life that's difficult, but rather doing it with a well-defined purpose, namely, preserve force and avoid war. *Le mot juste* over a slap across the face, a dagger over a nuke. Always the efficiency of it.

DON'T EXPECT TO LIVE UNTIL MORNING

Paris, July 13, 1793: The following story is familiar enough, but it's not without its lessons.

By 1793, the French Revolution's shine had definitely started to dim. The guillotine was no longer a novelty, and the rosy promise of *liberté, egalité,* and *fraternité* was seen for the charade it was. On top of everything else, Paris was oppressively hot that summer. Rain clouds squatted just west of the city, lightning spidered the sky, and thunder echoed through the streets like kettledrums. But it stubbornly refused to rain. Another unfulfilled promise.

On the morning of July 13, a beautiful young woman in white made her way through the brooding and ornate Palais Royal. Or maybe she was in blue, as some painters have portrayed her. Or maybe even in pea green. For that matter, who knows whether she was really beautiful or not. Doesn't political murder always assume a dramatic and exotic patina after the act?

What's for certain is that the young woman's name was Charlotte Corday. Of Norman gentry, she was a descendant of Corneille, one of France's greatest dramatists. Benefiting (or suffering) from a classical education, she would say afterward that her decision had been influenced by antiquity, namely Caesar's assassins who'd attempted to save the Republic. In one bloody act, she'd do the same for France.

At some point, Corday stopped to buy a black bonnet decorated with a green ribbon and a knife with a five-inch blade. The purchase of the knife would soon be explained, but why the bonnet?

From the Palais Royal she walked to the Cordeliers district, a part of Paris known for its radical politics. She was in search of the house of Jean-Paul Marat, a fierce, unyielding revolutionary. A doctor turned journalist, he wielded a pen dipped in acid. He believed that any Frenchman who harbored doubts about the revolution deserved to have his head separated from his neck.

Marat himself was something of an assassin. Before the revolution, he'd once applied to become a member of the Academy of Sciences, but being a doctor of middling ability who entertained bizarre theories about "animal magnetism," he was rejected. Antoine Lavoisier, one of the fathers of chemistry, was a member of the academy at the time, and, in what turned out to be a fatal mistake, he ridiculed Marat's theories—in public. Although Lavoisier was guillotined under the pretext of corruption, it was Marat's old grudge that sealed his fate.

As a Jacobin deputy, Marat should have been at the National Convention rather than at home. But he suffered from an acute case of psoriasis, a disfiguring and painful disease that forced him to spend days in a medicinal bath. Wrapping a vinegar-soaked cloth around his head also helped. But there was nothing to do about the heat, which made his psoriasis nearly intolerable.

Corday's original plan had been to assassinate Marat at the National Convention, resigning herself to certain arrest and the guillotine. But isn't self-sacrifice implicit in the deal? She only changed her plans after she found out that Marat was ill at home. So it was there she'd do the deed.

Marat's fiancée's sister turned Corday away at the door, telling her that he was too ill to see anyone. Corday went back to her lodgings and wrote a letter addressed to Marat, falsely claiming she had in her possession a list of names of dangerous counterrevolutionaries. When Marat didn't answer, she wrote a second letter, claiming she was being persecuted and needed his help.

It then occurred to Corday that she needed to write her final testament to the French people, explaining her motivations for murdering Marat. She pinned it to her dress, along with her baptism certificate, and retraced her steps to Marat's house.

Corday was again turned away at the door, but thanks to a distraction caused by a delivery, she slipped through the door and made her way to Marat's quarters. He was in his bath, a board across it covered with letters and papers.

Corday said something about the list of counterrevolutionaries. Looking at her with curiosity, Marat said something about how they'd soon enough lose their heads. Without warning, Corday produced her five-inch knife and plunged it into his neck, just above the collarbone. It severed a main artery and collapsed a lung. Marat quickly bled to death.

As portrayed in one nineteenth-century painting, the beautiful Corday stands behind Marat, staring away, the bloody knife about to drop from her hand. His lifeless body twisted over the edge of his bathtub. A beautiful murderess is a subject compelling enough. But wasn't Marat's murder also a cautionary tale to the powerful and arrogant that an innocent young woman, armed with only a common kitchen knife, is capable of striking at the heart of power? Corday might not have killed the French Revolution, but she did put it on notice.

THE ECONOMICS OF POLITICAL MURDER

Beirut, November 1986: It took me less than a week after I arrived in Beirut to decide my most valuable possession was a telephone that all on its own tirelessly dialed a number until someone picked up at the other end. With Beirut's telephone exchanges shot-up and barely limping along, it was the only practical way to make a call.

I kept the telephone in the middle of my desk as a reminder that my first chore every morning was to get ahold of at least one person. Normally, it was to set up a meeting with a source. I'd punch in the number, turn the speaker on, and go about my business, keeping one ear cocked for the sound of someone at the other end. It took me sometimes four or five hours to ring through to a telephone only a mile away. Reaching a number at the far end of Lebanon could take a week or more.

I knew it wasn't the best idea to call my sources from a telephone line connected to any American . . . if for no other reason than the United States was effectively party to the Lebanese Civil War. But for what it's worth, there wasn't in those days a functioning Lebanese government to eavesdrop on my calls. Even if by chance it did, the government was on our side. Or, as I'll get to, sort of.

But now that we'd made the decision to assassinate Hajj Radwan, it was time to cut out the lax bullshit. I had to anticipate that Hajj Radwan would start to hear echoes of my plans and then quickly move to tap my magic phone. It would have been as simple as recruiting a mole in the local telephone exchange, have him hang a wire on my line, run the wire to a tape recorder, and voilà, my Rolodex would be in Hajj Radwan's hot little hands. From there—if I was right about how smart this guy was—it wouldn't be long before everything unraveled. So, rather than call my sources from my trusty phone, I'd now have to adopt the practice of showing up at their front doors. Or signal them by moving a geranium pot in my window. Either way, the phone had to go.

By now the skeptical reader might start to wonder just how deep my paranoia ran in those days. But there's this in my defense: A year after the 1984 kidnapping of Beirut's CIA chief, Bill Buckley, we still had no idea who'd taken him or where he was being held. Then one day a friendly Arab government stepped forward to tell us in total confidence that it was someone called Hajj Radwan who'd grabbed him. We pleaded for details, but a name was all they'd give us.

At first, there was some doubt whether Hajj Radwan really existed. We'd never heard the name before, in any shape or form. So we ran it by the Lebanese police, who to our surprise said that, indeed, they did have a record for such a person—a passport application with a black-and-white photo attached. The police faxed us a copy of both. The photo was grainy, but staring out of it was a fierce, slender young man with a neatly trimmed beard.

The police agreed to let us photograph the original picture if we'd send someone down. But when one of our people showed up with a camera, the police red-facedly explained that in the interim both the application and the photo had disappeared. There was no point in rubbing their noses in it, but the only conclusion we could come up with was that Hajj Radwan had a mole inside the police, who was placed well enough to find out about our interest in him and who had enough chutzpah to steal his application and picture. It's sort of as if bin Laden were to have had an assistant FBI director on the books doing his blocking for him.

My paranoia about Hajj Radwan wasn't diminished by the fact that in a storeroom next to my office sat a suitcase full of Bill Buckley's clothes. They were kept there for when he was released. While no one put any real stock in that anymore, the suitcase was a daily reminder that Hajj Radwan could get to any one of us. (It would later be established that Buckley died of pneumonia in 1985 while still under Hajj Radwan's control.)

It was of constant interest to me how Hajj Radwan had been able to identify Buckley. As best I could piece together, he had someone at the airport able to observe the comings and goings at the VIP area, especially when Buckley accompanied his Lebanese counterparts to the airport to send them off to the United States. As I was told by my own source at the airport, Buckley might as well have tattooed his forehead: *Hey, guys, I'm a very important American spy with important friends.*

We also learned that Hajj Radwan could get into all immigration entry and exit records and flight reservations. Couple that with all of the other moles he riddled the Lebanese government with, and Buckley must have looked to him like a big fat fish in a very small fishbowl.

It didn't help that Buckley always wore a starched shirt, pressed suit, and tie. This was in crisp contrast to most foreigners in Beirut who favored the scruffy look—jeans, denim shirts, scuffed shoes. Buckley's living in a tony neighborhood in a grand apartment with a splendid view of the Mediterranean was another telltale marker. On top of it, Buckley kept to an unvarying schedule, leaving and coming home at exactly the same time. Even his most unobservant neighbors wondered who this disciplined man might be.

How exactly Hajj Radwan added it up to correctly pinpoint Buckley as the CIA chief, I don't know. It could have been thanks to tapping his phone. But it didn't matter because I'd firmly made up my mind to reverse Buckley's modus operandi by 180 degrees, to find a way out of the comfortable, habitual world most foreigners in Beirut so easily slip into. Part of it would be dumping my automated telephone. More strategically, I'd have to take a dive down the status ladder, turn myself into a complete nonentity, someone no one wanted to waste a good bullet on.

Although a proper assassination shouldn't come with a big price tag, and I was no Charlotte Corday, it definitely helped that money wasn't a problem. When I telexed Langley that I needed to buy a dozen old apartments in the bad parts of town to mix up where I slept nights, the money was immediately authorized. (If an expense was tied to a "security upgrade," Langley bitched but felt compelled to approve it.) It helped that in those days you could buy a bottom-end apartment in Beirut for under ten thousand dollars.

I asked a good contact to put the apartments in his name. With a reputation as a swordsman, he came up with the pretext that he needed them to "entertain friends." I directed him to neighborhoods along the Green Line, all more or less vacated since the start of the civil war. They were as disregarded and invisible as Hajj Radwan's slum.

It wasn't long before my trusted cat's paw came up with a half-dozen places no self-respecting Lebanese would set foot in—bullet-pocked, windows shot out, front doors blown off their hinges by rockets. None had running water or electricity. The dirt-poor refugees reduced to taking shelter in them minded their own business and pointedly ignored the odd foreigner (me) who'd show up from time to time.

Another way down the ladder was to buy a fleet of old Mercedes. They were chewed away with rust and dented, and their windows either stuck up (a sweltering ride in the summer) or stuck down (a wet ride in the winter). People looked right through them. And through me too, as if I were a homeless person. But in a country where a car is an unfailing class marker, it was well worth the discomfort.

It took about six months for me to establish a parallel existence in a world where the soft conveniences and amusements of civilization don't exist. I could disappear into it when I needed, cross over the tracks to the small, poor part of town. I knew I was nowhere near Hajj Radwan's standards, but at least I'd improve my odds over Buckley's.

I'll keep saying it, but the truth is you can't kill what you can't see.

FEAR MAKES US SEE CLEARLY

Assassination is a fine and subtle craft. Or to steal from Flaubert, the aesthetics of it are the highest form of justice. And in that sense it's an educative act: The assassin shows himself to be unsparing and hard in his clarity. He demonstrates how he's meticulously and correctly calculated the true value of the person he's about to murder, what his murder will accomplish, and what it will cost. He doesn't miss or unnecessarily take innocent lives. It's a leverage of force like no other.

Archimedes of Syracuse said that if he had a place to stand and a lever he could move the world. The assassin makes a similar claim: Give him a place to stand and a dagger and he'll move the world. Few have succeeded, but the ones who have, or came close, offer us a lesson.

On November 4, 1995, Yigal Amir assassinated Israeli prime minister Yitzhak Rabin, shooting two bullets into him from a semiautomatic pistol. Rabin bled to death on the operating table. Rabin's murder mattered because of who Rabin was—a highly decorated and brilliant military officer, a hero in a nation of heroes. Moreover, he had a long record of not playing politics with Israel's security. During the first Palestinian uprising (1987–1993), Rabin—he was then defense minister—ordered Israeli troops to go in and "break the bones" of the Palestinians. It was credentials like those that put him in a position to persuade a reluctant Israel to make peace with the Palestinians. Amir's calculation was that with Rabin gone there'd be no peace. So far, he's been right.

On July 20, 1944, Colonel Claus von Stauffenberg tried something similar when he made an attempt on Adolf Hitler with a bomb in a briefcase. Weighing about 2.2 pounds, the components were stolen from the Wehrmacht. In other words, they were free. His motivations were equally barebones: Kill Hitler and save Germany from certain destruction. One life's a small price to pay for one's country.

Amir turned, and Stauffenberg came close to turning, history on a dime for pennies. Their approach to violence was strictly instrumental—one act with one defined, absolutely clear objective. Expending great resources wasn't necessary, and neither was creating widespread symbolic destruction. Neither assassin derived any pleasure from the shedding of blood. And neither entertained grandiose visions: no bullshit about the Clash of Civilizations or Utopia. And like the Laotian assassins, they intended to preserve the body.

The most iconic assassinations in history have been spare, economical acts—Julius Caesar cut down by daggers, the archbishop of Canterbury by broadswords, Archduke Franz Ferdinand by a semiautomatic pistol. A psychotic, Lee Harvey Oswald murdered Kennedy with a $19.95 mail-order rifle. If nothing else, he demonstrated that changing history is within anyone's reach.

It's by one swift, precise, and violent act that the assassin demonstrates to the powerful that in spite of all of their money and phalanxes of security they're still vulnerable. They've picked the wrong side of history or the wrong enemy. What good did the terrible force of the French Revolution do for Marat? What good did the Gestapo do against Count von Stauffenberg? Only luck (a blocking concrete pillar) gave Hitler a year's reprieve.

In choosing the uncomplicated and inexpensive over the elaborate and expensive, the assassin reduces a struggle to two people. *Manu forti*, he imposes the ultimate submission on a victim, leaving no room for misunderstanding the stakes or the finality of the contest. It's akin to a dual at eight feet or a medieval knight unhorsing another. There can be only one winner.

Set against our conceits about Progress and World Peace, I recognize this will strike a lot of people as ridiculously primeval. Hasn't assassination gone way beyond its shelf life? No doubt about it. But the truth remains that murder conducted face-to-face still terrifies people a lot more than killing at great distances or with giant bombs. Which means assassination isn't going away.

The early Zionist organization Lehi, also known as the Stern Gang, taught itself to efficiently streamline assassination. At its largest, the group numbered only in the hundreds. It didn't keep offices or infrastructure. Some members were known to carry cots on their backs so they could sleep in a different house each night. Lehi's preferred weapons were knives, pistols, and crude bombs.

I interviewed a veteran Lehi bomb technician who did his best to make the case that Lehi was quite careful about the employment of violence: "We never tried to kill innocent people, not civilians, not children."

As evidence, he told me the story of when Lehi attempted to kill a British army major with a book bomb posted through the mail, but ended up accidentally killing his brother, the group immediately dropped the post office as a delivery system. Stamps might be cheap, but the savings was overridden by inaccuracy.

Lehi understood the tactical advantages of not wasting precious resources by taking and holding ground or planting a flag, or, for that matter, even owning a flag. It strictly "compartmented" everything: no employee newsletters, no staff meetings, no conferences. But of course, why would the right hand ever let the left hand know what it's doing if both hands share the same objective—to persuade Britain to abandon Palestine by murdering its officials?

Lehi knew better than to try to turn itself into something it wasn't, namely a conventional armed force. Armies are cumbersome and slow; they're expensive to feed and arm; they're easy for an enemy to corner and destroy. Not to mention that it's much easier to vet an assassin than a division of green recruits to determine who'll run at the sound of gunfire and who won't.

Lehi bookended its bloody run with two notorious assassinations. In 1944, two Lehi operatives gunned down Lord Moyne, British Minister in the Middle East, in front of his Cairo residence. In 1948, Lehi operatives shot out the tires of UN mediator Folke Bernadotte's car and then shot him dead as he sat in the backseat.

As Lehi intended, the British were forced to pull back into fortresses not unlike ours in Beirut. Which turned Britain, like it did us, into an isolated and detested occupying power. Although Britain had reason enough to abandon its Palestine mandate, assassination certainly played a role in the decision.

In the beginning, moderate Zionists condemned the members of Lehi as dangerous fanatics. But after independence, Israel soon came to embrace Lehi's assassins as heroic patriots. By 1949, Israel had granted Lehi a general amnesty. By 1980, it instituted a military decoration called the Lehi Ribbon. By 1983, Yitzhak Shamir, a Lehi leader who had green-lighted Folke Bernadotte's assassination, was elected prime minister. The assassin in history has often ascended to power thanks to ruthlessly murdering his enemies. But this is the first instance that comes to my mind where a democracy elected an assassin as a head of state.

After independence, Israel adopted the Lehi model as an instrument of statecraft. Late on April 9, 1973, a half-dozen speedboats riding low in the water with Israeli commandos put ashore just south of Beirut. They were met by Mossad agents in rented cars and driven to an upscale neighborhood of Beirut called Verdun. The commandos split up and entered two nearby apartment buildings. In minutes they assassinated three Palestinian leaders believed to have been in on the Munich massacre. Their work done, the commandos left on their rubber boats, returning safe and sound to their mother ship.

The Verdun assassinations left Palestinians in shock and numb with fear. Who were these supermen who could sneak into an Arab capital and with impunity murder well-protected people? It was all the more jarring because the commandos' leader and a future prime minister, Ehud Barak, had dressed as a woman. There are few things more unsettling than a cross-dressing assassin.

Not too many years after Verdun, I ran into the Lebanese businessman who'd unwittingly rented the cars to the Mossad operatives. He was still bitter they'd burned his cars on the beach, particularly because Mossad had canceled their American Express cards before he could collect on the insurance. But for him, it was Barak's dressing as a woman that was the icing on the cake. He was convinced the Israelis' intent was to rub the Lebanese's noses in their cleverness.

On one level, the Israelis demonstrated that they could exact their pound of flesh far short of war. On another, the Verdun assassinations rattled the Palestinians to their core. Where was any one of them safe?

Who knows for sure, but offhand I'd say the skill and efficiency of the Verdun assassinations intimidated the Palestinians more than a warship sitting off the coast. I can't say exactly why, but precise, efficient murder seems to carry some sort of terror multiplier effect.

What Lehi and the other successful assassins of history tell us is that the act is never improved by making things overcomplicated. The fewer the moving parts, the less likely it'll fail and the more likely it'll produce terror in the enemy. It's probably one reason we're riveted by Marat's meeting his end in his bathtub. The only thing more disturbing would have been if he'd been squatting over his chamber pot.

As I'll soon get to, Israeli assassinations eventually became large institutionalized affairs and the Lehi touch was lost.

THE ASSASSIN ALWAYS EXCEPTIONAL, THE VICTIM ALWAYS IRREPLACEABLE

The Bekaa Valley, November 1983: For a year the USS *New Jersey* pounded Lebanon with artillery rounds the size of Volkswagens. The boom of its guns is something a generation of Lebanese will never forget. But with the enemy burrowed deep into the fabric of the country, the front lines in those days were extremely fluid and the way the Reagan administration looked at it was what else could be done with a monkey house like Lebanon except try to flatten it.

One innocent day I was at a quiet lunch in the Bekaa when something that sounded like a freight train hurtling off a bridge passed over the top of us. The impact was miles away, but the glasses on the table trembled, and a serving cart started to roll across the floor. In less than a minute, the restaurant was back to normal, everyone picking up their conversations where they'd left off. I didn't get the impression anyone was much impressed by the *New Jersey*.

The Lebanese often complained to me that the *New Jersey* was firing blanks. Or if it wasn't, its gunners were very bad shots. Nothing I could say would convince them that the *New Jersey* was firing real ordnance. On the other hand, I couldn't explain why the *New Jersey* never seemed to hit anything. I didn't know who he was that early in the game, but later I've often wondered what Hajj Radwan had thought about the *New Jersey* and all of our flailing around in his country.

The restaurant where I'd had a ringside seat to the *New Jersey*'s show of force sat right off the main Beirut–Damascus road. It was a route Hajj Radwan took three or four times a week to see his people in the Bekaa. For all I know, he'd passed by as I ate lunch. And if he had, could he too have decided that big guns don't win wars?

If Hajj Radwan wasn't the most powerful man in Lebanon, he more than anyone understood the fine instrumentalities of violence. His clinical, meticulous, pared-down approach to assassination demonstrated that over and over. Again, it helped that he didn't care about the conceits and excesses of power—reality always trumped pretense.

Hajj Radwan didn't maintain offices, training camps, or anything that came with ground anyone could tie his name to. The size of his organization varied strictly according to need and never grew larger than the low hundreds. Like any capable guerrilla group, they never put themselves under the same roof. Instead, they met in twos and threes, alternating between one another's apartments, street corners, or dark stairwells.

Hajj Radwan detested the modern corporate circus, wanting nothing to do with anything that smacked of administrative drag. He didn't permit personnel rosters, telephone books, PowerPoint and Excel spreadsheets, press flacks, or event planners. And definitely no conferences, staff meetings, and corporate pep talks. If someone didn't like the way he ran things, he could quit and go work for IBM.

Hajj Radwan treated the Internet as if it were the bubonic plague. It might be newfangled, convenient, and entertaining, the delight of the lazy and shiftless, but he understood it for what it was—a central bus station easy for the cops to watch. The worst sort of flytrap. Even talking in chat rooms was strictly verboten for his people.

Inside Hezbollah, few people even knew Hajj Radwan's name or, for that matter, that there existed an ultrasecret cell. And those who did never mentioned it outside their tight, closed circle. And anyone foolish enough to ask around about Hajj Radwan was immediately pegged as a spy. It's a consensus of silence that is difficult for us in the West to understand, but for the assassin, it's a sine qua non for survival.

It greatly helped that Hajj Radwan was never tempted to brand himself or his organization. No catchy names, no commissioning of hip, edgy logos, no tagging on walls. Some attacks he claimed in the name of the "Islamic Jihad Organization." But that was nothing more than a name to serve the act, a confected mystery meant to let his enemies tremble at it in dumb dread.

Hajj Radwan intuitively understood that the capable assassin doesn't measure his worth by the size of his budget, how many people are under him, or the number of fancy gadgets he possesses. And he definitely doesn't play the numbers game. Toting up body counts is a mark of failure and impotence, like a waterfront whore counting her tricks at the end of a night. In political murder, no one gives a shit how hard you try or how many times you do something, but rather how well you do it.

Other professional murderers bring the same sort of asceticism to the act. The Mexican drug cartels behead their victims with axes and kitchen knives, deliberately leaving the remains by the side of the road to make people understand just how ruthless they are . . . and to send the implicit message they'll happily do it again.

I would like to have been a fly on the wall when Hajj Radwan watched news reports coming out of Iraq about our attempts to assassinate Saddam in the early days of the war. How our cruise missiles smashed up a lot of stuff and killed a lot of people, but never came close to Saddam. I also wonder what he said about our emptying the Treasury for the "Global War on Terror," the six trillion dollars we spent on it, or whatever the final tally is. Could it not have seemed a grotesque amount of money to assassinate one man, Osama bin Laden?

NOTE TO ASSASSINS: Like the economies of love and betrayal, assassination must be finely calculated.

ALWAYS HAVE A BACKUP FOR EVERYTHING

Count on the most important pieces of a plan failing at exactly the wrong moment. Double up on everything— two sets of eyes, two squeezes of the trigger, double-prime charges, two traitors in the enemy's camp.

NOTHING EVER WORKS THE FIRST TIME

I'll never forget when they walked us through a mock ambush at CIA boot camp. It was a muggy September night, the cicadas shrieking as if they were the ones about to be murdered. One of our instructors shepherded us, as if we were lambs, into a half-buried bunker. Its six-inch-slit Plexiglas window looked down on a concrete bridge spanning a shallow gully. He told us to put in our earplugs.

At first, there was only the pulsing blackness of night. Then came the sound of a chain dragging over concrete. I couldn't tell what was going on until a car came into view crossing the bridge in our direction. Its lights were off. Another one followed close behind. There were four cars in all, a single chain pulling them roughly across the bridge. It reminded me of an automated car wash.

As soon as the first car reached our side of the bridge, there was a piercing light, followed by a boom and a ball of flame that climbed into the sky and vanished. Flipped over on its back, the car looked like a smoking, dead roach. From the far side of the bridge came a second explosion, slamming the last car into the one in front of it. The two cars in between were now hemmed in.

From somewhere on the riverbank behind us, someone slammed a rocket-propelled grenade into car number two. A second rocket hit it, shoving the car back a couple of feet. A heavy machine gun pounded bullets and tracers into number two. A second machine gun followed suit. Number two shuddered and started to burn, revealing the landscape for the first time. It was one way to see Virginia's Tidewater.

The next morning they took us back to inspect the damage. The rubber dummy in the backseat of car number two was a melted blob. "I don't think this fellow had much of a chance, do you?" the instructor said, wheeling around to see if anyone dared challenge him.

He didn't use the word, but I knew he was talking about redundancy—the two initial explosions, the two rocket-propelled grenades, the two heavy machine guns. If one failed, the second one would step in to take over. It's basic tactics familiar to any soldier.

THE ASSASSIN WHO DANCES WITH A HUNDRED LEGS

The need to compensate for human shortcomings, frailty, and run-of-the-mill stupidity won't come as news to anyone. It's as basic as two eyes, two ears, and two kidneys. But a fail-safe redundancy is absolutely indispensable for the assassin, if for no other reason than he's unlikely to get a second chance.

Police SWAT teams build redundancy into their "entries"—two "flash-bang" grenades thrown in each room; two snipers; two shooters, one entering a room "high," the other "low"; two bullets into a perp. The Navy SEAL credited with killing bin Laden reportedly went by the book, shooting him twice. "Double tapping" the bad guy has entered Hollywood's pop vocabulary.

Redundancy has even been built into assault rifles. The Israelis have on the market a two-barrel, one-trigger assault rifle called the Gilboa Snake. According to the advertising, "The features of the Gilboa Snake enables operators to accurately deliver two rounds into a target without the delay of cycling and the felt recoil which make 'double taps' difficult to group."

Redundancy also fits in with general strategy. On August 23, 2013, two car bombs went off in a crowded neighborhood in Tripoli, Lebanon. On December 29, 2013, Chechen Islamic rebels blew up the main train station in Volgograd, and then a trolley bus the next day. And there was Hajj Radwan's twin attacks in Beirut on October 23, 1983, one against the Marines and the other against French paratroopers. The number two—or, even better, multiple attacks—advertises that you enjoy the advantage of military reserves.

The siblings of redundancy are speed, surprise, terrain, and faultless intelligence. The less redundancy built into an assassination, the more the other elements must compensate for it. The ultimate redundancy, although the least efficient manifestation of violence, is massive firepower.

Surprise, of course, is also critical. No wink and a nod beforehand, no foreplay, no threats. The dummy in car number two wasn't offered the slightest hint of what was waiting for him at the bridge. The attack occurring at night added to the element of surprise.

As for speed, the attack on the convoy, from beginning to end, couldn't have lasted more than two minutes. It unspooled much too quickly for the human mind to react in a coherent fashion. There wasn't even enough time to choose between fight or flight.

The terrain was also ideal. Once number two started across the bridge—a narrow defile without escape—his fate was sealed. It was like catching someone coming down an escalator, trapped on either side, and people blocking escape in front and back. It's as easy as shooting a rubber duck in a bathtub.

Precise intelligence is the icing on the cake. The composition of number two's convoy, his route, and his schedule were all known to his assassins. The only thing better would have been if the assassins had been informed in advance where the convoy would stop to let number two get out to take a piss.

Nothing I saw of assassination in the years since my training changed my view of it. Follow the elementary rules, build in redundancy and superb intelligence, and a mark doesn't stand a chance.

I was caught up in my first real assassination in Lebanon's Bekaa Valley, an Israeli one. It came with the three classic elements of political murder—surprise, speed, precision. The one thing I wasn't so sure about was the intelligence, my sole contribution to it.

It all started when a Lebanese cop I knew knocked on my door to tell me he'd discovered a notorious Palestinian militant living next to him. When I asked him if he was sure he had the right Palestinian, he shrugged his shoulders: "It's got to be him." He was able to pick out the man's apartment building from an aerial photograph.

Without a way to confirm or disprove the cop's story, I sent a message around the region to see if anyone had anything to add. My answer came back very early the next morning in the guise of a violent pounding on my door. The cop shouted through the door that the apartment building he'd flagged to me had just been hit and completely destroyed by two F-16s belonging to you know who. (Two for the redundancy of it.)

I quickly decamped, anxious that the next person pounding on my door would be a Palestinian assassin bent on vengeance. As we drove away into the night, I was all but certain the F-16s were dispatched based on good intelligence; mine only tipped the scale. If I was on to him, they had to be, right?

The other thing I thought about is that in a time of war it's an organic and slippery progression from spare, dagger-in-the-heart assassination to falling into the lazy man's trap of bringing to bear massive overwhelming force. For instance, two F-16s with big bombs. Like I said, it's the time-honored default when the other elements of assassination aren't possible.

At the beginning of the Iraq War in 2003, the American Air Force did its best to assassinate Saddam, launching six separate cruise missile attacks on sites where he was supposed to be hiding. (In Pentagonese, it's called "destroying command nodes" rather than assassination.) None, though, came even close. It was like hunting a rabbit running at full tilt with a .50-caliber machine gun: It tears up a lot of earth, but leaves the rabbit to make it back to its hole and have a good laugh about it. But when does blindly spraying bullets in all directions ever lead to a sought-after outcome?

A group of Libyan Salafis I used to meet in Khartoum once tried to assassinate Gaddafi. The best ruse they could come up with was to commandeer a trash truck as their Trojan horse. A half dozen of them hid in the back, while the driver went through the routine of a pickup at Gaddafi's main palace in Tripoli. Although not quite sure where they were on the compound, the assassins jumped out, guns blazing. Gaddafi was nowhere in the vicinity, leaving the palace guards to cut them down at their leisure. When I delicately asked my Salafi friend what they were thinking, he replied, "Allah told us to do it."

No surprise it was the Germans who brought Teutonic precision and fastidiousness to political murder. In 1979 the Red Army Faction (RAF), also known as the Baader-Meinhof Gang, made an attempt on Alexander Haig, NATO's commander at the time. The venue was a bridge, the weapon fifty pounds of explosives buried in the pavement. While the RAF understood the principle of hitting the mark while passing through a narrow defile, they mistimed the detonation and only wounded two of Haig's bodyguards. Everyone expected the RAF to get better, and that they did.

Deutsche Bank knew that its chairman, Alfred Herrhausen, like other captains of German industry, was a potential target for assassination and accordingly spared no money to protect him. It furnished him with a heavily armored car and an escort of bodyguards. But what Deutsche Bank couldn't anticipate was a military-style assault masked by the innocent and banal.

As Herrhausen's Mercedes pulled away from his house in Bad Homburg the morning of November 30, 1989, no one noticed the bicycle by the side of the road. Nor, of course, did anyone notice the infrared beam crossing the road at tire level. It was a typical morning, nothing out of place, nothing suspicious, another routine trip to work.

Herrhausen's Mercedes broke the infrared beam closing the bomb's electrical circuit, which in turn set off the ten-kilogram explosive charge hidden in the bicycle's saddlebag. Although the charge was relatively small, it was perfectly lethal thanks to the fact that the concave shape of the explosives projected a two-kilogram copper metal dish at something like three kilometers per second. The extreme heat caused the dish to melt into an elongated ball, a "carrot." The carrot passed through Herrhausen's door, severed his legs, and exited the Mercedes on the other side. Herrhausen bled to death.

Experts call the device that killed Herrhausen a "platter" charge. In the Iraq War such devices would become known as EFPs—explosively formed penetrators. With an explosive-to-dish ratio of 4:1, they're capable of cutting through the thickest of armor. They're the equivalent of a sniper's rifle, which for the Secret Service makes them one of its darkest nightmares. With properly formed explosives, a correctly shaped dish, and an infrared firing device, no president is safe.

So far so good, but how did the RAF learn about platter charges? They're not something you read about in *The Anarchist Cookbook*.

The CIA first introduced platter charges in the Middle East during the first Afghan war (1979–1989). By packing a small, locally manufactured stove with explosives, the mujahideen could drive the curved bottom through any Soviet armor plating. From Afghanistan, the technology passed through Iran to various parts of the Middle East, including Lebanon. Hezbollah picked up the technology and perfected it.

Some reports have it that the East German secret police, the Stasi, trained the RAF in platter charges. But there were other equally plausible reports that pointed to certain Palestinian explosives experts based in Lebanon. While I'm not certain how it would have worked, it intrigued me that the Palestinian group in question was at the time allied with Hajj Radwan. Did Hajj Radwan have anything to do with training the RAF? It's another one of those things easy to believe but impossible to prove.

The Lebanese first figured out how to defend against a Herrhausen-style attack by adopting a sort of reverse redundancy. Militia commanders would move around in convoys of identical cars, sometimes up to twenty. Smoked windows and no license plates made it impossible for any platter-charge-wielding assassin to determine which car the militia commander was riding in.

Short of being able to afford a twenty-car convoy, the next best way to avoid a military-style assassination is to build unpredictability and randomness into one's existence. In this regard, Herrhausen made every mistake in the book: He left home for work at the same time every morning, he lived at an easily located address, and his neighborhood was lightly trafficked, which offered the RAF a clear field of fire. (It's another reason not to live in the suburbs.)

Hajj Radwan understood that it's our little habits and routines that offer the assassin his best chance. He didn't do things like commute to work, visit his mother, or attend annual trade shows. If he had a regular barber or doctor, he didn't advertise it. He was nowhere to be seen on his birthday. But above all, he never strutted around like a peacock.

Various sources agree that in the early days Hajj Radwan led the most disciplined of ghostly existences, avoiding all repetitive practices. He never left by the same door he entered, never slept under the same roof two nights in a row, and never identified himself with a particular car or telephone number.

Hajj Radwan brought the same strict regime to everything else he did. There was no detail too small for him not to personally attend to, from making sure the charges were dual primed to making sure everyone got to an appointment on time. He knew a bad battery or someone falling asleep at the switch could change the course of history. He knew he was only as strong as his weakest link, and the weakest link was only as strong as its weakest link.

For the first year in Beirut, I'd come in early every morning to check the overnight chatter, looking for that little weak link. I filled my boxes with three-by-five cards. I got to know Hajj Radwan's voice so I could pick it out of a noisy room. I knew his wolf pack almost as well as he did. But it was soon apparent that the chatter alone wasn't doing it. For a start, it wasn't in real time. While the chatter was grabbed out of the air in Lebanon, it first bounced its way back to Washington and only after a twenty-four-hour turnaround did it come back to Beirut. I'd find out Hajj Radwan had been at a certain place at a certain time. But so what? It was too late to get there before him. It was the same with satellite photography, which we got long after the fact. Even if we caught sight of Hajj

Radwan's car at Ayn al-Hilweh, it only told me he'd come and gone, not where he was going next.

The longer it went without my stumbling across a single piece of "actionable intelligence," the more I understood how hard it was to hit a fast-moving and unpredictable target. While chatter put me in the picture, it didn't put me in the game. No, I'd need a body with a pulse and a brain to tell me where Hajj Radwan would be on a certain day at a certain time, just as Herrhausen's assassin knew with near certainty when he'd be coming down the street. I knew I'd need to recruit a source close to him.

ASSASSINATION BY THE NUMBER

Kigali, Rwanda, April 6, 1994: The assassin has to be able to play in every key and on every scale, and smoothly adapt to changing circumstance and opportunity, just as he must build in layers of redundancy into every moving part. While a blinkered, one-trick assassin might get lucky, it's the assassin prepared for every eventuality who's most likely to succeed.

The story has it that the night the president of Rwanda was assassinated, his wife was in their solarium, searching the sky for her husband's jet, a Falcon 50. It was due in from Dar es Salaam at any moment. Riding on the plane with her husband was the president of Burundi, seven other passengers, and three French crew.

She, like a lot of other people, had heard there'd been an important breakthrough at Dar—a power-sharing agreement that would reconcile Rwanda's two largest tribes, the majority Hutus and the minority Tutsis. She wasn't happy about it. While her husband was a moderate Hutu, she thought the despised Tutsis deserved nothing.

For neutral observers, an agreement between the Hutus and Tutsis would be a badly needed correction to Rwanda's unfortunate colonial past. During their nearly half-century rule, the Belgians took Machiavelli at his most cynical, favoring the minority Tutsis in a deliberate, invidious strategy of divide and rule—all so they could loot the country undisturbed. The losers, the Hutus, were left to simmer in fury and patiently plan their revenge. And, unlike their Hutu president who preferred the olive branch over the gun, few were in the mood for compromise.

At about twenty-five after eight, the Falcon 50's lights could be seen circling the Kigali airport. Because a Falcon's engines emit a distinctive whine, everyone knew it was the president's plane. And anyhow, Kigali isn't a busy airport, making a small passenger jet a rarity.

As the jet came in for a landing, a silver knifepoint raced up into the sky, heading right for the Falcon 50. As these things so often go, time seemed to slow down. Maybe they'd pass each other, people thought. Maybe it's a test or something. But the Falcon 50's and the missile's paths continued toward their fatal intersection.

Some witnesses said that the plane's lights went out first, the engines fell silent, and then a giant orange ball of flame filled the sky. But could it have really happened in that sequence? Others remember only an explosion and then silence. What everyone agrees on is that there was a second streak of light and a second explosion—a second missile.

Half the city watched as the fiery wreckage fell from the sky without a sound, ironically coming to earth in the presidential garden at the feet of the president's wife. Did she flinch or smile?

UN forces were blocked from entering the part of the airport where the two missiles apparently had been fired from. They could only assume Rwandan soldiers had fired them, and the Rwandans didn't want the UN poking around to confirm it.

When the Hutus started to systemically massacre the Tutsis, it was apparent the president's assassination had served as a prearranged signal for genocide. With anywhere from 500,000 to 1 million killed, it was the last great genocide of the twentieth century.

What did the wife know in advance? There are people convinced she was in on her husband's assassination. Why else would she have been in the solarium that night other than to witness with her own eyes her husband's end?

What is certain is that her husband's assassins knew what they were doing. They blended redundancy (two missiles), technical sophistication (the missiles' heat-seeking guidance system), and predictability (hitting the Falcon 50 on its approach path).

> **NOTE TO ASSASSINS:** As in love and war, assassination shouldn't be reduced to one dimension. It's a way of thinking broadly.

TEND YOUR REPUTATION LIKE A RARE ORCHID

Always appear to be rock steady, rational, bound by your word. It will terrify your enemy as much as the act itself. And when the shooting stops and it's time to talk, he'll welcome you as a trustworthy interlocutor.

NEVER TAKE SIDES IN A DOGFIGHT

Beirut, March 8, 1985: At a little after nine in the morning, a Lebanese general called his American contact in Beirut. There was an urgent piece of business they needed to discuss, he said. And it couldn't be done over the phone.

Since the name of the American isn't important, I'll loan him one, Charlie. His organizational affiliation isn't important either. As for the Lebanese general, I'll leave him as the General.

Charlie looked at the stack of unanswered cables on his desk and thought about how shitty the traffic would be this time of the morning. There wasn't a single working stoplight between his office and the

General's, which sat in the foothills overlooking Beirut. It would take him at least an hour to get there.

"How about later this afternoon?" Charlie asked.

"No," the General said.

"The traffic's—"

"No. Get up here. Now."

The General had never pressed Charlie like this, making him wonder what could've gone wrong. It was all the odder considering that the Lebanese army was officered mainly by Christians and was in those days fawningly beholden to the United States. They looked at us as the only thing preventing the Muslims from swarming over the walls and cutting their throats.

Charlie caught the first traffic on the coast road, then a bottleneck at Chevrolet Circle. It took him a good fifteen minutes to get through it, and another ten to get up the hill to the General's office. The General's aide was waiting for him and ran over and opened Charlie's door: "Hurry! Run!"

They took the stairs two at a time. The General was out on the terrace, looking through a pair of binoculars, Beirut spread out below him like a cadaver on a slab. A compact man with close-cropped hair, the General's French-tailored suit fit him impeccably.

Just as Charlie joined the General on his balcony, a flash of light shot out from a cluster of dun tenements in the southern suburbs, instantly followed by the crack of an explosion. A fountain of ash smoke rose from next to a mosque. Laundry that had been hanging from balconies floated languidly to the ground.

The General and Charlie watched silently as the smoke fanned out across the southern suburbs. Charlie estimated the charge at several thousand pounds—a blast radius of an entire city block.

Charlie waited for the General to say something, but he was absorbed, looking through his binoculars. The phone in the office rang. The General handed Charlie the binoculars and went inside to answer it.

The General came back out on the balcony smiling: "At least fifty."

"Fifty what?"

"Fifty of them for the two hundred forty-one Marines they killed."

With a sinking feeling, it occurred to Charlie that he'd just witnessed a revenge attack for the truck bombing of the Marine barracks in Beirut that had occurred a year and a half before. Although the General didn't say it, the only reasonable explanation was that the Lebanese army had been behind the bombing he'd just witnessed. But what had been the target?

While no one had been arrested for the attack on the Marines, the assumption was that Shiite militants in the pay of Iran had done it. The Marines would be claimed by the same fictitious group that claimed the April 1983 American embassy bombing, the Islamic Jihad Organization. As we'd come to learn, Hajj Radwan headed the IJO. Fine, but what Charlie couldn't understand was what the IJO had to do with the people who'd just been murdered. Had their office been bombed or something?

It wasn't until he got back to his office that Charlie found out that the target of the car bomb he'd just witnessed was Muhammad Husayn Fadlallah, Lebanon's only ayatollah. He survived only thanks to well-wishers delaying him outside a mosque where he'd just delivered a sermon. The final toll was never officially established, but it was put at about eighty, many of them women and children. (This is the same bombing that Hezbollah would accuse me twenty-six years later of orchestrating.)

As best Charlie could determine, the Lebanese army had decided to murder Fadlallah for no other reason than every Friday he would stand in his pulpit and rail against Israel, the United States, and the Lebanese Christians. A blowtorch of hate, he was Lebanon's face of militant Islam.

The problem was there was no good evidence Fadlallah had anything to do with the attack on the Marines nor, for that matter, with any other attack on the United States. As we would determine, he was only the militants' unwitting mouthpiece. Even more tellingly, the Iranians themselves at one point considered assassinating Fadlallah because he was an ideological rival to Iran's Supreme Leader, its ayatollah in chief.

And it only gets messier: At the time of the attack, Hajj Radwan was in charge of Fadlallah's security. Where he was when the bomb went off, we don't know. But what we knew for certain was that it was Hajj Radwan who led the investigation and the arrest and execution of some dozen suspects.

If the Fadlallah attempt had been purely a Lebanese affair, it would have been an obscure footnote in Lebanon's history. But almost immediately word went around that the CIA was ultimately behind it. Rumor was taken as fact when Bob Woodward came out with his book *Veil*. In it he recounts how President Reagan's CIA director, Bill Casey, confessed on his deathbed that he, Casey, had personally ordered Fadlallah's assassination.

The CIA was left scratching its head. It knew it hadn't authorized Fadlallah's assassination. Was it possible that Casey had really told Woodward this? On the other hand, it didn't make much difference: The CIA was now indelibly painted with the same brush as the Lebanese army—clumsy thugs who didn't give a crap who they killed and maimed. Just as damaging, the Lebanese decided if Casey couldn't keep a secret, no one in the CIA could. It was something I had to learn to live with in Beirut.

A CLEAN ACT GIVES YOU MORAL FORCE

Beirut, December 1986: The Colonel pulled out a piece of paper from his breast pocket, unfolded it, and smoothed it out on the coffee table between us. I got up and moved a table lamp closer for better light. It was a military map of downtown Beirut. Someone had drawn in the Green Line with a thick blue grease pencil.

The Colonel cut a distinguished figure—slim, graying at the temples, a granite jaw, starched fatigues. The only thing missing was a regimental mustache. He was a Sunni from the north. His unit, an infantry brigade, was now on rotation on the Green Line.

"Look at this," he said.

He followed the Green Line with a finger until he came to where it jutted into the Christian lines like a fist punching through a curtain. "I intend to straighten it out right here. What do you think?"

It took me a moment before I figured out that he wanted my go-ahead to launch an attack to "straighten out" the Green Line. I can't remember which Muslim militia was on the other side, but I do remember wondering what kind of hell it would unleash.

I looked over at the Colonel to make sure he was serious. I'd only been introduced to him a couple of months before, not enough time to take his pulse. Maybe this was his idea of a joke. He hadn't touched his drink and was sober as far as I could tell.

"Aren't you asking the wrong person?" I said.

"I can't go to my command because they would only say no."

The Colonel said he would pass off the attack as a firefight that had gotten out of control. No one would know any better. If I could get a green light, he'd make the attack early the next morning.

I was now thirty-four and should have been smart enough to tell the Colonel fuck no. Instead, I offered to meet back up at midnight with an answer. I didn't say it, but what I really wanted to do was let the deputy chief (the chief was out of the country) know that the Colonel was about to breathe life back into the civil war. We should probably give Langley a heads-up.

The deputy chief would have the right perspective on this, I thought. Like me, guns and violence didn't sit well with him. When he first arrived in Beirut and was given a standard-issue 9mm Browning, he started playing around with it and accidentally pulled the trigger and put a hole in the ceiling. A major from Delta Force detailed to us cut a heart out of purple paper and pinned it over the hole. (The deputy's Purple Heart was still there the day I left Beirut.)

I gave the Colonel ten minutes to clear the building and then left. My first stop was Chuck's. In Beirut in those days, it was always better to move around in pairs. Chuck rolled his eyes when I told him I needed to ask the deputy permission to start World War III.

The question now became how to find the deputy. He was in the middle of a messy divorce and spent his nights catting around Beirut with young Lebanese girls. He'd lately fallen for a genuine beauty, which in turn led to his turning off his Motorola radio. A girl with a lot of spirit, we called her Frittata. He would later marry her.

Frittata didn't like the deputy's regular haunts, which meant we had the entire Christian enclave to cover. It may have been tiny in terms of square miles, but it was thick with restaurants and nightclubs.

We started out with the French restaurants along the Dog River. They were mostly empty, and it didn't take long to figure out the deputy and Frittata weren't there. Nor were they at the usual places in Kaslik or the half-dozen seaside restaurants they frequented. It was time to recalibrate our sights.

The first strip club we stopped at was like a dank cave, a couple of lurid mauve bulbs hanging from wires behind the bar. In the back near the toilets there was a glass disco floor, colored strobe lights flashing underneath in time with ABBA's "Dancing Queen." A slender Filipina in a bikini was dancing by herself, a languid beat behind the music.

I spotted our administrative officer at the end of the bar. A short, heavyset man, he was in his usual mechanic's jumpsuit. He'd served a handful of tours in Vietnam where he'd acquired a taste for Asian girls. Lizard-still, he stared at the Filipina.

I sauntered over to him while Chuck stayed in the door, his hand under his vest, gripping his SIG Sauer semiautomatic pistol. I whispered in the administrative officer's ear that I needed to find the deputy.

Not taking his eyes off the Filipina, he said: "Do you see him? Go fuck off."

I was about to ask him if he'd help us look for the deputy—drinks on me—but Chuck in the meantime had decided he didn't like the looks of a pair sitting in a dark corner. I grabbed Chuck by the elbow and pulled him outside before the SIG Sauer came out.

A half-dozen girlie bars later, I decided I was too tired to care whether the Green Line was jagged or straight. Anyhow, I had to get back for my meeting with the Colonel.

The Colonel listened impassively as I suggested that it was his decision alone whether to straighten out the Green Line or not, but I added that, personally, I didn't think it was a good idea. Who cared whether the Green Line was straight or jagged? He threw down his scotch, then told me he needed to get back to his troops.

As I let him out the door, it occurred to me that, now he'd let me into his circle of violence, I'd let him into mine.

THINK TWICE BEFORE SUMMONING THE DEVIL

The apartment where I normally met the Colonel was in an upscale building about three miles up the coast from Jounieh. Designed in a quarter circle, every apartment faced the sea. It came with an elegant tiled pool and a small harbor for residents to dock their boats. As I figured out, most of the neighbors used the apartments as fuck pads. Fine, but what I couldn't figure out was why they called them "chalets."

By our meeting the following week, the Colonel still hadn't straightened out the Green Line, and he never would. I thought about asking why the change of heart, but instead I poured him a tall whiskey. I picked out a fresh cigar from the humidor, clipped off the end, and handed it to him along with a box of long matches.

As he lit his cigar, I slipped a plain envelope across the coffee table, noting that there was an extra thousand dollars in it. I didn't say why, and he didn't ask. I lighted my own cigar. Aren't these things meant to give you time to formulate your thoughts?

"Do you want some real work?" I finally asked.

The question wasn't without its archaeology. For some time now, the Colonel had been telling me he intended to retire to Atlanta but that he first wanted to do an important service for the United States. It was up to us to decide what that service would be.

I pulled out of my backpack an eight-by-eleven manila envelope and pulled from it Hajj Radwan's picture—a copy of the same grainy passport picture the police had faxed to us. Enlarged, it made Hajj Radwan look even angrier and more menacing than the original fax. I turned it around so that the Colonel could take a good look.

He held it up in his hand to study it, then looked over at me: "I don't know him."

I would soon regret it, but I decided that full disclosure was in order. I told him how Hajj Radwan had kidnapped Buckley and very well might have been behind the attack on the Marines and the two embassy bombings. I even told him the story of how he'd arranged to snatch the original application from the jaws of the police. As I went on, the Colonel never took his eyes off Hajj Radwan's picture.

I wrote out Hajj Radwan's name in Arabic on a three-by-five card and pushed it over the table to him. He picked it up and looked at it.

I filled up our glasses. "I need your help finding him."

"I don't know where to start."

"But you probably have soldiers who do, maybe even some from his neighborhood."

I already knew the Colonel had half a dozen Shiite soldiers from the southern suburbs in his brigade.

The Colonel whistled and turned his head to look out toward the sea.

I sensed I was losing momentum, but now wasn't the time to give up.

"Couldn't they be persuaded to look into it, give us something? I don't know, an address?"

He looked at me unwaveringly for a full five seconds before he asked, "Is your intention to kill this man?"

I hesitated a fatal split second before answering. "Right now, let's just find him."

He pushed the three-by-five card back across the table toward me.

I didn't pick it up: "Keep it."

"I will remember the name."

I took the card and put it in the envelope. "So what do you think?" I said.

"Let me think. Maybe."

In Lebanon, you never hear "no." "Maybe" is the polite, perfectly serviceable stand-in for it. But in as much as I could read the Colonel's body language, his "maybe" was more like a "fuck no."

I thought how here's a military man who's been on the front lines of war for the last ten years, produced the deaths of an untold number of people, and now refuses to help hunt down a man who wouldn't hesitate to murder both of us. Did I scare him with the story about Hajj Radwan stealing his papers from the police?

After the Colonel left, I took my drink out onto the balcony. A young girl in a bikini was swimming laps in the pool. The underwater lights were on. She looked too poised and classy to be someone's mistress. But who knows; there's so little I understand about this country.

SOMETIMES RAKING THROUGH THE ASHES ONLY GETS YOU MORE ASHES

Beirut, October 2009: On a trip to Beirut for the Hariri Tribunal, I call the Colonel to catch up on old times. He's now retired, but instead of immigrating to the United States, he's in business here. We meet in the restaurant on the rooftop terrace of a fancy boutique hotel in Ashrafi-yah, not far from where the Lebanese president-elect was assassinated in September 1982.

The Colonel has exchanged his starched fatigues for an expensive Italian suit and a hand-sewn silk tie. He's as slim as ever, his upright bearing still intact. He's apparently done well, a man no longer in need of the CIA's money or, for that matter, me.

We laugh about old times, how posh and intolerably chic Beirut's become, how the Lebanese have shed bloodlust for money. But isn't that the way these things usually go?

When we get around to political gossip, I drop it in—as naturally as I can—that it's something the way Hajj Radwan was caught red-handed in the murder of Hariri. The Colonel pretends not to hear and looks around for the waiter. "Sorry, I have an appointment. Maybe we can have dinner one night." He catches a waiter's eye and makes as if he's scribbling on his hand.

I know there's no point in drilling a dry well, but I've come a long way and don't intend to let him go without something: "So, no opinion about Hariri?"

"I believe your question should be why Israel decided to kill Hariri." When I look at him in disbelief, he says: "You know as well as I do that the Israelis will never leave us in peace."

The cockeyed conspiracy theory that Israel killed Hariri started even before the smoke cleared that Valentine's Day. The truly inventive souls swore they'd seen the Israeli F-16 that had bombed Hariri's convoy. And now with news of the tribunal's indictments, the latest twist is that Israel somehow manipulated Lebanese telephone records in order to frame Hezbollah. Could the Colonel possibly believe this crap?

But never one to abandon a lost, dead, and buried cause, I ask, "So how then did the Israelis get to Hajj Radwan and murder him?"

"May I invite you to come up to my village?"

And there it is, I think: a genuine offer of hospitality to avoid the truth.

As I watch the Colonel disappear into the elevator, I think how you should never underestimate the upside of ostentatious savagery. Even from the other side of the grave, Hajj Radwan still terrifies the crap out of the Lebanese.

DON'T NEGLECT THE LOCAL MUSEUMS

Now that I've been publicly linked to Hajj Radwan's murder, I'll never get a chance to visit his mausoleum in Nabatiyah. This leaves me to picture it as something like the Gothic reliquaries my mother used to drag me through when I was a kid in Europe—hushed, dark, eerie. A peephole into a very alien world.

But I didn't need to see Hajj Radwan's tomb to know that he lived in a world where moral ambivalence doesn't exist. There's no kicking the can down the road, no twiddling your thumbs waiting for bad karma to catch up with your enemies. It's a world of brutal calculations, where every important decision comes with a built-in on/off switch. Murder is like breathing—no blessing or license needed. It may all sound tribal, primeval, and repugnant to us, but it's the way many parts of the world work.

People who live close to the bone don't have a choice other than to preserve their reputations. Call it honor, a culture of shame, or whatever you like. The point is, you don't go around making empty threats, you don't miss, you don't kill the wrong person, and you don't wander into quagmires you don't know how to get out of. And God forbid, if you ever do, you never acknowledge the mistake.

The brutal economy of life means you can't afford to become tethered to a failing enterprise. There's no tolerance for thoughtlessly flipping the on/off switch up and down, no changing horses midstream, no waiting around for a better opportunity to come along.

So it is, the assassin, with each and every act, demonstrates he's capable of bringing a quick, discrete, cathartic end to an enemy. Doing it expeditiously and right the first time gives him moral force; there are no points for a good try. You don't threaten to get bin Laden "dead or alive" and then wait a decade to do it.

It's with his reputation in mind that Hajj Radwan never advertised an assassination in advance. While he, of course, didn't want to lose the element of surprise, he also didn't want to make a promise he very well might not be able to keep. There is little doubt that this is what was at play with the first American embassy bombing in April 1983. By never acknowledging it was an attempt on Ambassador Habib, he let people believe it was a straightforward attack on the American embassy. And indeed, it's the way it's going to go down in history.

Like the Colonel, Hajj Radwan could only have shaken his head in disbelief at the failed attempt on Fadlallah. He couldn't have missed the sheer ineptness of it: an ally out of control, the wrong target, bad execution. Could it only have served as an encouragement to him to press on all the harder against the United States and its impotent Lebanese allies, the Maronite Christians?

No doubt he took away the same lesson from the two Iraq wars where the United States tried and failed to assassinate Saddam Hussein. Its shiny and expensive technology counted for nothing. Again, the same went for bin Laden. How could the United States lose the tallest Arab in the world and then flail around in Afghanistan for no purpose at all? It clearly had failed to heed that old piece of Persian wisdom: When you decide to kill the king, kill the king.

SUCCESS IS THE KEY TO LEVERAGE

And by the way, never underestimate good old garden-variety ruthlessness. Sadly, it's what keeps a lot of us in line and society running smoothly.

I'll always remember the time the local florist assassinated one of my uncles (by marriage). She was good, bringing to bear impeccable intelligence, lightning speed, and total surprise. It came out of nowhere too, and in its fashion proved lethal.

To all appearances, my uncle was a happily married man. His wife was a class act, his children polite and dutiful. He often went on about the sanctity of marriage, how through thick and thin a man must stick with his wife, how monogamy is of a piece with the underlying order of the universe. My uncle worked hard. On his time off, he paraded his family around town. His wife turned their Santa Monica house into a gem of propriety and order.

One Valentine's Day, my uncle was jammed up between appointments but had just enough time to drop by the florist around the corner from his office. He asked for her twenty-four freshest red roses—twelve to be sent to his wife at home and twelve to another address.

The florist asked my uncle whether he wanted cards to go along with the bouquets. He thought about it for a second before he picked out two cards and jotted down quick notes on each. He licked the envelopes closed, making double sure there wasn't a mix-up with the addresses.

As soon as my uncle was out the door, the suspicious florist opened the envelopes to take a look. Confirming one bouquet was for my uncle's mistress, she switched the cards and sent the bouquets on their way.

By the end of Valentine's Day, my uncle's life came crashing to earth: His wife divorced him, and his mistress left him. (The wife got the Santa Monica house.) As for the florist, anyone with a secret steered well clear of her.

From time to time I wonder about her and all the other people with moral on/off switches. How is it that as soon as she decided my uncle deserved it she didn't hesitate to pull the trigger?

I used to think the ability to make instantaneous decisions was encoded in our DNA. You're either fast on the trigger or you're not. But a Navy SEAL told me that, in fact, it's possible to condition your brain to speed up your reactions. It has something to do with adjusting the amygdala. At the sound of gunfire, you either run or fire back, not stand there with your hands in your pockets.

Or maybe it's just plain common sense. After the botched Fadlallah attempt, how could the Colonel take the CIA seriously? Its putative henchmen didn't even know how to use a weapon thousands of Lebanese had mastered, the car bomb. Was this the best the CIA could do?

If I'd sat the Colonel down and told him the Lebanese army did it all on its own, I'm sure he wouldn't have believed me. Wasn't the Lebanese army an American proxy, at our beck and call? Surely, the General would first have come to Charlie to ask permission to kill the man. If we couldn't arrange that, we shouldn't be in the game.

And it wasn't as if I had a good argument on my side: The United States has a long, miserable record of mismanaging foreign proxies. Take Vietnam. By 1963 the Kennedy administration had had it with Ngo Dinh Diem, South Vietnam's inept and stubborn president. But rather than do the job itself, it started a whisper campaign that we'd all be better off with Diem out of the game. And indeed, it wouldn't be long before the generals overthrew and murdered him. But as it turned out, Diem's successor was worse, proving the dictum you can't put political murder on remote control. You're either all in or not at all.

I also have to wonder whether the Colonel didn't look at Hajj Radwan as something of a Robin Hood, a man who served all Lebanese, not just his sect. He had given the Lebanese a sense of agency, one that they'd been without for thousands of years. He'd turned violence outward, away from civil war, and directed it at foreigners. In spite of being a

Christian, could the Colonel not have had a grudging respect for Hajj Radwan?

This is all to say that the night I pitched the Colonel to help assassinate Hajj Radwan, I suspect he thought it was a lot more likely Hajj Radwan would get to me before I got to him. The Colonel may have been fast on the draw, but it didn't mean it was a good idea to sign up with the gang that couldn't shoot straight.

NOTE TO ASSASSINS: Just as you wouldn't buy a pig in a poke or go on a wild-goose chase, pick your fights judiciously.

RENT THE GUN,
BUY THE BULLET

Just as there are animals that let other animals do their killing for them—vultures and hyenas—employ a trusted proxy when one's available. If the plot's uncovered, you'll have someone to sacrifice.

EVERYBODY TALKS ABOUT THE WEATHER . . . WE DON'T

Paris, December 1988: Mother was an industrial smoker. Whenever she'd visit me on an overseas posting, she'd always get off the plane with a carry-on full of Marlboros, a dozen cartons or so. How she made it through customs all those years, I'm not sure. It probably had something to do with her being built like a squat castle and possessing a bright, open face. She looked nothing like a smuggler.

As soon as I'd install her in her hotel, she'd insist on an elaborate lunch, bottles of both white and red wine. She usually wouldn't touch her food, though, instead she'd sip her wines, smoke one cigarette after another, and listen to how exactly I intended to entertain her during her visit. Although, by anyone's standards, her idea of "entertainment" was more like a forced march.

Mother didn't tour so much as she carpet-bombed. She insisted on missing nothing, on and off the beaten track. We had traipsed through some of the world's most accommodating and posh capitals and a few of its more exotic sumps—Dushanbe, Tajikistan, for example—but Mother's visits to Paris were always a nightmare.

The trouble was, she knew the place too well. She had dragged me there as a child so she and her bohemian friends could spend their days in faux-serious discussions in Left Bank cafés. Nights, it was usually a seedy transvestite bar they'd taken a liking to. In May 1968, she hauled me back again so I could see firsthand what a revolution looked like. She'd countenance nothing less than authentic Paris, but my portfolio was the Middle East, not France. The handful of French *authentiques* I knew weren't interested in entertaining mothers. I knew a few down-at-the-heel bistros, but that was it. No, I'd have to come up with a serious expedient. And then I got this blade of an icy thought: Why not borrow Mother to help recruit la femme Nikita!

This part takes a bit of background. A few months earlier, as I was about to transfer from Beirut to Paris, I made the rounds of my Lebanese friends to cadge names of people I could call on to jump-start my tour. A journalist who liked a good prank thought about it for a moment before he asked, "Do you want to meet an interesting French girl? She eats only what's alive."

He'd first heard of her—I'll call her Alice—by reputation. It was in the early days of the Lebanese civil war when she showed up in Beirut to fight for the Palestinians, for Yasser Arafat's Fatah, to be precise. She must have been something like eighteen at the time and, from the descriptions he heard, a real thoroughbred—beautiful and precociously well educated.

Eventually, the journalist saw a TV clip of her running out into the street, firing her Kalashnikov in the direction of a Christian position, a bandolier of ammunition draped over one shoulder. After she'd empty her Kalashnikov, she, like her young Palestinian comrades, would duck back behind a building to reload. "Her eyes were creased, smiling," he said. "You just knew she loved it."

For a time, Alice dated the Red Prince, the notorious Fatah security chief who ruled Beirut with a bloody, iron fist. He had a reputation for killing anyone who appeared to be even a remote threat to the Palestinians. After the Israelis found out the Red Prince had been one of the masterminds behind the Munich Olympics massacre, they assassinated him with a car bomb—en route (ironically, given my current intentions) to his mother's birthday party.

I wrote down Alice's name, reminding my journalist friend to see if he could find a Paris telephone number for her.

Not long after I arrived in Paris, I ran a trace on Alice. Langley fired back what's called a "screamer." Alice wasn't just a pretty girl with a colorful past, she was an in-the-flesh Angel of Death, almost certainly connected to a half dozen assassinations. One of her boyfriends came out of her apartment and put the key in the ignition only to have the car explode, killing him instantly. At some point, she joined the armed French leftist group Action Directe and then somehow ended up connected with the German Red Army Faction, the assassins of Deutsche Bank chairman Alfred Herrhausen. Her new friends, as they prided themselves, were the kind of people who spend their days plotting murder rather than standing out on the front lawn talking about the weather. There also was the little question about whether she had set up the Red Prince for assassination.

The more I read about this female hyena, the straighter my hair stood on end. I couldn't understand why she wasn't in jail. By the time I got to the end of the cable, I decided the last thing I needed on a new tour was to hang out with this girl. But with Mother on the way, I had a change of heart. And who could tell whether she might get me back into the game in Beirut.

Alice's radical past would still be a fresh memory in Beirut. I'd have to actually meet her to find out if she was in a position to dig up a lead on Hajj Radwan. Or, who knows, she might be prepared to serve him up on a platter à la (maybe) the Red Prince. Or, what the hell, pull the trigger herself if she could get close enough. And as long as I'd gotten this far, what better way to approach her than hiding in the wake of Battleship Mom?

When I asked a French police contact to help me find Alice, she looked at me as if I'd lost my mind. It took her a couple of days before she came back with a phone number for Alice, a Left Bank bookstore.

I had no trouble getting Alice on the phone, but when I did, my French, a language I'd never quite mastered, failed me. Mercifully, she switched to English: "Please, what is it that you want?"

I mumbled something about having a common friend in Lebanon. The icy silence that came back down the line suggested I wasn't retaking ground. So I blurted it out: "My mother's in town. Would you like to join us for dinner?"

I knew I sounded like a total idiot, maybe insane. I waited for Alice to slam down the phone. Instead, she asked, "Where?" I let her pick.

And that's how I ended up on a date with an authentic Femme Nikita, with my mother as chaperone and (although she didn't know it) a beard in the bargain.

Mother and I got to the restaurant first. She immediately decided she didn't like the place, if for no other reason than that it was full of tourists happily consulting their guidebooks and chatting about Paris's splendors. She took pointed offense at a table of older Germans in pastel and earth tones. (They looked pleasant enough to me.)

Mother put on her tortoiseshell reading glasses and picked up the wine list. After a moment, she looked up: "And who is this woman we're having dinner with?"

Before I could answer, I spotted a middle-aged woman stalled in the front door, obviously looking for someone she didn't know. Even in the dimness, I could see Alice's days as a siren were long past: She was syphilitic thin and hard as flint. I half stood up and waved. Alice came over to our table.

She coldly shook my mother's hand, looking her up and down with what I took to be a sneer. Alice sat down and half turned in her seat to look for a waiter. Not seeing one, she sighed. My mother asked if she could pour Alice a glass of wine. Alice looked at her with a painted smile: "I don't drink."

I looked over and caught Mother sniffing the way she does when she suspects something is off. She started to rummage through her purse, but rather than her claws, she pulled out her silver etui and her cheap Bic lighter. She lit a Marlboro and for what seemed an eternity inspected the lighted end.

Through dinner, the conversation was painfully ordinary—the weather, Paris prices, the hideous traffic. I tried to get in a couple of questions about Beirut, probing for something I could pry open with Mom safely back across the Atlantic, but Alice ignored my every foray. For a second, I wondered if my cop friend hadn't put me on to the wrong Alice. I had to remind myself that my friend had assured me the police knew exactly who she was.

Her chicken fricassee done, Alice abruptly stood up and announced she couldn't stay for dessert. She had a rendezvous, she said. She left us to pay the bill.

THE KEY THAT OPENS IS THE KEY THAT RUSTS

If I'd had a traditional romance in mind, that one dinner was more than enough to cool any ardor. And not to mention that I, no doubt, was too clunky for Alice's tastes. But what I couldn't get out of my mind was the outside chance that Alice had run across Hajj Radwan during her Beirut days. The Red Prince—her ex-boyfriend—had initially recruited Hajj Radwan into Fatah and had served as his mentor during his rookie years. Had the Red Prince introduced Hajj Radwan to Alice? Had Hajj Radwan fought side by side with Alice? Unlikely, but I'd never know until I could sit Alice down again and ask her.

A couple of weeks after my mother left, I called Alice. She sounded friendlier this time and even suggested we get together. She said she was at a conference the following day in the late afternoon. Maybe we could meet for coffee afterward?

"On second thought," she said, "why don't you come along and sit through it with me?"

I had to wonder what sort of conference a French assassin would attend, but I immediately agreed. She gave me the address of a hotel in Montparnasse I'd never heard of. Little did I know that three blocks away, less than a year later, a wonderful lead to Hajj Radwan would go up in smoke, literally.

When I left work to meet Alice, it was raining, traffic at a standstill. By the time the taxi finally made it across the Seine, I was already twenty minutes late. In frustration, I jumped out and half ran down the Boulevard Montparnasse.

When I got to the address, I found a modern, boxy hotel, the kind of place Parisians have fought valiantly to keep out of their city. But if banality truly is the essence of a good smoke screen, the place couldn't be beat. Who would think of looking for la femme Nikita in France's version of a Motel 6? The concierge directed me to the conference room on the mezzanine level.

The door was closed. I could hear a man's voice inside hectoring a hushed room about something. I was about to let myself in when I noticed next to the door an easel with a placard on it. There were three small letters at the bottom right, EST.

Vaguely familiar, I leaned over to read the fine print: Erhard Seminars Training.

Fuck.

The little I knew about est was that it was some New Age, California-based cult where you aren't allowed to piss for hours so you can have the pleasure of being verbally assaulted for every real and imagined character flaw inflicted on you at birth. Enlightenment through bladder distress. Okay, I had enough flaws for est to incarcerate me for life. But now wasn't the time I needed to be reminded of it.

I let go of the knob, turned around, and slinked away like a bilge rat abandoning a sinking ship. I never called Alice again.

How could I have been so stupid to think Alice would ever be able to help me hunt down and murder Hajj Radwan? I should have seen right away she was a flake who couldn't be trusted with a sensitive mission. If I'd sent her to Beirut to help me find Hajj Radwan, she would only have kept looking for herself. I'd have done better recruiting Mom to do it. At least she and I had had a womb in common.

THE RIGHT STUFF

When I was a young man, an old family friend once put his hand around my shoulder and offered me a little piece of wisdom. "Finding the right girl is like testing a used car. The first thing you need to do is take her out on a hard drive to see what parts fall off." He was half serious.

Before deciding whether he would make it with a girl or not, he'd take her on a long brutal road trip to Baja California . . . usually in a small sports car. They'd camp along the way, whatever the weather. If she survived the scorpions that crawl around Mexican beaches, there was a chance they might have a good run.

"Most didn't," he said, squeezing my shoulder. "You find out pretty quick who the batshit crazy ones are."

Hezbollah has a more conventional way of selecting new recruits.

They'd line them up on a very hot day, warning them to remain rock-still. Just as the first of them would start to succumb to the heat and wobble, a drill instructor would fire a Kalashnikov down the line—at eye level. In the tape I saw, one of the new recruits is hit in the ear, falls to the ground, writhing in pain and holding the bloody stump where his ear used to be. For his efforts, he was selected out because he didn't have the fortitude to fight in a war.

Hajj Radwan had more of an artisan's touch to hiring his people. Corporate America would call it an "internal referral"—someone already working for a company who will vouch for an applicant. The idea is an insider is not about to recommend a dud and risk losing his job. Or in Hajj Radwan's regime of discipline, his life.

Hajj Radwan only took in people who were an open book to him. Many of them he knew from birth, had grown up with, and/or was bound to by marriage or blood. The point is he needed to be able to examine a person's entire life cycle before he could ever trust him—how he coped with extended families, how he did in pre-K, who he dated, how he related to Islam.

As the Lebanese police discovered from analyzing telephone data, all of Hariri's assassins were in one way or another attached to a small town in southern Lebanon called Nabatiyah. Hajj Radwan's brother-in-law was from there, as were a lot of the street men who tracked Hariri the morning of his murder. (Hajj Radwan's own village is close to Nabatiyah.)

But none of this is to say Hajj Radwan engaged in nepotism. He wasn't a godfather who reflexively took family into the business. He knew relatives, as well as anyone, can get you killed. As for friends, Hajj Radwan looked at them as a frivolity and a self-indulgence, never as ready-made recruits.

Hajj Radwan also very early on learned he could dispense with the social conveniences and arrangements most of us take for granted. He strangled in himself any inclination to believe anyone could ever truly like you. It's a comforting delusion, and nothing more. For Hajj Radwan, the only true bond is the threat of pain.

As rigorous as his selection system was, Hajj Radwan understood that Laws #7 and #8 (Vet Your Proxies in Blood) come as a pair—you test, you recruit, you test. A candidate's advertised qualifications might look fabulous on paper, but only in the crucible of war will you know for sure. Let someone spend weeks under Israeli bombardment and not end up cracking, and you just might have the man you need.

As far as I know, Hajj Radwan's system never failed him. There is no record of malingerers, traitors, or defectors from his ranks. In other words, Hajj Radwan would never have gone near a flake like Alice, let alone taken her on as part of his organization.

WHERE THERE'S SEX, THERE'S DEATH

Marrakesh, January 22, 1983: It's not generally well-known, but Hassan II, the late king of Morocco, was one of the most proficient and prolific assassins of modern times. His customary practice was to drop his victims out of a helicopter over the Atlantic and let the sharks conveniently dispose of the remains. But when the occasion called for it, the king knew how to improvise.

As the official version went, on the evening of the twenty-second, King Hassan's security chief, Ahmed Dlimi, was driving outside Marrakesh when his car was broadsided by a truck traveling at high speed. Dlimi died instantly, and the truck's driver immediately was detained for reckless driving and manslaughter. The police quickly closed the case as a simple accident. But it was the naive Moroccan who didn't suspect the king had had his security chief murdered.

But Dlimi's murder nonetheless came as a surprise to many Moroccans. A faithful subject and an efficient intelligence chief, Dlimi had kept Morocco in good order for more than a decade. He'd assassinated his predecessor on the orders of King Hassan and strangled many a coup attempt in the cradle. It was Dlimi who'd overseen the notorious murder of a Moroccan dissident in Paris in 1965. Dlimi wasn't the king's personal assassin, but he came close. In other words, King Hassan had to have had a very good reason for murdering him.

The suspicion was that the king had caught Dlimi plotting against him in some sort of palace intrigue, maybe planning some sort of putsch. But because of the political delicacy of the matter, the king, rather than jail Dlimi, felt he needed to foreshorten the course of justice. Again, it was only a theory.

If there was one thing that Hassan had learned over the years, it was to keep his own counsel, especially when it came to foreigners. One rare exception was his good friend General Vernon Walters, the former CIA deputy director and ambassador to Germany. The king never forgot that Walters had given him a ride on a tank when the king was a child during World War II, and their friendship remained uninterrupted ever since.

A few years after Dlimi's death, on a visit to Rabat, Walters asked the king about him. The king chuckled: "My friend, if you only knew what I have had to endure. I shall tell you."

The king said that he had started to hear stories that Dlimi's drinking had gotten out of hand. On occasion, he himself could smell liquor on Dlimi's breath. The king knew he couldn't have a drunk as his security chief, but on the other hand, he wasn't sure exactly what to do about it. Simply firing Dlimi would set off a flight of unsettling rumors about coups and so on. Even the intimation of disloyalty in the royal inner circle doesn't serve the interest of an absolute monarch.

One night at a little after two in the morning, Dlimi called Hassan and excitedly told him that he'd caught the king's wife sleeping with a captain of the palace guard. Dlimi was obviously drunk, his words slurred and incoherent. The king didn't know what to think and told Dlimi they'd talk in the morning.

The next day the king discreetly looked into Dlimi's charge and found out there was no truth to it. The king started to think about the best way to ease out Dlimi. But before he could come to a decision, he heard from a good source that Dlimi had told a Saudi envoy about the queen's infidelity. Hassan didn't need anyone to tell him that his rivals, the Saudi royals, were now tittering about King Hassan's unfaithful wife. Thus, with his honor at stake, he had no choice.

Hassan, of course, knew he could get away with it. He controlled the entire food chain, from the police to the press. He had plenty of people he could trust to do the job right, just as Dlimi once could have.

> **NOTE TO ASSASSINS:** When it comes to looking for a proxy, don't forget that a dead lion is always better than a living dog.

VET YOUR PROXIES IN BLOOD

Assassination is the most sophisticated and delicate form of warfare, only to be entrusted to the battle-hardened and those who've already made your enemy bleed.

A DREAM WITH DARK EDGES

Omagh, County Tyrone, August 23, 1974: In the IRA's eyes, Detective Inspector Peter Flanagan was a traitor. Not only was he a Catholic who'd gone to work for the Royal Ulster Constabulary (the Protestant-controlled police in Northern Ireland), he'd also made the inexpiable sin of going into the Special Branch. The Special Branch had a well-earned reputation for helping Britain's Special Air Service finger IRA operatives for assassination. In other words, Flanagan had written his own death sentence.

The IRA selected Sean O'Callaghan to assassinate Flanagan for no better reason than that O'Callaghan was on active IRA service, a so-called volunteer. Although he had never assassinated anyone before, O'Callaghan's mettle had been tested in a mortar attack on a British army base that resulted in the death of a female soldier. The IRA told

O'Callaghan that Flanagan deserved it because he'd participated in brutal interrogations of IRA operatives.

A man of habit, Flanagan would eat lunch every day at the same Omagh pub, a place called Broderick's. He always parked his VW Beetle in the same spot on Georges Street and sat on the same stool at the end of the bar. He read the *Irish Independent* as he ate.

O'Callaghan knew enough about an operative's work to know he needed to reconnoiter Broderick's in advance, map the place out in his mind. He also needed to see Flanagan with his own eyes. When the gunplay starts, there's no time for dithering or making the mistake of shooting the wrong person.

Flanagan was at the far end of the bar on the day O'Callaghan cased Broderick's, right where he was supposed to be. O'Callaghan ordered a half pint of Guinness at the opposite end. Having finished his beer and seen what he needed to, O'Callaghan left.

When it came to putting a team together, the IRA produced Paul Norney, a sixteen-year-old boy from Belfast. It didn't care that Norney was on the run, suspected of the murder of a British soldier. The other accomplice detailed to O'Callaghan was a young girl who he knew only by the name he loaned her, Lulu. The IRA told him she could drive, and that's all that mattered.

O'Callaghan had his doubts, though. He'd heard of another operation where a young girl was recruited to drive for a job, but in fact she couldn't shift gears. O'Callaghan made Lulu show him she could drive. She did fine.

The guns were hand-delivered a couple of days before they were set to go: two new snub-nosed Magnum .357s.

The night before, O'Callaghan, Norney, and Lulu spent the night at an IRA safe house in Carrickmore. Everyone stayed up until early in the morning. At one point, things got tense when Lulu started to tease Norney about his age. Norney didn't take it well, and O'Callaghan had to pull her out in the hall to tell her to knock it off. "It was a prestige operation and we wanted it to go well," O'Callaghan would later write in his memoir.

In the morning, all three went to a garage, where O'Callaghan walked up to the owner and identified himself as an IRA volunteer. O'Callaghan said he needed to borrow a car. Intimidated to the bone by the IRA, the garage owner didn't ask why. As they left, O'Callaghan told him to hold off reporting the theft to the police.

As they set off for Omagh, another car went on ahead to check for patrols and flying roadblocks. O'Callaghan had told the driver of the other car to signal by tapping his brakes if he saw anything O'Callaghan needed to worry about.

As they got closer to Omagh, the lookout car raced ahead and then came back flashing its lights: It's a go.

Lulu parked in the no-parking zone next to Broderick's. O'Callaghan and Norney got out to check to see if Flanagan's Beetle was there.

Norney looked in first to make sure Flanagan was in his spot at the end of the bar. He told O'Callaghan he was.

O'Callaghan: "You sure?"

Norney was.

O'Callaghan: "Okay, let's go."

O'Callaghan went in and spotted Flanagan sitting at the end of the bar, reading the *Irish Independent*.

As soon as Flanagan saw O'Callaghan and Norney coming toward him, he understood what was about to happen. "No . . . please . . . no!" Flanagan said.

O'Callaghan started jerking the trigger of his revolver. Flanagan stood up and staggered back in a futile attempt to save himself. He stumbled and fell through the bathroom door. O'Callaghan continued shooting bullets into him.

Flanagan was still, face-forward on the bathroom floor. O'Callaghan instinctively knew Flanagan was dead.

As O'Callaghan reloaded his gun to calm himself, he only now noticed everyone in the pub staring at him. The owner stood frozen, an empty glass in his hand and a towel in the other. A woman said something he didn't catch. O'Callaghan turned to her: "Just sit down, shut up, and nothing will happen to you."

O'Callaghan and Norney came out of the bar and crossed the road to the getaway car. Norney climbed in first. But before O'Callaghan could get in his door, Lulu pulled away, dragging O'Callaghan down the street. He shouted at her to get it together. She stopped, and he got in. He turned to Norney and told him to reload his gun.

Lulu was far down the road before O'Callaghan realized she was heading down a one-way street. He told her to turn around. He didn't care that they'd have to drive back past Broderick's.

"Is he dead?" Lulu asked.

O'Callaghan: "Yes, he's dead all right."

Norney giggled: "Dead? 'Course he's fucking dead."

After they abandoned the stolen car by the side of the road, an IRA team collected them with a van and drove to a cottage in the country.

It was only then that O'Callaghan took stock of the truth that he'd just murdered a man in cold blood. He wrote in his memoir that it was something he'd spend the rest of his life thinking about.

After three hours, all three were moved again, this time to a house near Carrickmore. When they arrived at the back of the house, a middle-aged priest came out to meet them. It was a man O'Callaghan knew, someone who'd loaned his house to the IRA before.

The priest knew that they'd just murdered Flanagan. As they entered the house, he blessed all three with holy water. The priest told O'Callaghan over dinner: "Flanagan was an abominable man who sold his soul to the devil." As they were about to move yet another time, the priest again blessed them.

Lulu went back to Belfast, and O'Callaghan never saw her again. Norney and a couple of other IRA operatives were later arrested in Manchester after firing shots into a restaurant that had just given them bad service.

In 1988, a depressed O'Callaghan turned himself in to the police. He received a sentence of 539 years, including time for Flanagan's murder. He was released from prison in 1996 by royal prerogative.

S ean O'Callaghan is a gaunt man, caved in as if life's eaten him away from the inside. One moment he's leaning against the kitchen counter, immobile, a cup of coffee steady in his hand. The next he's pacing back and forth like a caged animal, as if he's in a hurry to say what he has to and get away.

O'Callaghan, in fact, has been confessing for years. In his memoir, he spares himself and the IRA nothing. It reads like something you'd tell to a priest in the privacy of a confessional rather than a mea culpa for an unsympathetic and uncomprehending world.

O'Callaghan joined the IRA in 1969 when he was sixteen. A bomb he was making exploded in his parents' house. He was sent to jail for it. After his release, he did one odd job after another for the IRA. But mostly he mixed up chemicals for car bombs.

O'Callaghan resigned from the IRA in 1976 and moved to London where he married and opened a cleaning business. When the IRA tried to reenlist him, he decided to turn informer for Irish intelligence. He would say later it was the 1979 assassination of the queen's cousin Lord Mountbatten that had finally turned him.

The exact nature of O'Callaghan's service to Irish intelligence is unclear. One version has it that O'Callaghan tipped the authorities off to a shipment of seven tons of Kalashnikovs sent to the IRA by the Irish-American crime boss Whitey Bulger. In 1984, O'Callaghan supposedly helped foil an assassination attempt on Prince Charles and Princess Diana during a Duran Duran and Dire Straits concert.

Down on his luck, O'Callaghan tried to retool himself as a security consultant. But business was never good, and his fortunes continued to slide. In 2006, a year after I'd interviewed him, two young men he'd met at a gay bar in West London tied him to a chair with electrical wire while they robbed the apartment he was temporarily staying at.

The occasion for my meeting O'Callaghan was to interview him for a documentary on car bombs. Camera on, O'Callaghan described how he could mix enough material for a car bomb in one day—about five hundred kilos of nitrobenzene fertilizer. It was the same chemical composition responsible for turning Northern Ireland's cities into smoking ghost towns.

O'Callaghan insists that the bombs he made were designed to destroy empty buildings rather than people.

When I asked him whether he'd personally set off a car bomb, he answered: "I did, yeah, um, well in the country, quite a few of them."

When I asked if they killed anyone, he said: "No, no, there was nobody killed or injured in any of the car bombs I was involved in." But he quickly added he would have been very happy to kill a cop or a British soldier.

O'Callaghan's ambivalence about violence reminds me of the Italian Red Brigades, another set of Catholics who turned to violence in order to right a political wrong. Although dyed-in-the-wool Marxists, they never could bring themselves to entirely abandon the Catholic faith. The two founders of the Red Brigades, Renato Curcio and Margherita Cagol, married in a church. And like the European bourgeoisie, they took August off.

It seems to me both O'Callaghan and the Red Brigades lacked the will and stamina to see things through to the end, to do what had to be done. They certainly never showed they were prepared to meet the end Hajj Radwan met in Damascus. They were weakened by some indefinable ambivalence about violence, all but ensuring they would fail at it. Hajj

Radwan's suicide bombers' deaths were an absolute given, but they never lost their way, stalled, or turned around.

There are other little things that tell the same story. For instance, IRA "volunteers" see no problem living in British government–subsidized housing or taking unemployment checks. It's something Hajj Radwan never would have considered, no matter how short on money he got. For him, any dependency on any enemy for anything is a sign of weakness and vulnerability. How do you convincingly conduct a rebellion when you're on the dole? Or, for that matter, how do you put yourself beyond compromise? Not only does it send the wrong message to an enemy, it also offers him innumerable portals of entry.

Did the IRA's ambiguity about violence—and in particular the belief that blowing up buildings wins wars—fatally undermine its cause? I suspect so. Destroying other people's stuff rarely turns the tide of battle. It's the same with symbolic violence. O'Callaghan was right when he said the IRA had made an unforgivable error in murdering Lord Mountbatten, a man without power. It won them nothing, but it cost them a lot.

SEND ONLY YOUR VERY BEST

There was a time when I still believed in the possibility of repairing relationships. What it meant for me in Beirut was that every couple of weeks I'd catch a ride on a Black Hawk helicopter over to Cyprus to see my wife and children. Langley had kindly allowed them to set up in Larnaca to be near me but out of the line of fire. They thought it would keep the embers of marriage alive.

Like any plan infallible on paper, this one fell apart at first contact. A Libyan assassin with American blood on his hands moved next door to my wife's apartment, giving Langley a case of the vapors. My wife and children were bundled off to Brussels on the first flight out. My visits became less frequent, and the marriage suffered accordingly. (It was okay, I reassured myself. Life could damn well take a break while I was on the hunt for the world's greatest assassin.)

One Christmas, Mother decided she would fix things. With no advance warning, she gathered her grandchildren around her: "My dears, I've made a decision."

She turned first to my eldest, Justine. She knew Grandma well enough to know something was up. She'd recently overheard me calling Mother a spiteful old cow, but she didn't understand the language of adulthood well enough to not take me seriously.

"Come sit by me," Mother said, patting a place on the sofa next to her for Justine to sit. "I have something to ask you."

Justine did as she was told, not saying a word.

"Tell me who Philip of Macedon was," Grandmother said.

Justine, only eleven, had no idea.

"He's Philip the Second, Alexander the Great's father." Mother lit a cigarette, tilted back her head, and blew a thick cloud of smoke at the ceiling.

"He had a broken tibia," she resumed. "And surely you know he was assassinated."

"Who?" Justine asked.

"Philip. And what do you think about the theory that Alexander himself was assassinated?"

When Justine didn't say anything, Mother guffawed: "Your parents are so pitifully ignorant. Do they teach you nothing? That does it—this summer I'm coming back to take you to Pella so you can see for yourself Philip's leg."

I'd grown up with Mother's Alexander the Great stories and how she'd embraced the Great Men school of history, a world of honor where men did their duty, no questions asked, no dithering. But this was all new to Justine, and she had no idea why she was going to be dragged off to Macedonia.

I had no great hope that a quick trip to Macedonia to look at Philip's skeleton would turn Justine into a classics scholar or make her mindful of her duties. But she did come home with another lesson of sorts.

While transiting the Frankfurt airport, Mother decided she needed to stock up on cigarettes. The duty-free queue snaked around the store, putting everyone in a foul mood. That is except for the cashiers, who, unperturbed, worked at their usual plodding pace. When my mother finally got to the front, she graced the cashier with one of her indulgent and endearing smiles, then patiently explained that the magnetic strip on her Visa card wasn't working properly—the cashier would have to manually enter the card's number.

Things went downhill from there when the cashier pretended she didn't hear Mother and pointlessly continued to swipe her Visa card. Mother asked if she spoke English. The cashier looked up for an instant. "My English is very good." She went back to swiping the card.

Mother puffed herself up like a blowfish for the one and only main assault: "You *fucking* Nazis. You never learned anything!"

The duty-free shop fell dead quiet, no one even thinking about a counterattack.

Shakespeare's *Hamlet* bounced around in my head from the first time I read it. It makes a wonderful argument for doing nothing—I don't know—take your trust fund and go off someplace quiet and tend to your comforts and hobbies. Or in my case, bide my time until I could collect my pension. And while I'm at it, who granted me the divine-like power of determining life and death? It's something I tried not to think about in Beirut.

There's few of us who don't suffer the qualms of taking another's life. Assassinating Hitler is one thing, but when it comes to political murder in general, there just isn't a manual for it. Our DNA just isn't designed to coolly parse through the pluses and minuses of it. Only psychopaths are truly capable of cold-bloodedly pulling the trigger on a stranger. Nor, for that matter, are we even inclined to talk about it. Try raising the merits of assassination at the next office Christmas party.

O'Callaghan wrote in his memoir that later, after Flanagan's assassination, he heard Flanagan hadn't, in fact, been involved in the torture of IRA prisoners. It made him wonder whether working for the Special Branch, an organization that helped Britain assassinate members of the IRA, was enough to justify his murder. By that standard, anyone working for any institution associated with the British government would be a potential target.

In my hunt for Hajj Radwan, I had to take my lessons where I found them. It would have helped had my conscience been a completely empty vessel. Assassination isn't something you work yourself up to in installments. There is no *Assassination for Dummies*.

Anyhow, as the attentive reader has probably caught on by now, Mother was in her own right something of an assassin. When it came to fight-or-flight, she never dithered. Intuitively, she grasped the tactics and, in particular, how, with an uncompromising coup de main, it's possible to seize the field of battle, letting your enemy know flight is his only option.

When my attempt on Saddam was about to blow up in the press, I called her to give her the quick and dirty. She got through the decision to murder Saddam fine, but when it came to the circus I'd let it turn into, she snorted. Was that the best the CIA could do? And when she heard about the FBI investigation, her only question was whether that other set of fools didn't have something better to do with their time.

Mother was born with an on/off switch, while most of us have to build one from scratch, then keep it from rusting.

HOLD 'EM DOWN IN THE CRUCIBLE UNTIL THEY CHAR

There are few things more fatal to your cause than an incompetent assassin. If he fails spectacularly, you fail spectacularly. Which means a hard vetting of an assassin is absolutely critical.

As I've said, Hajj Radwan got all of his best people off the front in the south. The crucible of war is the most reliable guide to who's got the right stuff and who doesn't. And then, of course, there's the Darwin effect—the truly incompetent are self-selected out. It's a harsh regime, but it's the only one that works.

Not that this will come as news to anyone who needs solid people on a team, but the Navy SEALs will run a new recruit through a grueling basic-training course not so much to count the number of push-ups or sit-ups he can do but to see at what point he will crack. But it wouldn't be until they got to Afghanistan or Iraq and saw combat before the real vetting was complete. New York investment bankers will test an intern by sending him out to buy lunch, the idea being that if he can't keep a dozen sandwich orders straight in his head, he'll never be able to juggle millions of dollars of complicated trades. But the real vetting comes when he's sent off to play with real money.

What it all comes down to is examining a person's flaws and weaknesses rather than his advertised strengths. In battle, or when the world otherwise starts to go to shit, straight A's and paper credentials count for nothing. A Harvard MBA won't tell you whether someone's going to run at the sound of gunfire. Nor will it tell you who's inclined to betray you and who won't.

It might be different the day we're able to bar code people—I don't know—pull up on our iPhones their genome sequencing, grades, rap sheets, credit history, SAT scores, applications for unemployment, and every relevant e-mail and text, both sent and received. Or even better yet, when they make an app to image someone's neural networks in order to tell us exactly what he's thinking. In the meantime, the only thing we can count on is that the person in front of us isn't the person we see. Which means there's no getting around compelling a new recruit to leap through burning hoops at a full-tilt run to see how he fares. The only truth, as Hajj Radwan would have told us, is pain.

To be sure, it's not a matter of only a one-time early vetting. For instance, there's nothing more corrosive than the twin evils of money and narcissism. The kind of person who reads *Wine Spectator*, treats his instincts as adventures, looks for the perfect four-hour-a-week job, and, failing that, marries into money is too distracted to be a good assassin. Whatever serious vetting he got early on no longer counts.

It's something Hajj Radwan couldn't have missed. He had a front seat to the Red Prince's loud and fiery end, saw how he'd gone soft and lax and paid the price. Like so many other Palestinian exiles, the Red Prince treated Beirut like a bordello and spa rather than a military base. Unable to resist fast cars, fast women, and grand apartments on the Corniche, the Red Prince was tied up attending to his comforts instead of the mechanics of murder and survival. Coddled and inattentive, he offered himself up to the Israelis on a silver platter. What a dumbshit, Hajj Radwan must have thought: You never, ever let your guard down in this business.

Again, it goes back to the fact that the assassin is only as strong as his weakest point. When it fails, so does the whole enterprise. It's a lesson the IRA had a hard time learning.

NOTE TO ASSASSINS: If assassination is a telegraph sent to an enemy to let him know the game has changed, you'd better be sure your telegraph operator knows how to work the key.

DON'T SHOOT EVERYONE IN THE ROOM

Exercise violence with vigilant precision and care. Grievances are incarnated in a man rather than in a tribe, nation, or civilization. Blindly and stupidly lashing out is the quickest way to forfeit power.

LIFE'S NOT A FREE-FIRE ZONE, SO DON'T LEAVE IT ON AUTOMATIC

I'd learned the hard way in Beirut that Hajj Radwan's front door was bolted, sandbagged, and trapped. And if somehow I did miraculously blast my way through it, the place for sure would be empty. No, I'd have to up my game to beat the bastard, find a better iteration of Alice. She or he would also be from Hajj Radwan's old days, only still active. And of course, more worthy of confidence than Alice—grounded, steady on the trigger, ready to sacrifice himself. Okay, it's a résumé befitting the second apparition of the messiah. But I didn't see an alternative.

Not long before Hajj Radwan was assassinated, I was in Gaza making a documentary for British television about suicide bombers. One thread we followed was the 1996 Israeli assassination of a young Palestinian engineer turned Hamas master bomb maker. In sheer number of kills, the man ranked up there with Hajj Radwan. Inside Hamas, he was known simply as "the Engineer."

As a teenager the Engineer had taught himself to repair electrical appliances, which proved useful for making car bombs and suicide vests. His technical abilities, combined with a wanton cruelty, put him at the top of Israel's kill list.

A fixer in Gaza arranged for our crew to film the apartment where the Engineer had met his end. With the neighborhood's cheap, exposed cinder-block construction, potholed streets, and vegetable pushcarts, we could have been anywhere in Gaza. There was no address on the apartment building or, for that matter, any other good way to distinguish it from the neighboring buildings.

A young man and an elderly woman showed us into a small bedroom at the back of their second-floor apartment. It was spare, clean, the walls newly whitewashed. The bed was neatly made. I walked over to the window to see what the Engineer's last view of life would have been. It looked down on a pile of broken masonry and trash. Prisons have better views.

I suspected only a handful of people knew the Engineer had been holing up here, and visitors must have been extremely rare. Cut off from family and friends as he was, I wondered whether he came to regret the path he'd taken. Or did it only deepen his hate?

I examined the bed more closely. The mattress obviously had been replaced, and someone now slept here. I sat on the bed exactly where he'd sat the last moments of his life, my back also against the wall. There was no sign of spalling from the explosion on the wall; someone had done a good job patching up.

The young man told me what happened that day.

Not having a cell phone of his own, the Engineer would from time to time borrow the phones of visitors. When an uncle of the apartment's owner came to visit, he agreed to let the Engineer borrow his phone so the Engineer could talk to his father. The phone soon rang. The uncle listened for a moment and turned to the Engineer. "It's your father," he said. "He wants to say hi."

Not getting up from the bed, the Engineer reached for the phone and held it to his ear. "Abi?" My father?

Did the Engineer notice that the uncle's cell phone was a bit heavy? Or did he even stop to think the Israelis were eavesdropping on his father's telephone?

Before the Engineer could say another word, the telephone exploded, taking off a quarter of his head. He died instantly.

No one else in the room was injured. The uncle, to whom the Israelis had given the phone, fled Gaza for Israel before he could be arrested.

The point of this story is that I needed someone like the uncle, someone able to put himself in the same room with Hajj Radwan.

WE ALL HAVE OUR ACHILLES' HEEL

Paris, June 8, 1992: The man at the center of this story is still in the game, so I'll do him the service of loaning him an alias, Claude. It wouldn't be the one he'd pick, but it's better than reminding people he'd gotten caught up in a notorious assassination in central Paris.

It was a colleague who'd first introduced us one wet October afternoon at what's called in espionage a "turn-over" meeting, the occasion when the old handler passes off an informer to the new handler.

Turn-overs can be dicey. The new handler's never sure the informer will take to him, while the informer's never sure whether the new handler will keep him on the books. Money's the most common problem, but so is "production." Like most plodding bureaucracies, Langley suffers from the what-new-have-you-told-me-today syndrome. If a new handler starts to hit that note too soon, it's not unknown for the informer to storm out of a meeting and never come back.

Not that Claude ever considered himself an informer, at least in the sense that the CIA wanted him to be—i.e., its exclusive property. Claude, in fact, didn't take a salary, but he was more than happy to play the role of a high-end connector useful to a lot of people but beholden to none. How he made his money wasn't our business.

The appointment was set for three at a café on Avenue Friedland, two blocks down from the Étoile. My colleague and I took a table in the glassed-in front part of the café. We didn't care who saw us, including French intelligence. We assumed that sooner or later they'd find out about our association with Claude, if they didn't know already. So why make it look sinister by meeting in a dark alley or something?

The rain started again, black umbrellas unfurling on cue. My colleague pointed out a round, shortish man coming our way. His umbrella was up too. He was in an expensive mouse-gray cashmere coat, a silk scarf at the neck, and a Borsalino sitting squarely on the top of his head. He had a dead cigar in his free hand. He grinned broadly when he caught sight of us.

As he pushed through the door, Claude caught the waiter's eye and ordered a *serré*. A triple espresso. We stood up to shake his hand. He sat down, offering us cigars from a leather case—Cubans, Romeo y Julietas. In those days everyone in Paris seemed to smoke, including enjoying cigars in cramped cafés. If you didn't like it, you could take your coffee and sit outside in the rain. Neither of us took a cigar.

I don't remember what we talked about; it was more than twenty years ago. But I do remember liking Claude right away. Like me, he was a man curious about the world. He cast his net as far as it would go, always on a plane to go meet some exotic character.

After I got to know Claude, I wondered if there was a bottom to the well of people he knew. He'd met Hajj Radwan in the early eighties in Beirut, and later ran into him in Tehran from time to time. A couple of times I tried to persuade Claude to help me against Hajj Radwan, but he categorically refused. Didn't I understand that this was a bright red line in our relationship?

I'd normally meet Claude at least once a week, either over drinks or dinner. Or sometimes at his apartment. Yeah, I know, for amateur espionage aficionados, this isn't a practice a smart operative would follow with a real informer. But like I said, the French probably knew about us. If we had something we didn't want them to eavesdrop on, we'd go outside on the street to talk.

One day Claude mentioned in passing that he would be shepherding around town an official from the Palestine Liberation Organization. He was a rising star in the PLO, and Arafat supposedly considered him like a son. There was even talk of his one day taking over PLO security. His name was Atef Bseiso.

Atef may have been a man worth knowing, but he came with some serious baggage. The Israelis privately accused him of helping plan the kidnapping and murder of eleven athletes at the 1972 Munich Olympics. I never got a good look at the Munich evidence, which left me basically agnostic on Atef's role. Not to mention that the Israelis aren't exactly infallible when it comes to the Palestinians: They infamously assassinated a Moroccan waiter in Lillehammer, Norway, mistaking him for the Red Prince.

Either way, my real interest in Atef was his connections to Hajj Radwan. For a couple of years now, we'd been picking up pretty good chatter that Atef's man in Lebanon met Hajj Radwan fairly regularly. The venue was the same Palestinian refugee camp I'd visit years later as a journalist, Ayn al-Hilweh.

When I asked Claude about the relationship between Atef and Hajj Radwan, he said that Atef would only tell him they'd meet from time to time in Algeria. But nothing more. Did Claude know more than he was saying? I could only guess.

Atef was the real thing, the latchkey to Hajj Radwan's back door. I didn't tell Claude what I had in mind and only asked him to set up a dinner with Atef.

In the taxi there, I asked Claude about Munich. "He was a kid," Claude said. "He had no idea what was going on. It's bullshit."

By the time we arrived at the restaurant that Claude had picked in the Bois de Boulogne, Atef was already sitting at the table. A bear of a man with beetling brows and a strong handshake, he had the manners of a diplomat rather than a spook. His English was good. School-learned, I guessed.

It was a long, cheery dinner with lots of wine. It was 1991; the first intifadah was winding down, and the PLO was waging a charm offensive on all fronts; we talked politics, batting around this one question: If the PLO was to really put down the ax, would Israel forget the past?

My impression was that Atef was one Palestinian ready for peace. But that didn't necessarily mean he was ready to sacrifice Hajj Radwan to further the endeavor. In any case, it was too sensitive a question to ask at the first meeting and definitely not in front of Claude.

As we waited outside for our taxis, Atef promised to come back to Paris the following month to continue our meetings. But as Claude would relay to me, Atef got busy and had to postpone. But I didn't care: He was worth the wait.

What I still had to do was figure out whether Atef had any inclination to play Trojan horse to Hajj Radwan's Troy. Did he have a price like so many Palestinians? Or would it be a case of making some political trade for his betraying Hajj Radwan?

This is another gross and unfair generalization, but we looked at the Palestinians as a biddable people. Beaten down, desperate, and poor, they're quick to betray their own, even family. That someone sold out the Engineer didn't come as a surprise to anyone. Just as it didn't come as a surprise that we were able to buy our way into filming the room the Engineer was assassinated in. It only cost a couple hundred dollars. By comparison, no amount of money would have persuaded Hajj Radwan's people to show us the spot where he'd been assassinated in Damascus. His staged martyrdom museum was all we'd get.

But it wasn't as if Hajj Radwan didn't understand the Palestinians, and all their shortcomings and weaknesses and the lethal trap they represented. He'd grown up with them, fought alongside them, and knew how with the right incentive they'd turn on him in an instant; they were his soft underbelly.

My problem now was determining Atef's price. I'd need a lot more time with him to figure that out. In the meantime, though, I'd need to put the other pieces together.

THERE'S NOTHING LIKE THE MOB FOR A QUICK FIX

In Paris, I made a habit of meeting every raving lunatic, criminal imposter, and common fraud who happened to knock on the CIA's front door. They all had some fantastic story to tell, which almost always came with a demand for money. But since ninety-nine percent of the stories I heard were unadulterated bullshit, the tale-tellers never got a penny out of me. But I do have to admit some stories were truly entertaining.

One day in December 1990, a diviner showed up with his divining rod. His proposal was straightforward: If we supplied him with maps of Baghdad, he and his rod would point us to the bunker where Saddam was hiding. Considering that President George H. W. Bush badly wanted to assassinate Saddam rather than occupy Iraq, my genius boss thought we should look into it. It was the no-stone-unturned philosophy. But common sense prevailed back at Langley, and we were instructed to take a pass.

It's not to say that all "walk-ins" were total dead ends. Two months after my meeting with Atef, I got a call from the front gate guard to tell me a "Mr. Walker" wanted to see me.

Standing at the front desk was a rainspout-thin man waiting for me. He looked more Italian than French. In fact, as he would tell me, he was Corsican.

We sat on a bench out front, the din of traffic from the Place de la Concorde forcing us to lean into each other to be heard. I noticed his shoes were scuffed and worn down. How long would it be before he hit me up for money?

To make a long story short, the man, whom I'll call Mario, said he wanted to help the United States against terrorism. His ace in the hole was his large extended "family." They lived in a lot of interesting parts of the world and knew a lot of interesting people. "People who could greatly help us," he said. Mario didn't put a name to it, but I knew he was talking about the Corsican mob.

I knew nothing about Corsican mobsters other than their tentacles were into all sorts of very dark places in France. I was intrigued enough to invite him to lunch the next day. I picked a chic restaurant in the Fifth Arrondissement, a place expensive enough to keep away the low-end tourists and cops.

We talked politics, with me quickly getting around to Algeria, where Atef supposedly met Hajj Radwan.

"We've got people there," Mario chimed in. "Right where they should be."

I was comfortable with Mario, his French almost as accented as mine. As we parted in front of the restaurant, I gave him my telephone number and told him to call as soon as he was ready to introduce me to the Algerian side of the "family."

The next day at noon, my phone rang. But rather than Mario, it was my boss: "If you wouldn't mind, please come up."

Standing next to the boss was a beefy man with a buzz cut. Right away I pegged him as a DEA agent.

"Bob, our colleague from the DEA has a few questions for you," my boss said. "But first look at these."

He pushed across the desk a stack of glossy black-and-white photographs. One was of me shaking Mario's hand in front of the restaurant we'd just come out of. There were more of me, arriving at the restaurant and later walking to the Métro. The quality of the photos was good. I could tell they'd been shot from a tricked-out surveillance van.

I had to laugh at the fop I looked in my thin-soled Italian loafers and double-breasted washed-silk suit. It was an outfit that had set back my mother at least one thousand dollars when she was here.

"Do you know who this man is?" the DEA agent asked.

I gave him Mario's name.

In return, the DEA agent gave me a quick summary of Mario's DEA file, which ranged from his involvement in a Corsican settling of accounts that ended up in a wild shoot-out in a nightclub off the Champs-Élysées to a massive swindle against the French government. Mario would be in jail for life if he wasn't so slippery, he said. By the time the DEA agent finished, Mario sounded like the true lynchpin behind the French Connection. *Shit,* I thought, *Mario is a real player.*

After the DEA agent left, the boss asked me about Mario. When I told him he was a walk-in, he asked what I intended to do with him. I said I wasn't sure yet, neglecting, of course, to tell him about Algeria and Atef. There was no way I was going to include this man in my plans to get Hajj Radwan.

As I was about to leave, he stopped me by saying I'd be well served to be a little more wary of walk-ins. *Yeah, ain't that so,* I thought. He was the naïf who cabled back to headquarters about the diviner.

"As a matter of fact," he said. "Don't see Mario again, even to say good-bye."

"Of course."

The following week, I met Mario at a café close to where we'd had lunch. There was no van in sight, but I went in the back entrance anyhow. And when we finished, I left the same way.

It wasn't as if I thought I could beat the DEA at this game. They had to be all over Mario, including his phone. I momentarily thought about bringing the DEA agent into my scheme, lying to him that Hajj Radwan was in the middle of a drug deal. He would have done half the legwork for me. But I decided against it because political murder's already hard enough without bringing the narcos in as co-conspirators.

I met Mario a couple more times before he offered to take me "right to the top." His "boss," he said, had a "proposal" for me. I didn't know who he was talking about or what the proposal might be, but assuming it had something to do with Algeria, I agreed.

The office I followed Mario into was furnished in elegantly distressed Louis XV and a couple of ultramodern marble statues. Recessed lighting set it off nicely.

We waited in the anteroom, the secretary studiously ignoring us. It was fifteen minutes before a man who could have been Mario's cousin walked up to us. His suit made Mother's look like she'd bought it off a sales rack at T.J.Maxx. He stuck his hand out as if he were about to stick a knife in my gut: "Jean-Charles Marchiani."

Although I'd never laid eyes on the man, I knew exactly who he was. In fact, most politically sentient Frenchmen did. Formerly a French intelligence officer, he now was the sidekick of Jacques Chirac's ex–interior minister. He was a Corsican from Bastia.

The details have never been completely aired in public, but it was Marchiani who negotiated a French hostage deal with Iran. Boiled down to its essence, the deal stipulated that in return for Iran's promise to stop killing and kidnapping Frenchmen, France would open its wallet to Iran.

What few people wanted to consider was that on the other side of the deal was ultimately Hajj Radwan: He was the one killing the Frenchmen and holding French hostages. In fact, as part of Marchiani's deal, a huge one-time payment was directed to Hajj Radwan in return for releasing the French hostages. Who says political murder doesn't pay.

When Washington heard the terms, it gasped. It was a deal even more flagrantly dirty than Iran-Contra. (No one was so insensitive as to point out that with Iran-Contra we'd also indirectly rewarded Hajj Radwan.) But the deal worked as advertised, and Marchiani would climb the ladder, eventually winning a seat in the European Parliament. Though one day he would end up in jail for corruption.

Back to the story: Marchiani wasn't interested in wasting any time pussyfooting around: "So whaz it you wanna see me about?"

I turned around to have Mario explain that I'd thought it was Marchiani who wanted to see me. But he was gone.

The only thing to be done at this point was throw caution to the wind: "We have a problem with a certain man in Lebanon. His name is—"

"I know exactly who you're talking about."

Of course he did; he'd personally sold France's soul to Hajj Radwan.

"The United States has a sealed arrest warrant for him and needs help executing it."

Marchiani made his hand into the shape of an imaginary pistol, then pointed its imaginary barrel at the temple of an imaginary man. He then curled his forefinger to make as if he were pulling the trigger of his imaginary pistol.

Since it was more likely that Marchiani would offer me up to Hajj Radwan rather than the other way around, I was reduced to doing a riff on Hajj Radwan—what a cold-blooded murderer he was, etc. Marchiani sensed I was going nowhere with it and shooed me out of his office.

Outside on the sidewalk I looked around for Mario to wring his neck for setting me up with Marchiani like this. But then considered that, thanks to his little stunt, I now had some leverage over him, i.e., I was in a position to ask him to find me a real Corsican assassin for a job in Algiers. But of course, only if I could first persuade Atef to come on board.

THE SOUND OF A KNIFE THROUGH THE TEMPLE

Atef never did make it back to Paris before I was transferred out. It was Claude who told me what happened on the night of June 8, 1992.

Atef had called Claude that morning to say he'd be coming to Paris to see French intelligence. They agreed to have dinner that night. They'd pick up Atef at his hotel, the Méridien Montparnasse, and from there the three would drive to a nearby Chinese restaurant Atef liked.

The Méridien is an atrocity, a soulless high-rise gouged with a soulless lobby meant to give you the feel of airiness. Instead, it puts you in mind of an abandoned warehouse.

Claude called Atef in his room from the front-desk phone. A couple of minutes later, Atef came out of an elevator in the wake of a clutch of tourists. As Atef made his way across the lobby, Claude caught sight of a man sitting on a divan and pointedly staring at Atef. When the man noticed Claude looking at him, he turned away, pretending something fascinating on the other side of the lobby had caught his attention.

Claude pointed the man out to Atef, who by now was staring at the wall as if he were searching for a hole to disappear into. Claude told Atef to wait while he went to look for a pay phone. He found a French intelligence contact at home and told him about the man, saying he looked like a tail. The contact said he was pretty sure it wasn't French intelligence. Either way, there was nothing he could do about it that late in the evening. He advised Claude and Atef to go ahead with their dinner plans, but right after, Atef should go back to his room and stay put for the night. They'd sort it out in the morning.

Over dinner, Atef and Claude talked about the suspicious man on the divan, but they agreed to treat it as a coincidence and nothing more. It wasn't until after eleven they headed back to the Méridien.

When Claude pulled up in front of the main entrance, the lobby was full of Japanese tourists who'd just been dropped off by a tour bus. Claude got out of the car to say goodnight to Atef.

As Claude shook hands with Atef, out of the corner of his eye he caught a glimpse of two men walking down the sidewalk in their direction. Dressed in short black leather jackets and with their heads shaved, they looked like skinheads. One had an athletic bag in his hand. They were walking fast as if they were late for something.

Now on guard, Claude noticed the two skinheads exchange a look. Without warning, they lunged at Atef. One embraced Atef from behind, while the other raised the gym bag and positioned it to the nape of Atef's neck. Inside was a 9mm pistol. There were two quick muffled cracks. The man holding Atef let him slump to the ground.

Claude looked around for help. It was only then that he noticed the two trucks blocking either end of the street. A precaution in the event the police happened on the scene? Claude watched as the skinhead assassins disappeared down into an underground garage. There had to be an exit on another street, he thought. They would be long gone before the police showed up.

Like most everyone, Claude assumed Atef's assassins were Mossad agents who'd just taken revenge for Munich. He was no doubt right. But I still wonder if part of it didn't have something to do with Hajj Radwan. If I knew about Atef's association with him, so did Mossad. Either way, Claude is lucky the assassins were professionals, otherwise they'd have murdered him too.

THE ON-RAMP TO THE APOCALYPSE AND OTHER LETHAL CERTITUDES

If there's one lesson to be learned from Atef's assassination, it's this: Don't unnecessarily waste bullets. There was no point in Atef's assassins killing Claude, and they didn't. Why irritate the French for no purpose at all?

While writing this book, I happened to be on the phone with a Homeland Security official, explaining how I was struggling to come to terms with how some people narrowly channel violence and others kill indiscriminately. He cut me off, saying he knew exactly where I wanted to go with this. He had noticed the same phenomenon with South American narcotics violence.

Colombia's Medellín cartel, for instance, normally sends an assassin into a restaurant with a silenced pistol to murder the intended victim and with orders not to kill anyone else. On the other hand, the typical Cali cartel assassin will spray an assault rifle around a restaurant, killing as many people as he can. It's almost as if he doesn't care whether he hits the intended victim or not.

"The reason for it is pretty clear," the official said. "The Cali cartels are a lot weaker than Medellín's, which leads them to believe they need to instill dumb fear in everyone. It's their way of establishing 'respect' for their power."

When you think about it, the nineteenth and twentieth centuries are replete with insecure people who inflict as much violence as they can to "instill respect." It's the only way they know how to shore up their power. Anarchists, nihilists, the Chinese Cultural Revolution, the Khmer Rouge, and the Taliban are cases in point. But it doesn't stop there.

In the final months of World War II, the British and American air forces unleashed one of the largest and most controversial bombardments of Nazi Germany. Over three years, they destroyed Dresden, a baroque gem of a city. The problem was that Dresden possessed no clearly discernable military or strategic significance. Did the Allies hope that in euthanizing Dresden they would somehow euthanize Germany? If so, it didn't work.

Let me go back to the Engineer and all the dumb blood he spilled. Like the Cali cartel, he believed that when Israel was forced to understand the terrible random violence he was prepared to rain down on it, it would see no choice other than to alter course—in the Palestinians' favor. But what occurred, in fact, was that Israel opened up the stops, grimly determined to destroy the Engineer and everyone like him. The Engineer didn't liberate a square inch of Palestine.

"Fairness" is not a word normally associated with political murder, but when the Palestinians heard about the Engineer's assassination, I would imagine they grudgingly recognized that from the Israelis' point of view the man deserved it. And they could only have been impressed that the Engineer was the only one killed in the room. No F-16s, no tank fire, no collateral murder.

And let's throw al-Qaeda into the mix. Al-Qaeda's objective on 9/11 was to kill the largest number of people possible. It made no difference who they killed, in uniform or not. And just like the attackers of Dresden and the Engineer, al-Qaeda failed to alter the course of events in their favor. The United States, in fact, was moved to come after it with a meat cleaver. But considering the kind of people al-Qaeda attracted, that wasn't much of a surprise.

When bin Laden set up in Peshawar in the eighties, he attracted one of the most bizarre and feckless potpourris of true believers to ever gather in modern times. While they professed they'd come to drive the Russians out of Afghanistan, anyone could see they weren't battle worthy. They were too coddled and soft to survive an Afghan winter, let alone a firefight with the Red Army.

Bin Laden's acolytes kept to their expensive Peshawar villas, endlessly smoking water pipes and arguing over the meaning of jihad. The closest they came to hardship was flying back home to plead with their families for more money so they could return to the "front." They only understood violence and war in the fuzziest of abstracts.

The presumed 9/11 mastermind, Khalid Sheikh Muhammad, was of the same stripe. Born in Kuwait to a relatively well-off Pakistani family, he came to Peshawar to find something to do with his life. Not exactly a man of colossal genius or courage, he stayed in the rear, raised money, and fantasized about war.

KSM first appeared on America's radar when he was caught sending money to his nephew Ramzi Yousef. At some point, the two of them hatched a plan to knock down a high-rise full of people as an act of pure annihilation, somehow believing it would persuade the United States to stop supporting Israel. They couldn't understand that it was like dropping a cat in ice water hoping to improve its disposition.

In 1993, Ramzi Yousef would go on to blow up a van in the underground parking garage of the World Trade Center. He managed to kill six people, but the bomb wasn't large enough to bring down the building. He was run to ground in Pakistan and extradited to the United States to stand trial.

The absolute vacuousness of Yousef's mind came out in court. "You [America] were the first one who killed innocent people, and you are the first one who introduced this type of terrorism to the history of mankind when you dropped an atomic bomb which killed tens of thousands of women and children in Japan and when you killed over a hundred thousand people, most of them civilians, in Tokyo with fire bombings."

Never taking his oar out of those shallow waters, Yousef said that in bringing jihad to the United States he was "bringing the fight to the Jews." There are a lot of Jews working in the World Trade Center, he said, and killing them would force America to change its policy.

Both uncle and nephew demonstrated a complete callousness toward life, an unfocused and undiluted hate that destroyed but did nothing else. They practice-bombed a Manila movie theater, injuring seven.

They left a bomb under an airliner seat, which killed a Japanese passenger. At one point, they considered blowing up eleven airliners over the Pacific.

Political naiveté like this is most often born out of a mix of ignorance and inexperience. It's particularly lethal when it involves a civilization in peril. Take, for example, the Khmer Rouge, the Palestinian militants, Peru's Shining Path. All three believe they are skirting extinction and have no choice but to lash out at their enemies. They are fixated on the vague possibilities of violence rather than its finer calculations.

Another way to look at mindless violence is to compare it with the mindless destruction of architecture. An insecure people will destroy an enemy's architectural heritage and other cultural symbols as a means to deny its existence and thereby shore up its own. This is exactly what al-Qaeda tried to do when it destroyed the Sufi tombs in Timbuktu. Or when the Saudi Wahhabis systemically razed ancient Mecca to efface Islam's pagan past.

In comparison, Mossad meticulously planned and carried out Atef's murder, employing the least amount of violence necessary. Not to mention accomplishing it with a cold, irremediable efficiency: There's no way to survive two 9mm bullets into the medulla oblongata (the nape of the neck).

Hajj Radwan also brought to bear accurate, proportionate, and discriminate violence. When Israel invaded Lebanon in 1982, he attacked only Israeli army targets, not civilians. He attacked the Marines rather than just any American. And he definitely didn't bother with symbolic targets, such as synagogues or churches.

Hajj Radwan would resort to slaughter only when it was in direct response to slaughter perpetrated by the other side. It was only after France supplied Iraq with the munitions used to bomb Iranian cities that he set off bombs in Paris and indiscriminately killed civilians. In his eyes, a justified and proportionate application of violence.

Applying the word "fairness" to Hajj Radwan isn't going to fly. But what he did have was an uncommon ability to distinguish between man and function. Given the opportunity, he always went after the man rather than the title. He murdered Hariri not because he was a former prime minister but because of who Hariri was—a rising threat. It's just as Caesar's assassins didn't pick him because he was just any Roman general, but because of who he was and what he wanted.

Unlike the Engineer and KSM, Hajj Radwan, like an insurance company, knew how to accurately model risk. He recognized that societies have only a fixed tolerance for absorbing violence. While you never want to apply too little of it, applying too much of it is even worse. While Hajj Radwan could get away with killing Frenchmen, he knew when to stop in order to leave room for a deal with the likes of Marchiani. It's always about the deal to be had, not the quantity of blood spilled. It's something the Engineer and bin Laden couldn't figure out and consequently they got nothing for their efforts.

> **NOTE TO ASSASSINS:** It's a fine line between instrumental and random violence. But like it or not, it's pretty much up to the victim to decide when the line's been crossed. So never ignore an enemy's sensibilities. And never forget there's no such thing as a silver lining to a massacre.

NEVER CEDE TACTICAL CONTROL

The eye behind the scope decides whether to pull the trigger or not. Committees, bureaucracy, and collective decision making are guaranteed to spoil the broth.

If I could find a way to get him out of there, even putting out a contract on him, if the CIA still did that sort of thing, assuming it ever did, I would be for it.

—RICHARD M. NIXON ON SADDAM HUSSEIN

Salah-al-Din, Iraq, March 4, 1995: When the CIA sent me to northern Iraq, my orders were chiseled in stone: Keep a low profile, don't get killed, come home, file report. I also need to state for the record that no one said a word about assassinating Saddam Hussein. Or, for that matter, starting World War III. But as these things so often go, fortune had its own plans.

In my defense, we're talking about Iraq 1995. The place was a howling madhouse. In the north the Kurds were slaughtering one another in droves, if only for the stubborn joy of it. Saddam's rump state was one vast gulag, his prisons booked to capacity, people starving in the streets. With Saddam unable to meet the payroll, his beloved army was starting to crumble. He ordered deserters rounded up and their ears amputated. Saddam himself showed every sign of cracking, from time to time threatening to reinvade Kuwait or even rocket Israel.

Seeing opportunity in chaos, Congress showered money on the CIA in the hope it could turn the Iraqi exiles on its payroll into a military force capable of unseating Saddam. But what Congress couldn't understand was that those same exiles, to a man, were a pack of swindlers, thieves, and freebooters. No amount of money was going to pry them out of their posh CIA-paid-for apartments in London's Mayfair and Paris's Sixteenth Arrondissement.

At the same time, there were those of us who often wondered if Congress's enthusiasm for getting rid of Saddam wasn't only for show. It wouldn't, for instance, do anything to repeal Executive Order 12333, President Reagan's 1981 ban on assassination. It meant the CIA was left with the sugar-plum-fairy dream that some Iraqi general on a white horse would ride over the hill and overthrow Saddam in a military coup d'état. Or, equally fanciful, his valet would grow a pair of balls big enough to put a bullet between the boss's eyes.

When the CIA sent me to Kurdish northern Iraq in 1994 to babysit two Congressional aides—it was my on-the-ground debut for things Iraq—it took me a nanosecond to decide we needed someone up here permanently. The way I looked at it, it was the only way we'd ever embolden a general on a white horse. I promptly volunteered to become the CIA's Man in Kurdistan.

There's something I should note here. Having served in Paris for three years, I wanted to go back to Beirut to get back in the fray. But after my misadventures there, Langley wouldn't consider it. Which made Iraq the next best thing. And, in the interests of full disclosure, my pitiful thinking went no deeper than that Iraq and Lebanon had to share the same operating manual since they were both part of the Levant. = Syria / Lebanon

Knowing Lebanon the way I thought I did, how hard could it be to figure out Iraq?

Another thing I learned in Paris played into my decision. After Atef
was assassinated, I'd foolishly clung to the hope there might be something to be done with the Algiers angle. I'd asked Claude to fish around,
and it wasn't a week before he came back with an intriguing tidbit that
one of Hajj Radwan's old mentors, a retired Algerian intelligence officer,
still kept in touch with him. When Hajj Radwan traveled to Algiers to
see Atef, he'd always drop by to see the mentor. Claude gave me the mentor's Algiers home phone number . . . and from there it was a matter of
waiting for what the French call an *aubaine*—a godsend.

It came a month later in the guise of a bearded, fire-breathing Algerian Salafi. He told the guard at the front gate he wanted to tell the CIA
something in the strictest confidence. My enthusiasm for walk-ins un-
dampened, I volunteered to meet him.

The Algerian looked crazy, and he was. There was something very
combustible burning inside him. Every time he wanted to make a point
he'd grab my hand in an attempt to crush it, his eyes blazing red. He
kept yelling about some proto-Nazi group in Lyon having bulldozed his
mosque. "Allah will not let this stand!" he screamed. I kept looking over
my shoulder at the guard, afraid he would pull out his sidearm and
shoot both of us.

I took the Algerian out front to the park to the very bench Mario and
I once had borrowed. He said he wanted only one thing from the CIA:
help in overthrowing the military junta in Algeria. There was no chance
of that, but I strung him along until I could figure out whether he might
have people in Algeria capable of running down Hajj Radwan's mentor.
It was all a long shot, but at that point, it's all I had.

The Algerian Salafi and I met once a week, and the more time I spent
with him, the more convinced I became that he was truly insane. Worse,
he'd taken a liking to me. But why was I surprised? The mentally dis-

turbed come to me like birds to a lighthouse. Eventually he told a French magazine he intended to murder the Algerian ambassador to Paris. The same day, the police ran him in, which, in turn, led him to call me for help. The cad that I was, I didn't take his call.

The Algerian wasn't the only dead-end lead to Hajj Radwan that floated to the surface during my Paris days. A walk-in claiming to be in touch with Hajj Radwan showed up at our embassy in an Eastern European country I'm not allowed to name. Anyhow, thanks to its efficient intelligence service, which seemed to have every phone and hotel room in town bugged, it quickly became apparent that the man was a swindler. Or, as they're called in the business, a fabricator.

I'd burned through a lot of CIA money in my lonely hunt for Hajj Radwan, and the only thing I had to show for it was the epiphany that there was nothing to be had in Europe. The exiles who take up refuge there live off stale reputations and imagined importance. They're all desperate to latch on to a sugar daddy like the CIA. But when has it ever been any different?

After the revolution in 1917, the British fell into the same trap, believing White Russian exiles could do something about the Bolsheviks, namely assassinate Lenin; the British got absolutely nothing for their efforts. The CIA tried to do something about Mao and the Chinese Communists using the Taiwanese, but fared no better than the British did in Russia. Machiavelli got it right when he said exiles are a worthless bunch.

NEVER TAKE IN STRAY CATS

When five of us pulled up in front of the dun two-story cinder-block house in the one-mule shithole of an Iraqi village called Salah-al-Din, my first question was: What's going to keep Saddam from assassinating us?

The house we were meant to live in for the next six months sat on a bald, windswept saddle. Its living room fronted a bleak hardscrabble field. To paraphrase someone I can't remember, there wasn't a tree to hang Judas from. Which meant any would-be sniper had a clean shot through our front window. And it wasn't as if Saddam's assassins had far to come: On a clear day, you could see the Iraqi front lines from our roof. Hajj Radwan would rather have opened his wrist than set up camp here.

In fact, there wasn't any protective coloring to be had. We were the only foreigners within a thousand parasangs, or whatever measurement the Kurds go by. And the way we were outfitted in a rainbow of Gortex parkas, hiking books, and Kalashnikov assault rifles we might as well have had "CIA" emblazoned across our fronts. For a moment, I stupidly thought about our dressing up like the Kurdish *peshmerga* in their exotic turbans and sashes. But we'd have given off the malodorous scent of imposters and been shot on sight.

It wasn't as if we could trust our hosts, the Kurds. Not only were they slaughtering one another, their ranks were riddled with regime spies. Trust me, it occurred to me more than once that if Saddam recruited a Kurd to kill us, it would be me, the chief, at the top of his list. It left me with the dumb hope that Saddam would decide I wasn't worth the candle.

My days were spent shuttling between the Kurds, urging my old Toyota Land Cruiser to go faster than it knew how. A moving target's harder to hit, right? Nights, we stayed home watching satellite TV, everyone drifting off to bed at about nine. I couldn't imagine why I ever thought Iraq would put me back inside the Arab mind.

Life in the north would have passed by in a mix of dull anxiety and unrelieved boredom had not an Iraqi general crossed over from Saddam-held Iraq bearing a "message" for "the CIA spies." I was alarmed that news of our arrival had spread so far and wide, but I agreed to meet him.

With the general's bushy mustache, squat neck, and black pools for eyes, he could have passed as Saddam's doppelganger. With his throaty Arabic, he even sounded like him. Not exactly thrilled to be sharing the company of a CIA agent, the general kept craning his neck as if he were trying to crawl out of a noose.

After a lot of hemming and hawing, and half a dozen cups of coffee, the general finally got it out that five senior military officers had sent him north to offer us a plan to get rid of Saddam. What they had in mind was a classic coup d'état, very much like the one we'd been dreaming about for so long. They would commandeer a battalion of tanks, seize the strategic points around Baghdad, and invite Saddam to step down. The whole thing would be over in a couple of hours, and with any luck, no one would die. All they wanted from the United States was a sign of support, like an F-16 flyover at a certain time.

Their plan sounded reasonable enough to me. On the other hand, the general hadn't offered me the details. He wanted Langley's initial reaction first. As soon as the general was out the door, I wrote up the meeting in a succinct telex for Langley. The way I looked at it, wiser heads back there would prevail. They'd either green-light it or take a pass. How hard could that be?

Foreknowledge cannot be had from ghosts and spirits.

—SUN TZU

When I didn't get a response to the general's plans after a week, I started to get nervous. And when one week turned into two and three, I started to wonder what in the hell was going on. Didn't the dolts back home understand by now what a mistake it was to leave me in a vacuum to figure out things for myself? By week four, I decided all on my own that the problem had to be that Langley preferred something cleaner and more expeditious.

I sat the general down and told him he had to come up with something, well, more "streamlined." Capturing Baghdad sounded too messy. A week later the general relayed to me a message from his rogue officers: They were now prepared to suborn twelve tanks and drive on to Tikrit, where they'd pulverize Saddam in his palace. Since the palace sat by itself on an outcropping of rock, it would be a fairly clean job.

I was encouraged that the putschists weren't talking about an assassin's high-powered rifle or poisoning Saddam's espresso. Though I should concede that a tank's main gun is a fairly precise weapon, which might even leave some to characterize it as a weapon of assassination. Not my problem, though; I wrote up the new plan and sent it back to give Langley a chance to weigh in on whether or not the "Tikrit plan" sounded like a violation of 12333. Wasn't it exactly for something like this that Langley kept all of those smart lawyers on the payroll?

In the meantime, the general duly sent a message to the rogue officers, letting them know we'd probably be going with the twelve tanks on Tikrit option.

It also finally dawned on me that it truly was time to start tightening things up. What would Hajj Radwan do in my shoes? Okay, he would never have allowed himself to be put in my shoes, but beyond that, I knew it was high time I deprive Saddam of a sitting target. I exchanged our Toyotas for a fleet of old dented-up cars. I broke us up into two teams and made sure we changed houses every night. Some nights we slept in caves. But I still felt like whitey at the oasis, the restless natives out there in the black night waiting for their chance to pounce and cut our throats.

I also decided we'd better seriously arm ourselves. One of my guys, an ex–Army captain, went down to the local arms merchant and bought a Russian Dragunov sniper rifle. He couldn't wait to test it. But when he came home, he had a bloody circle around his right eye. With Dragunovs, as he figured out too late, the scope isn't meant to rest against your face when you fire it.

Just when I thought I was getting a grip on things, a woman showed up at the local Kurdish intelligence office, claiming she needed to tell the Americans something. Before anyone could get over to see her, she blew herself up, leaving fragments of her skull embedded in the concrete ceiling. Was she a counterassassin sent to interrupt our plans? There was no way to know. I took it, though, as an evil omen that the deck wasn't cutting in our favor, and then was certain of it when the notorious Iraqi exile and convicted swindler Ahmed Chalabi charged onto the stage. Frankly, Chalabi was the last thing I needed.

A University of Chicago and MIT grad, Chalabi had been convicted in Jordan for bank embezzlement. Resurrected by the CIA after the Gulf War, he now owed his political existence to Washington. It was our F-16s that kept Saddam from grabbing and lynching him; it was the United States he ran to when things got ugly. By rights, Chalabi should have been America's obedient proxy who slavishly followed my orders. Instead, he treated me as if I were the mad uncle in the attic. He would pretend to listen to me, but as soon as I was out the door, he'd revert to his old conniving self.

I could have tolerated Chalabi had he known anything about his own country. But he hadn't lived in Iraq since 1958, which meant he didn't have a clue about how the fine gears of Saddam's regime turned. Like every other exile I'd ever run into, Chalabi was all smoke and mirrors. To make matters even worse, he had a political following in Washington, mainly neocons.

Getting wind of the twelve tanks on Tikrit plan, Chalabi decided his face card in the game would be to forge a letter making it appear as if the National Security Council had enlisted him in the plot against Saddam. The forged letter helpfully laid out the specifics: An "NSC assassin" by the name of "Robert Pope" was on his way to northern Iraq to carry out the deed. And—surprise, surprise—he couldn't accomplish it without Chalabi's help.

As we'd later determine, Chalabi had forged the letter for the benefit of two Iranian spies who'd crossed over the border to pay him a visit. Leaving the letter out faceup on his desk, he arranged to be called out of his office, giving the two Iranians the chance to read it. After having read the letter (upside down), the Iranians raced back to Tehran to report that the NSC was about to put a limit to Saddam's days. As far as anyone was able to determine—Chalabi denies the whole thing—Chalabi's ploy was to make himself appear in Tehran's eyes as an indispensable player.

As we also found out later, the Iranians were never fooled. But what did happen was that the Iranian military went on full alert, moving armored units to its border with Iraq. Saddam followed suit, putting his army on full alert. (It was the first time he'd done so since the Gulf War.) Joining the party, Turkey put its army on full alert and closed the border crossing into Iraq. I knew it was only a matter of time before Washington finally stirred itself awake.

As my little house of cards started to come down, it occurred to me that Hajj Radwan would have blindfolded Chalabi, marched him out into the main square, and executed him without ado or ceremony—for everyone to take note and pay heed. But of course, unlike me, Hajj Radwan didn't have a flock of know-nothing neocon chicken hawks sitting on his shoulder. Nor, for that matter, did he have to answer to a moribund institution like the CIA.

Not that I'm without guilt in any of this. Even at the time, I knew I should have sat down the rogue officers for a face-to-face meeting. Since they couldn't cross the front lines into the Kurdish north, I should have insisted we meet in Amman, Jordan.

I should have also made the generals take some concrete action that would demonstrate that they, in fact, were prepared to harm Saddam—

mortar his Baghdad palace or something. It's just elementary gang wisdom that you don't trust anyone until he's made the enemy bleed. Blood in, blood out, as they say.

What it all comes back to is you can't make something like assassination work by remote control. Not from a comfy office on the Potomac, not from a café in Europe, and not even from the mountains of Kurdistan. It's just another sine qua non that you see the guts of it with your own two eyes, get out on the field and sweat it out with your guys.

But none of this changes the fact that if I couldn't get an answer out of Washington about the Tikrit plan, even a simple yes or no, there was no way I was ever going to get them to let me go to Amman to meet the generals. So I was left to wait in grim anticipation for this little baby to run off the tracks.

At four in the morning on March 1, there was a knock at my door. I opened it to find my radioman. He said: "Want to read a message from the White House?"

In my long, checkered CIA career, I'd never seen a piece of correspondence sent directly from the White House to a CIA station, let alone to a pissant unit like mine. I found a flashlight and sat down at the end of my bed to read it.

It was a curt message to all of the plotters, including Chalabi. It said something about how the action "you have planned" had been "compromised," and "proceeding" would be at "your peril."

To be sure, the White House's prose was nuanced and businesslike, but by the time I got to the end of it, I didn't need to decipher Linear B to get the drift: *Knock the fucking assassination thing off.*

It wouldn't be until I got back to Washington that I found out that Chalabi's fabrication—the tale of the faux "NSC assassin" aka "Robert Pope"—had reached the White House's ears and set its hair on fire. The White House knew for a fact that it hadn't dispatched this Pope to Iraq to assassinate Saddam. Who else could it be other than the CIA?

It also didn't help that the chairman of the Joint Chiefs had called

Clinton's national security adviser in the middle of the night, demanding to know what in the hell was going on in Iraq. From where he sat, it looked as if the three largest armies in the Middle East were on an apocalyptic collision course. And by the way, if there really was a plan afoot to assassinate Saddam, shouldn't he know about it?

In the fog of bureaucratic battle, the White House called the acting CIA director, who mumbled he didn't know anything about a Robert Pope. Now panicked, the acting director called the FBI director to investigate. Ignorant of the facts, the FBI opened a criminal investigation. (It's what they do for a living.)

A platoon of FBI agents beat the bushes up and down the Potomac looking for Robert Pope. But since he didn't exist, they couldn't find him. By default, they turned their attention to my team and me. Which was how we became the first American officials criminally investigated for an assassination attempt on a foreign leader.

Meantime, back in Iraq: The general showed up in front of our house in an ancient Russian jeep driven by a very old Kurdish *peshmerga* warrior. The general was decked out in the elegant full-dress uniform of an Iraqi major general, a sword clanging at his side. With a gleam in his eye, he told me he was about to march on Tikrit, meet up with the main force, and deal with Saddam. But as soon as the general drove off, a Kurdish militia arrested him. (The Kurds later told me that they'd done it because of the White House's message to them that "my plan" had been "canceled.")

There was no sign that anyone had moved at the appointed time on March 5. And now with the general hors de combat and my only conduit to the putschists lost, there was no way to find out what had happened to the colonel and his tanks. It left me with the unhappy thought that Saddam had decapitated us instead of the other way around.

When I got back to Washington, two FBI agents badged me and read me my rights. The charge? Crossing interstate borders to commit murder, to wit, Saddam Hussein's. The two agents were genuinely curious about what exactly had gone on in Iraq. Was there a reason one of my guys had an injury from a sniper rifle? Any lingering doubts I still had that not everyone in Washington shared my enthusiasm for the attempt on Saddam now completely evaporated.

It took the FBI about a month to decide that there hadn't been an NSC assassination plot, that Robert Pope was Chalabi's invention, that we were all innocent of murder and attempted murder. Why they decided to overlook the twelve tanks on Tikrit plan, I don't know. I imagine they realized it would look ridiculous prosecuting CIA operatives for an attempt on America's number-one enemy.

Cleared, we went back to our lives. Or sort of. Like I said, I had a lot of time to think about the folly of it, how I'd flagrantly violated every rule in Hajj Radwan's book. Had I learned nothing in Beirut? Or, for that matter, anything about life?

AN INTERLOPER IN THE TENEMENTS OF WAR

Actually, Mother taught me a lot about life, that things like having a mouth full of straight white teeth, owning at least thirty-six button-down dress shirts, and not marrying a tramp were important. But not the least of it, she taught me that when it comes to a nasty fight always pick the time and the terrain.

When Mother was in graduate school, she lived in a generally sedate apartment building, but on the other side of one wall from her was a middle-aged man with a taste for younger women. He'd stay up late into the night partying, music radiating through the wall. When it became apparent a polite knock on the wall wouldn't do it, Mother moved to act.

One afternoon she called the local hospital to find out the name of the doctor on duty that night. Waiting until the music started next door, she called the morgue, evoking the doctor's name. There was a stiff that needed to be picked up, she said in a businesslike manner. She gave the name and address of her partying neighbor.

When two morticians showed up at his door, asking for him by name, his little soiree came to a quick end. Although Mother's neighbor couldn't pin down the identity of his foe, he accepted defeat gracefully and moved out. Mother went back to her studious life.

"Know what fights to pick," she told me. "And never, ever let your enemy pick the ground."

Too bad Mother wasn't in Iraq with me.

Here's why my Saddam plot failed:

One: The Iraqis are not wired to conspire with outsiders. For lack of a better explanation, I blame it on the Mongol invasions, which turned them—this is another unfair but serviceable oversimplification—into possibly the most xenophobic people in the world. It translated into the truth that if there were any Iraqis inclined to assassinate Saddam, the last thing they'd do is share their thoughts with the CIA.

Two: The CIA didn't possess anything like a friendly tribe in Iraq, nothing close to Lebanon's Christians. Even the Kurds didn't like or trust the United States, as I figured out when they arrested the general on D-day. Did they do it at Saddam's behest or as a matter of caution? I don't know. But looking back on it now, what's clear is that I'd have been lucky to find a Kurd agreeable to driving down to the local 7-Eleven to buy me a tub of ice cream.

Compared with Hajj Radwan's experiences in Iraq, our isolation was all the more apparent. When his cell showed up there in 2003, it quickly recruited a large pool of young men prepared not only to undertake murder at Hajj Radwan's direction but also to risk their lives. We saw it in the attack on Karbala and the execution of five American soldiers.

Three: In spite of my best efforts, there was nowhere for us to hide in the north, certainly nothing like Hajj Radwan's Palestinian refugee camps. There were some hollow-eyed Christian visionaries in a village near ours, but it was strictly a no-no borrowing them for cover. If I had tried, Congress would have repealed EO 12333 as a one-time exception to come after me for endangering the Christian base. Left to the elements, we were like squids in a snowstorm.

Finally: I was a finch imprisoned in a bureaucratic cage. I had to ask Langley for all things small and large. If I wanted to recruit a new informant, I'd have to go through a long song and dance to get an okay. It could take weeks or months. Hajj Radwan never had to ask for permission for anything. Either the mission was on or it wasn't. Either he could do it or he couldn't. He lived in a binary, unencumbered world I sorely envied.

At bottom, my problem was I was playing in Saddam's backyard. His spies were everywhere, and no part of Iraq was out of his sight. He personally knew every important player in the country. Who drank too much, who had a hernia, who was sleeping with whom, etc. For one year he'd sat across a conference table from the general, my cutout to his would-be assassins. He also knew the Kurds like the back of his hand, namely that they wouldn't support the twelve tanks on Tikrit plan; that they were perfectly happy in their crappy little enclave; that they lived by the homespun wisdom that you don't try to fix something if it's not broken. I'm all but certain Saddam wasn't surprised when the Kurds balked and arrested the general. Saddam's understanding of Iraq and its people was one I could never come close to replicating.

Adding to it, Saddam was in undisputed control of his rump state, he was his own man. He alone decided who deserved it and who didn't. He didn't have to put up with the likes of Langley's bureaucrats or EO 12333.

The United States, of course, was no more clairvoyant than I when it invaded Iraq in 2003. No one even entertained the possibility that Iraq might be worse off without Saddam. With nearly a half million killed at this writing, clearly his murder wasn't a good social bargain for all. But when does blindly thrashing around in the exotic parts of the world ever make things better for the locals or, for that matter, the thrashers? As Sun Tzu put it, war can neither be avoided nor won without knowledge of the enemy.

NOTE TO ASSASSINS: Don't pick a fight on the wrong side of the tracks. Or as any grunt will tell you, Never move beyond your artillery fan.

OWN THE GEOGRAPHY

Immerse yourself in your enemy's world before deciding whether to act or not, especially in those places where truth is determined by power. And definitely don't take any blind shots.

Rule number one in politics: Never invade Afghanistan.

—HAROLD MACMILLAN

Khost, Afghanistan, December 30, 2009: Forty-five-year-old Jennifer Matthews, mother of three, was the unlikeliest of assassins. Or for that matter, of targets. Born to a strict evangelical family from suburban Harrisburg, Pennsylvania, she was raised and remained a believer her entire life. She attended Ohio's Cedarville University, an evangelical college where Bible study is mandatory and creationism is taught to the exclusion of Darwin. She married a devout boy from the same school, and their first child was soon on the way. Like a lot of people from small-town America, Matthews felt a strong pull to raise a family close to home. But she decided there had to be more to life and applied to the CIA.

Hired in 1989, she and her family moved to Washington, D.C.; they bought a home in Fredericksburg, Virginia. Like all new émigrés, they had to learn to cope with the high cost of living and the shitty traffic that comes with northern Virginia's unremitting vinyl-sided suburbs. But working for the government had its attractions—steady employment, regular pay raises, good health insurance. So northern Virginia was where they'd settle down, she making a career at the CIA and he as a chemist.

At Cedarville, Matthews had majored in television journalism, so it made a certain sense that the CIA would turn her into a photo analyst, someone who typically spends a career poring over stacks of glossy black-and-white satellite photographs. She'd do well if she could learn to write succinctly and quickly, churning out a regular stream of finished intelligence reports. Promotions would come with predictable regularity.

Matthews entered the CIA near the end of the Cold War, an era when a lot of people thought it was high time to cage the beast. The CIA had never gotten over its 1961 half-baked "invasion" of Cuba, the Bay of Pigs. Or its half-baked attempts on Castro's life. So when it came time to arm and train the mujahideen to fight the Red Army in Afghanistan, the CIA gladly handed the task off to the Pakistanis. No new Bay of Pigs equaled no wrecked careers.

In the same spirit, a great cultural shift started to sweep across the CIA, the bureaucrats triumphing over the field operatives. Things such as modern management, cost-benefit analysis, and balancing budgets were prized over classic espionage. It wasn't exactly thought through, but the basic idea was that a corporate sensibility would file the rough edges off the CIA, clean it up enough so it could go out and mix in polite company.

Soon enough, the writing was on the wall: If you wanted to get to the top, you'd better punch your ticket behind a desk at Langley. And sure enough, it wasn't long before manicured, deskbound bureaucrats started to be promoted faster than field operatives. The notion of rubbing shoulders with foreigners and parachuting into foreign jungles was now as quaint as a top hat.

Soon people who'd never served in the field were put in charge of the field, allowed to call the shots in a country they'd never laid eyes on. The analyst who oversaw the CIA teams tasked with tailing people around the world was confined to a wheelchair from a boyhood accident. Although he himself had never tailed anyone, he was expected to advise people who did.

The patently unqualified were sent out to the field. In the middle of the hunt for bin Laden, the CIA sent a career logistics officer to Islamabad as the boss. No one bothered to ask how, with absolutely no understanding of South Asia, he was supposed to comprehend one of the most opaque countries in the world.

An analyst was appointed as head of all CIA clandestine operations. His first and only act of significance was to sever all CIA connections to the dark side—swindlers, dope dealers, mercenaries, religious fanatics, assassins, forgers, the mob, or anyone else who didn't share America's ideas of decency and propriety. For the old-school operatives, it came as a neck-wrenching, 180-degree reversal from a practice of keeping in touch with the world's scum, if only to keep a pulse on it. Arms dealing, money laundering, and all the other black arcana now became terra incognita for the CIA. It was as if the Mayo Clinic had stopped seeing sick people.

The CIA also decided it would make itself as politically correct and vanilla as the rest of America. It introduced things such as "off-sites," management gurus, and casual Fridays. For the adventuresome, there were Outward Bound–like "bonding" weeks on the Pecos River—hikes, singing around the campfire, rappelling off cliffs. Cultural barriers came down too. When America stopped looking at homosexuality as moral turpitude, so did the CIA. It even introduced LGBT seminars. Could transgender bathrooms be far behind?

In the great leavening, operatives were expected to spend the bulk of their careers in Washington learning the bureaucratic ropes. It all worked out nicely. While the ambitious, smart operatives came home to fight on Langley's bureaucratic battlefields, the analysts could go overseas to get their tickets punched. It was the CIA's version of the World Is Flat.

There was an undisguised sigh of relief when the old-school operators who knew their way around guns and explosives finally decided to shuffle into retirement, taking along with them the oddballs who'd spent their careers in the exotic parts of the world and spoke exotic languages. Who needed some sad bastard whose only talent was to speak fluent Baluchi? The new mantra was if a foreigner couldn't speak English, he wasn't worth knowing.

A ct Two: The CIA would have been completely out of the rough trades if it hadn't been for 9/11 and drone assassinations. Never mind that EO 12333 was never rescinded. The way I read it, the same lawyers who'd ignored me in Iraq finally got off their asses and, rightly or wrongly, conjured up the semantics to authorize political murder.

Before I get any further, I need to make it crystal clear that I separated from the CIA in December 1997 and haven't read a piece of classified information since. In fact, I've steered well clear of my still (serving) ex-colleagues in order to keep CIA security off their backs. In other words, what I know about drones and the Khost tragedy I've learned as a journalist (i.e., you're getting my opinion). Whether it's more worthy than Main Street's, I leave it up to the reader.

I also should add that from what I've gleaned over the years, the people doing most of the targeted killing is the Pentagon rather than the CIA. After all, it's the military that pulls a drone's trigger rather than the CIA. I'm told that thanks to the military's "waived special access programs"—i.e., no congressional or judicial oversight—we don't hear much about Delta Force and the Seal assassinations. It's a detail, though, that doesn't matter for this book. Again, it's a rulebook rather than a survey.

It's been reported in the press that CIA drones killed more than two thousand people, mostly in the tribal areas of Pakistan. The unit responsible for them, the Counterterrorism Center, became the CIA's fixed center of gravity. If you wanted into management, an assignment there was a de rigueur rite of passage. But it didn't mean the old-school operatives were brought back. Thanks to brand-spanking-new technology, drones are flown and monitored remotely, from even as far away as the continental United States. Anyone who could work a mouse and had the patience to sit in front of a flat-panel screen for hours on end could get into the drone assassination business.

The CIA's analytical side was completely swept up in the drone craze. Overnight, analysts went from paper pushers to high-tech assassins. According to *The Washington Post*, twenty percent of them were turned into drone "targeters." With godlike powers of life and death, they were now the CIA's new operatives.

Drones came as a nice fit for the CIA, seamlessly folding into its tight-lipped and cloistered little world. Targeters could send out for Chinese takeout and lattes, and never have to take their eyes off their screens. The most dangerous part of their day was the drive to work and back home. As for the grunt work, it was left to the contractors in the field who repaired and armed the drones.

One side effect of drones was that an overseas career pretty much became irrelevant. A six-month stint in a war zone such as Iraq or Afghanistan was enough to classify you as a seasoned field officer. Never mind that these tours amounted to being locked up in fortresses like Baghdad's Green Zone.

No surprise, drones did wonders for cleaning up the CIA, wiping away a lot of the Bay of Pigs stain. After all, interacting with the world with a mouse is pretty much risk-free, sort of like fishing in a septic tank with a mechanical arm. Even better, it was the White House and the bloodless lawyers who slavishly do its bidding that made the final decision on the "kill lists." The moral hazard of assassination was on its back rather than the CIA's.

In a town that feeds on hard power, the CIA's sudden rehabilitation was easy to gauge. A CIA tech could run a drone video feed into the White House's subterranean Situation Room and offer the president and his cabinet a front-row seat on what's so quaintly called a "kinetic action". It has probably occurred to Langley that it is more relevant today than it ever was during the Cold War.

I'll get deeper into drone assassinations in Law #12, but the point here is that when the CIA sent Jennifer Matthews to Khost, Afghanistan, it was pretty much a bureaucratic exercise—a ticket-punching. Never mind that she was just as unprepared for the shit mist she was shoved out into as I was in Kurdistan. And as I've come to realize, there but for the grace of God go I.

THE FLESH AT THE END OF THE ASSASSIN'S BULLET

Samuel Johnson: "Nobody can write the life of a man, but those who have eat and drunk and lived in social intercourse with him."

By that measure, getting to know the Pashtuns isn't possible. They neither want to drink nor eat with us, and most definitely they don't want us wandering around their backyard. Throw in the fact that these people have no fixed addresses, no fixed telephone lines, and that they behead people like pollsters and marketers and are all seemingly named Khan, and the chances of an outsider's ever getting to know them is zero. Which translates into the related truth that the chances of ever conducting a successful campaign of political murder against them is also zero.

Political murder in Pashtunistan is all the more impossible because there's no one Pashtun head to lop off. The one-eyed Mullah Omar is only a public face, pretty much disconnected from the thousand-headed hydra that runs the Pashtun resistance, or as it is commonly referred to, the Taliban. The only people in history who've ever been able to make the Pashtuns properly submit were the Mongols, and that was only thanks to genocide.

Adding to the complexity, rural Pashtuns have a reputation for being unfathomable, primitive, and superstitious people. They imbue time with mysterious properties. Such as believing that in the winter at midnight, witches will call to them with voices stolen from someone they know. During the last two hours of daylight, a Pashtun will refuse to loan milk from his cow for fear it will leave a curse on the cow and cause it to go dry.

Pashtun society is dominated by low technology, small landholdings, small workshops, and trade carried out on the street. Most houses aren't hooked up to the electrical grid, and their only source of light is kerosene lamps. Water is drawn from wells; there's scant medical care; goats and sheep are the main source of protein.

People who have the misfortune of going to war against the Pashtuns characterize them as an unforgiving and belligerent people. Seemingly, a man will sire a large family because he knows he stands to lose half his boys in war. When the Pashtuns don't have an outside enemy to fight, they fight one another. Like the ancient Greeks, they find self-worth in killing other men.

Pashtun politics are pretty much indecipherable to outsiders. Strictly organized along tribal and kinship lines, all power is personal and contingent. A patriarch or a militia commander often will have no public title or position.

Important decisions are made in what's called a *loya jirga*, an impromptu congress. No minutes are taken, and a very rough nonbinding consensus prevails. Its proceedings are invariably opaque, with even participants unsure of why or who made a particular decision. It's as if Congress debated and voted blindfolded in a mosh pit.

Pashtun politics are all the more complicated because there are nearly four hundred Pashtun tribes, each occupying a place with stable boundaries. Within them, there are hundreds of important clans and extended families. As I said, there's no preeminent leader of the Pashtuns, often not even in a particular district. Ties between distant tribes and clans are irregular and sporadic, or sometimes there are none at all.

The British Raj spent nearly a hundred years attempting to subdue the Pashtuns, alternating brute force with bribery. During tribal uprisings, the British conducted punitive raids in an attempt to put them down, blowing up houses and often destroying entire villages. They called it "butcher and bolt."

Like Julius Caesar in Gaul, the British marched up and down the Pashtun tribal belt desperately trying to put down one revolt after another. Although some British officers spoke Pashto and were familiar with the Pashtuns, they never discovered a way to convince them of the benefits of empire. In the end, unlike Caesar, the best the British could hope for was a truce, a temporary and fragile one at that.

Between 1919 and 1947, the British Royal Air Force relentlessly bombed Pakistan's tribal belt in hopes of forcing the Pashtuns to submit. It was a strategy founded on nothing more than the untested hypothesis that a spectacle of force would do the job. The British would have accepted symbolic submission for the actual act, but they didn't even get that. When they finally gave India its independence, the British left the Pashtuns as ungovernable as when they arrived.

After partition from India, the Pakistanis also never found a way to subdue the Pashtuns. Even today Pakistani military and Frontier Corps patrols rarely stray far off the main roads for fear of ambush. From time to time, the Pakistanis launch punitive raids, with a lot of air power and bluster, but with no more success than the British. (Why exactly the

United States thought that drones would succeed where the British and Pakistani air forces failed I'll get into in Law #12.)

A fortress is taken most easily from within.

—JOSEPH STALIN

In a lot of ways, Afghanistan reminds me of Lebanon. For one, its modern history's been one long and uninterrupted negotiated compromise. When the British gave up the ghost in 1919 and granted the Afghans their formal independence, the two main linguistic groups, the Tajiks and the Pashtuns, saw no point in forming a let's-get-along, homogeneous nation. Combine it with the Afghans' deeply rooted tribalism and, like Lebanon, Afghanistan becomes a perfect emporium for political violence . . . a place where one murder does end a conversation.

Also like Lebanon, Afghanistan is the victim of colonial cartographers who drew its borders in the interest of the metropolitan centers rather than local sensitivities. Take a look at a map: Matthews's new posting, Khost, is a thumb stuck in the eye of Pakistan's Pashtun tribal badlands. Legally speaking, it may sit on the right side of the border, but with the way Pakistan's North Waziristan province loops around it, it's a hangman's noose.

For true believers like the Taliban—a people who only care about divine demarcations—borders are of no importance. Which means they went to bed and woke up dreaming of ridding Allah's sacred vineyards of the American base at Khost. But with its high dirt berms, Jersey barriers, floodlights, machine-gun emplacements, and helicopter gunships flying night and day, Khost was a fortress as impregnable as any Crusader's castle. There was no easy way to sneak in and slaughter the infidels.

According to the newspapers, stopping the Taliban from coming over the walls was the military's problem rather than Matthews's. The CIA had its own security people attached to the base, but they were meant only to keep the curious from poking around the CIA's little corner. In fact, the more deeply embedded and out of sight its people were, the happier Langley was. Whose orders, incidentally, were unambiguous: No one from the CIA was allowed to set foot outside Camp Chapman, not even for afternoon shopping in Khost. The CIA people arrived at base by helicopter or plane and left the same way. If they needed something from town, they'd send a local Afghan employee for it. If Khost felt like a prison, it's because it pretty much was. Stuck watching DVDs and eating communal meals in a trailer didn't improve anyone's mood.

And neither did the daily work routine. Days were spent reading through hundreds of intelligence reports, most of it pap. In between times, it was waiting for the occasional Afghan source to show up. They all arrived with big promises, such as they could find bin Laden if they had only a little more money. Since no one at the base spoke Pashto, there was no three-cups-of-tea chitchat. Which meant that the people who lived around them on that high Central Asian plain, with all of their bizarre tribal politics and ideas of justice and reprisal, were an alien and threatening mystery.

Matthews coped with the boredom by taking a daily run around the airfield. There were regular Skype calls home. On her first one, she posed for her children in a flak vest and toting an M4 assault rifle. But mostly life at the Khost base was a matter of dull endurance. Until, as it did to me in Kurdistan, fate found a way to turn the tables on Jennifer Matthews.

ANOTHER STRAY CAT LET IN THE TENT

As the Jordanians told the story, they'd caught the young Palestinian doctor secretly writing for a militant Islamic blog. They knocked on his door, offering him the choice of either infiltrating al-Qaeda on their behalf or rotting in jail. To spare his family, the doctor agreed to become a mole inside al-Qaeda. He even proposed moving to Pakistan to improve his chances.

It was only after the doctor was taken in by al-Qaeda in Pakistan's tribal areas that the Jordanians decided to come to the CIA. Having no station of their own in Pakistan, the Jordanians needed the CIA's assistance to meet the doctor. And as always, they hoped to curry favor in Washington with a potential goldmine of intelligence.

The CIA's seventh floor could barely hide its glee. The CIA had never had an al-Qaeda informer before, not even a foot soldier. And not only was the Palestinian doctor inside, he was where it counted: al-Qaeda's rear base in the Pashtun tribal belt. How could the White House not hope he'd be the one to finger bin Laden for assassination, fulfill Bush's promise to get him "dead or alive"?

Any lingering doubts about the doctor's bona fides were put to rest when he reported back that he'd started to treat Ayman al-Zawahiri, the Egyptian doctor who then was al-Qaeda's number two. The doctor described Zawahiri's condition in enough clinical detail to corroborate it using old Egyptian medical records.

Zawahiri may not have been the prize bin Laden was, but there was nothing to stop the doctor from worming his way into bin Laden's circle, and, the way these things work, give the White House the option of assassinating both of them. All that was needed was for the Palestinian doctor to leave behind concealed beacons in their residences. (Beacons would emit signals for the drones to follow.)

The plan fit in nicely with the new cleaned-up and chlorinated CIA. There was no need for long-term vetting of the doctor, nor all the mess that comes with handling informers. Either the doctor would plant the beacons or he wouldn't. And if he planted them in the wrong house, who cared? It wasn't as if anyone was going to sue the White House or the CIA.

The only question now was where to meet the doctor. The CIA wasn't about to send an operative into North Waziristan or anywhere else in

Pakistan's tribal areas; the chances of a kidnapping or an assassination were too high. So why not let the closest CIA outpost in the region meet him, the one at Khost? It was only a short ten-minute drive from the border.

I can only imagine what went through Matthews's mind when she read the cable from headquarters informing her that she'd be the one meeting the doctor to start to organize the assassinations. She'd spent a career behind a desk and now she was handed a bat destined to hit a grand slam in the World Series of the Global War on Terror.

When the doctor e-mailed the Jordanians that he was ready for the meeting, his Jordanian handler started making preparations to fly to Khost. In the meantime, the CIA quickly started to prepare to debrief the doctor. If things went according to plan, Zawahiri's days were numbered . . . and just maybe bin Laden's were too.

Everything was set for the meeting with the doctor at the end of December. But a revolt had started to boil up in the ranks. Matthews's security chief wanted to run the doctor through a metal detector at the front gate, then search him by hand. He said it was the only way to treat someone who'd been living in a place where young men stand in line to go on suicide missions.

The security chief also didn't like Matthews's plan to have the entire CIA base turn out to meet the doctor. Were they hosting a diplomatic reception or something? When she announced she intended to throw a birthday party for the doctor, he shrugged his shoulders in resignation. Who bakes a birthday cake for an al-Qaeda mole?

There was also the creeping realization that the doctor was calling all the important shots about when, where, and under what circumstances the meeting would occur. The doctor had stubbornly refused to meet in Amman and now insisted that if he was to come onto an American base he must be treated with "respect" and not searched like a common criminal. To the jaundiced old hacks, the doctor was starting to smell like a "dangle." A Pashtun Trojan horse.

Matthews didn't pay attention, and neither did anyone else up the line. The problem was that the president had already been briefed. How do you now tell the president that the whole thing had been called off because of a funny feeling about your best mole inside al-Qaeda? (Incidentally, cluing in the president is a flagrant violation of Law #10 about never ceding tactical control.)

The doctor was already a day late, and now the day was wearing away fast. But at 4:40 p.m. the Jordanian handler's cell phone finally rang. He listened for a moment, unable to hold back a grin: The doctor was en route. Matthews moved fast to assemble everyone for the meeting. In ten minutes, there were sixteen of them milling around the motor pool. There were only two officers missing: the two girls in the kitchen baking the doctor's birthday cake.

They all saw the base's old red Subaru station wagon at the same time as it nosed through the main gate. *Good*, Matthews must have thought. *They didn't ignore my orders and stop them.*

They kept their eyes on the Subaru as it skirted the airfield and picked up speed as it headed in the direction of the CIA's side of the base. Only the driver was visible. *It's okay*, Matthews must have thought. The doctor would be slouched down in the back behind the driver to keep him out of sight of the Afghans.

When the car pulled up in front of the motor pool, the Afghan driver shut off the engine and got out. It was a second before the doctor let himself out. Matthews had seen the doctor's picture, and this definitely looked like him—the CIA's first and only mole inside al-Qaeda.

The doctor unfolded himself and climbed out of the car. He looked uncertainly around himself at the dozen faces that couldn't help but stare back. He was half bent, a little unsteady, supporting himself on a metal crutch. He adjusted his crutch to better walk. When he was on the phone with his handler, he had told him that he'd been injured in a motor scooter accident in North Waziristan. So that explained the crutch. No one thought twice about it, and it wouldn't be until the postmortem that it was concluded that the crutch was a prop to explain why the metal detector went off—that is, course, if he'd been run through one.

The doctor looked over at his Jordanian handler, but the doctor didn't seem to recognize him. Something was wrong. The handler stepped forward, his hand raised to shake the doctor's. But the doctor kept his hand inside his *salwar kameez*. The doctor started to mumble something. The handler couldn't understand him. He then realized the doctor was muttering a death prayer—*La ilah illa Allah*. There is no God but God.

The doctor looked up at the sky. He fumbled under his *salwar kameez*. Two of the security contractors lunged at the doctor to wrestle him to the ground. The handler hesitated, and then he too jumped on the doctor, grabbing for his arm. But it was too late. They call it the "great white light." But is that really the last thing you see when you die of an explosion?

Matthews died in the helicopter on the way to surgery. Not counting the doctor, nine people died. It was the CIA's worst loss of life in a single attack.

THE BARBARIANS AREN'T LIKE US

In his Spanish Civil War memoir, *Homage to Catalonia*, George Orwell describes how one day a fascist soldier jumped out of a trench in front of him. The man was holding his pants up so they wouldn't fall off, which is what saved his life. "I did not shoot, partly because of that detail about the trousers. I had come to shoot at 'Fascists,' but a man that was holding up his trousers isn't a 'Fascist,' he's visibly a fellow creature, similar to yourself, and you don't feel like shooting at him."

Orwell was thrown by the realization he didn't really know the enemy. Which brings me to the question, Shouldn't we be killing people we know and all of the really evil shit that comes along with them? Isn't it the enemy you know, with a face and a past, you want to destroy, instead of the one you don't know? You're certain he's either done you harm or is about to. What I'm trying to say is that killing total strangers, especially at great distances, is something other than proper assassination. It's more like—I don't know—spraying insects from a crop duster.

Let me go back to the Lao assassins. There was no misidentifying the victim or mistaking the crime. The locals knew everything there was to know about the victim, in particular how exactly his murder would better everyone's chances of survival. They were able to put both a face and a price on blood.

At the other end of the scale, the CIA can murder as many Pashtuns as it likes, but with the Pashtuns' horizontal power structure and their opaque politics, it could never know what it was getting out of it. With a faulty understanding of an enemy, murder is a blind shot. Which in turn means we're making more enemies than we're eliminating.

Our military faces the same problem. While the Pentagon has permitted targeted killings in Afghanistan and can do things like number each and every house in every suspect Taliban village—they call them "battlefield maps"—it hasn't been able to identify the Taliban command well enough to eliminate it. Indeed, when U.S. troops do finally withdraw from Afghanistan, they'll be leaving the country in the same state as they found it—with the Taliban in charge.

It would be a mistake to lay the entire blame at the feet of the American military or the CIA. Washington is a capital so far from an age when assassination was the common fate of leaders that it's unable to understand its rules or workings. Couple that with Washington's devouring lack of interest in anything foreign and its near-sighted, one-dimensional view of the world, and it is all but inevitable that complicated, nuanced political murder is beyond its grasp.

KEEP IT IN THE FAMILY

In ancient Rome, prominent families kept mounted in the atrium of their houses what's called a *tabula patronatus*. It was a sort of brag wall, a certification of influence and wealth that let visitors know exactly who they were dealing with and what sort of respect was due them. Though it was never the intention, a *tabula* was a handy road map for exterminating a particular Roman clan, ruthlessly moving down the *tabula* until the clan's power was destroyed. A victim was ostracized, sent into exile, or assassinated.

In India, when the Gandhis started to mistake themselves for royalty, assassins stepped forward to erase the line, killing Indira and then her son Sanjay. In Pakistan, Prime Minister Ali Bhutto and his daughter met the same fate. (Ali was hanged, and Benazir Bhutto was blown up by a suicide bomber.) Should we include the Kennedys in the wiping out of a charismatic line?

Hariri was the only truly important figure in his clan. But in his enemies' eyes, he was an oversized and dangerous one. He'd purchased political loyalty across Lebanon, taking under his wing parliamentary deputies, army officers, judges, and clerics. He was often on the phone with them to make sure their bank accounts were doing well and, more important, to make sure they were doing his bidding. Hariri's *tabula* was starting to look like Caesar's, which is one reason Hajj Radwan decided to take a sledgehammer to it.

Hajj Radwan generally never moved against anyone until he fully understood his pedigree, his influence, and who stood where in his family. When Hajj Radwan decided to close down the Hariri investigation, one of his first victims was the nephew of the Lebanese president assassinated in September 1982. It was a message to his clan that it had best back off pushing the investigation. And that it did.

I suspect something similar was at play when Hajj Radwan made an attempt on Ambassador Habib. The way Hajj Radwan looked at it, with Habib having a reputation for being close to President Reagan, his murder would have struck at Reagan's base of personal power—i.e., whittled away Reagan's *tabula patronatus*.

As long as I'm on ambassadors, I wonder if Hajj Radwan didn't succumb to the common error of overestimating the true significance of American ambassadors. Although Habib indeed may have been close to Reagan, and while the State Department may bill an ambassador as a personal representative of the president, the truth is most are either political hacks or bureaucrats with fancy titles. The president would be hard put to even remember their names, let alone take the assassination of one of them as a political defeat.

Make no mistake, Hajj Radwan would have fared no better than the United States in the Pashtun tribal belt. With no understanding of Pashtun politics, he too wouldn't have known where to start with political murder. But at least he would have had the sense not to try.

> NOTE TO ASSASSINS: When an assassination is incomprehensible to Main Street—or, even worse, to the assassin— the chances of it producing the desired result are slim. It's best when an assassination is embraced by a wide swathe of people.

MAKE IT PERSONAL

Drones, Hellfire missiles, and sniper rifles may give you the illusion of supremacy and easy victory, but it's only when you're able to look the target in the eye that assassination really stands a chance of working.

THE FINE CALCULUS OF MURDER

The face of modern assassination that Washington would like us to see is one of cool, flawless, empirical efficiency. Like some all-seeing space-age pterodactyls, drones prowl America's battlefields, relentlessly hunting down its enemies. We're all but promised that nothing eludes a drone's camera or its missiles. Which means that anyone with an X on his back and stupid enough to show his face in the open isn't long for this world. It may sound like cruel geometry, but the point is we're told that drones unerringly cull out the guilty from the innocent.

An official involved in drone assassinations in Iraq told me that a drone's TV guidance system is accurate enough to drop a one-hundred-pound Hellfire missile inside a target as small as a medium-size pizza. It doesn't matter whether the target's moving or hiding behind a rock. It's a big plus that a drone camera's resolution is high enough to make out a man's face from ten thousand feet above.

"The fucker won't look up until he hears the incoming missile's buzz," my ex-colleague said, "and then you see this horror on his face as he realizes what's about to happen. The last you see of him is a bright flash."

It was thanks to drones that the U.S. finally ran to ground the Jordanian-born head of al-Qaeda in Iraq, Abu Musab al-Zarqawi. As the official told me, the initial break came when the man's mentor, a radical Sunni cleric, was identified. From there it was as simple as keeping an eye on him, waiting for Zarqawi to pay him a visit. Which he couldn't resist doing.

It did Zarqawi no good that he understood the threat of drones, and did everything he could to stay out of their sight. He moved locations on the hour, slept in a different house every night, and continually switched out cell phones, even then limiting his calls to a minute or two. In the end, he simply couldn't beat the drone's eye.

"I had working for me this woman named Margaret," the official told me. "She lived and breathed Zarqawi. She spent eighteen hours a day glued to four flat-panel screens, telling the drone pilots what angle she needed, how long she needed it over a target. You should've seen her eureka moment when she finally put Zarqawi in our crosshairs."

The honor of vaporizing Zarqawi fell to an F-16 because a bomb bigger than a Hellfire missile was needed to destroy the building he was hiding in. But the consensus soon became that it's more efficient to arm a drone with a missile and cut down the time between lock-on and launch. It was a case of dumping the middlemen—the F-16 and its pilot.

Another advantage of drones over jets is that they're able to hover over a target for days at a time. It would take a serried array of jets constantly up in the air to replicate them, burning up hundreds of thousands of gallons of fuel and running the Air Force into the ground.

Drones are also more versatile, allowing an operator to easily make a last-second change to a missile's course, if need be, diverting it in mid-flight and exploding it harmlessly in a field. Drones also are easy to maintain: They're powered by high-performance snowmobile engines.

But what really sparked the love affair between Washington and drones was a promise that new sophisticated data analytics would bring near divine infallibility to political murder. It was a brilliant marriage between advanced algorithms, unlimited computing power, intercepts, and drone camera feeds that brought a speed and precision to assassination never before seen in the history of man. Instantaneous justice at the click of a mouse.

It was all the more seductive because data analytics had already started to drive everything that touches our daily lives, from managing electrical grids to long-term weather forecasting. As one computer executive told me, it's now possible to run an algorithm through Twitter feeds commenting on movie trailers and then be able to tell a studio how many days it should keep a new release in theaters. Or whether it should let the movie go right to DVD. If data analytics are able to predict our tastes, why can't it sort out the good guys from the bad guys?

Data analytics also took a lot of the moral hazard out of political murder. If IBM's Deep Blue can outthink the world's best chess players, it certainly can distinguish between right and wrong, who's been naughty and who's been nice. And woe to anyone foolish enough to suggest justice can't be left to a computer, a modern-day deus ex machine; he'll instantly be dismissed as a Luddite.

How far off is the day when killer drones will "own" America's "battle spaces"? Or, as the NSA analysts colorfully put it, the NSA is now in the business of putting "warheads on foreheads." Fighting war won't be any harder than performing a Chopin sonata on a player piano—plug and play. Even better, no more of our girls and boys storming the shores of Tripoli; and no more Vietnams, Iraqs, or Afghanistans either.

———

Washington's faith in computers goes back to American cryptogra-
phers' informing everyone too late that the Japanese navy was
about to attack Pearl Harbor. Since then, there's been an unshakable
belief that a better handling of chatter won't let it happen again. Suck
everything out of the air that's to be sucked, instantly process it, and
we'll be as safe as a baby with a mother's love.

Of course, 9/11 took a lot of wind out of that sail, but America's intelligence agencies doubled down anyway. The National Security Agency
turned its Big Ears on Afghanistan and Pakistan, scooping up trillions
upon trillions of intercepted phone calls, e-mails, electronic money
transfers, airline manifests, Facebook and Twitter feeds. Sophisticated
new software allowed it to churn through the zigabytes upon zigabytes
of intercepted data with lightning speed. NSA's new, advanced algorithms ensured that the smallest speck of gold didn't slip through its net.

If a prepaid cell phone in Karachi talks to a prepaid one in Peshawar,
a digital red flag shoots up. If the Peshawar prepaid cell phone then calls
a number in North Waziristan connected to the Taliban, another flag
shoots up. From there, an algorithm brings divine clarity to it all: Innocent or guilty? Live or die?

The NSA hasn't been too shy to whisper around Washington that its
targeting is only getting better with time and money. Things like
"self-learning algorithms" and "evolving databases" have mammothly
improved the scope and accuracy of its software, instantly shaving
off the random and the inconsequential. The implicit promise is that
there'll come a time when the NSA will be able to instantly and finely
process billions upon billions of telephone calls and never introduce a
human being into the process . . . until it comes time to pull a drone's
trigger. How far away can it be before the NSA's last analyst is shown
the door?

The same is true for monitoring the Web. At first, the NSA was able to read only e-mail "packets"—the so-called meta- or routing data. But now it can get into the "payload"—NSA's shorthand for the text of a message. It's also able to scan broadband Skype calls. With virtually free "cloud" storage, everything we ever write on a computer or talk about over a phone is somewhere out there in the ether, waiting for the NSA to scoop up and download into its giant "data farm" in Utah. Who knows what bit of random information will help call in a drone strike?

Similar advancements can be found in related fields, such as video forensics. By extracting digitally embedded data from images, it's possible for a video sleuth to tell the temperature and humidity of a room where a DVD's been filmed—whether it's been shot in humid Karachi, for example, or the dry mountains of North Waziristan.

I've never myself seen it, but there's apparently been an eerie science-fiction twist to it all, what's called "data visualization." The way I imagined it is that as algorithms pile suspicion on suspicion, a promising candidate for a kill list will go from a cold cobalt-blue dot to a canary-yellow one and then, if he's particularly unlucky, to a bright burning-red one. Since, I've been told we're not quite there with the color scheme. But the point is that while a human being may still decide whether to pull a drone's trigger or not, it's a computer doing the thinking—all of it—right before our very eyes.

The implicit promise with these fully automated killing machines is close to the Philip K. Dick classic short story "The Minority Report." Only rather than predict future crimes it will mete out instant and terminal punishment. Is this what the end of history looks like, killer robots flying the skies and rendering justice?

John Brennan, President Obama's first-term drone commander and now CIA director, has claimed that drones have broken al-Qaeda's back. What's left of its networks exists underground, completely neutered. And it's all been accomplished with divine-like precision. Brennan: "There has never been a single collateral death because of the exceptional precision of the capabilities we've been able to develop."

The machine victorious, political murder fully automated and scrubbed clean.

BEAUTIFUL LIES SLAIN BY UGLY FACT

True, blasting al-Qaeda out of its lairs in Pakistan, Yemen, and every other rat hole they've scurried down into has all worked out nicely for us: no lost airplanes, no dead pilots. But in the headlong rush to automate political murder, we've forgotten one essential element of assassination: The more intimate the act, the more unambiguous the message.

Drone assassinations are like—I don't know—phone sex. They solve the immediate problem, but they leave you unsure of what exactly you got out of it and hungry for more. Whether we're talking about the little death or the big one, the act is only complete when you're able to look your partner in the eye.

A couple of days before Hariri's assassination, the head of Hezbollah, Hassan Nasrallah, and Hariri sat down for tea together. Tea, for God's sake! We'll never know, of course, whether Nasrallah was aware of the plans to assassinate Hariri. But if he was, I'd guess that rather than size Hariri for a coffin, Nasrallah was giving himself a last chance to decide if murder was the only recourse. Whether Hariri could have said anything that would have stayed his execution, we also don't know. But we do know that Nasrallah and Hajj Radwan knew Hariri as well as they knew their own—all his failures and successes, the ins and outs of his crooked business deals, his acts of selfless charity, his brilliance and his stubborn and pointless grudges. They'd finely calculated what Hariri alive cost them, and how they'd be better off after his passing. In the end, it was murder, sure, but it was also a deeply personal affair, closer to the divorce from hell than letting an algorithm pick your next movie.

The other great assassinations in history were also close-up, personal affairs. Supposed friends and colleagues murdered Julius Caesar with daggers. Archduke Ferdinand's assassin pulled the trigger from only five feet away. One plan to murder Hitler was for the assassin to wear an explosive and all but embrace the psychopath before blowing himself and his Führer to kingdom come.

And now that I've brought up that iconic attempt, isn't assassination something of a twisted Freudian act of love? The true assassin, à la Charlotte Corday or Colonel Claus von Stauffenberg, is prepared to freely and gladly sacrifice himself in order to save society, to completely submerge his ego into the common good. In his attack on two American embassies and the Marines, Hajj Radwan employed suicide bombers to remove any doubt about the sacrifice, dedication, and intractability on his side. And by the way, paying the ultimate price has nothing to do with Islam per se. Japanese kamikaze pilots and Tamil suicide bombers also took their own lives for what they believed was a higher good.

Drones, algorithms, and Cray computers may have promised us Cartesian clarity, but in eliminating the human factor, they've greatly diminished the primeval force of political murder. But at bottom, isn't it all beguilingly too easy, like shooting buffalo from a train?

Drone assassinations got off to a rocky start. The first attempt occurred on February 4, 2002, when the press reported that a drone flying over Afghanistan fired a missile at a man who appeared to be Osama bin Laden. Like bin Laden, he was unusually tall, and the two men with him were showing clear deference to him.

As soon as the Pentagon acknowledged the strike, reporters descended on the site. But rather than bin Laden, they found the bodies of three Afghans who'd been rummaging around for scrap metal. The tall man turned out to be only five-eleven, not bin Laden's six-four. Bin Laden apparently had been nowhere near the site of the missile strike.

The botched attempt on bin Laden was noteworthy because it was the first and only time the American government publicly acknowledged the specifics of a drone assassination attempt. But lesson learned: No more details for the untutored.

The first apparently successful drone assassination came nine months later, in November 2002. A Predator drone flying over Yemen killed a suspected al-Qaeda member and five other passengers riding in a car. Among them was an American citizen. The attack was widely reported in the press, but there was no official confirmation other than whisperings here and there that the U.S. had gotten its man. But by no means did it mean that drones were now foolproof.

Among the many missed strikes, a drone attempt on bin Laden's deputy Zawahiri at a place called Damadola, Pakistan, ended up killing eighteen local Pashtuns rather than Zawahiri. A Predator drone killed two Marines in Afghanistan, mistaking them for Taliban. Innocent Bedouin on the move in Yemen were cut down by a drone. One botched attack kept following another.

And then reports started coming out of Afghanistan's and Pakistan's tribal regions that suggested there were an alarming number of drone strikes widely off target. Wedding parties and houses full of children were being hit instead of al-Qaeda. Even reportedly accurate strikes were way off the mark.

Pakistani photographer Noor Behram had already pretty much decided on his own that politics was driving the strikes rather than anything like mathematical precision. He knew he couldn't trust the wild rumors filtering out of the tribal areas or, for that matter, the official statements out of Washington and Islamabad. So he went up into the tribal areas to see for himself and photograph the results.

Behram started to show up at drone attack sites in 2008, doing his best to get to them before the bodies were dragged out and the sites were cleaned up. Before Behram could start taking pictures, he'd often get on his hands and knees to help dig out the survivors. It wasn't risk-free work: Often there would be follow-up drone strikes at the same site. The locals admired his courage and welcomed him at the sites.

After three years of gruesome work, Behram claimed to have the proof on film that more civilians were being killed than the United States and Pakistan admitted. His pictures depicting dead children and old people seem to bear him out. (Custom in the tribal area will not let him take pictures of dead and injured women.)

"For every ten to fifteen people killed, maybe they get one militant," Behram said. "I don't go to count how many Taliban are killed. I go to count how many children, women, innocent people are killed."

A lot of other stuff bubbling up in the press made one wonder exactly who it is we're killing with the drones. In February 2011, for instance, *The Washington Post* reported that 581 "militants" had been killed the previous year by drones in Pakistan. But only two were on any "most wanted" list. Nine months later the *Post* reported that in the previous three months, sixty people had been killed in fourteen drone attacks. But the White House would put a name to only one victim, who, by the way, no one I knew in the intelligence world had ever heard of.

It's hard to come up with a good explanation why the American public isn't offered the identities of these people. The locals presumably comb through the rubble and charred cars and know precisely who's been killed. Is the reason Washington can't tell us is that it doesn't know? Or does Washington know drones are killing civilians and doesn't want us to know?

What Washington always seems to miss is just how tricky eavesdropping can be. When it's good, it's very good; I'd go so far as to say there's no better firsthand intelligence. It's just a fact that when two people are on a phone call foolishly expecting privacy, they'll say things never meant to be said in the open or to a stranger. It's even better when they're angry and blurt out some hideous truth.

But for the unwary, chatter is a treacherous snare. Often what's plucked out of the ether is two people speculating about something they know absolutely nothing about, like whether it's going to rain the following week or not. Having myself been caught in a chatter trap, I have a good idea about the pitfalls.

One day something I took as unimpeachable chatter put Hajj Radwan in a certain hotel in Paris on a certain day. We even had a room number for him. We persuaded the French police to do the needful and arrest him. But when French commandos fast-roped down the side of the hotel and crashed through the windows, they interrupted a Spanish family taking an afternoon snack instead of Hajj Radwan. To this day I don't know what went wrong. Did the French betray us? Or was it because we'd misread the intelligence?

One reason Washington fell in love with chatter is that it takes the hard work out of intelligence, letting it turn off its brain and abdicate all human agency and judgment. It's all the worse these days because Washington is politically and financially invested to the hilt in drones, data analytics, and the fantasy there is such a thing as mechanical justice. Never mind that a lot of innocent people are being slaughtered.

According to a lot of accounts I've recently been reading in the newspapers, Washington doesn't seem to care much that al-Qaeda has started to catch on and do things like constantly switching out phones. They've even taken to throwing their cell phone chips into a bag, shaking them up, and then redistributing them so the U.S. has no idea who is who. It's left it with "signature" or "pattern of life" strikes. They're based on nothing more sophisticated than a drone catching three young men in a field doing exercises, their AKs by their sides. If the three repeat it the next day and in the days after—giving the semblance of organized training—they've all but signed their own death warrants. Who cares that the condemned are without face or name.

The Darwin effect also seems to have kicked in. Smart al-Qaeda types now stick to Karachi and Peshawar, urban areas too densely packed to employ a drone missile. Even worse, many have stopped talking on telephones altogether. As one military intelligence officer responsible for drone targeting told me, in the years since drone strikes began in earnest, the leadership of our main enemy in Afghanistan—the so-called Haqqani network—only "spiked" once on cell phones. They've otherwise turned themselves into phantoms beyond the reach of our technology. Unconnected but alive.

And finally even our best software apparently sucks. It came to light in 2010 that drone target–acquisition software was sending drone missiles off course by as much as thirteen meters (forty-three feet). In a built-up area that's well within the kill radius of a lot of innocent people.

If there's a moral to the story, I suppose it's that the chances of automating assassination are about equal to the Plenty of Fish website finding us the perfect soul mate. But what do I know.

CORRELATION ISN'T GUILT

The more I heard about things such as data visualization and self-learning algorithms, the more it sounded like a bad science-fiction version of the Spanish Inquisition. I needed someone smart to show me where I was wrong.

I managed to run down the noted physicist Tsutomu Shimomura, who's an expert in the mathematics of link analysis—the same algorithms and data visualization reportedly use to draw up kill lists. Among other credentials, Tsutomu studied under Richard Feynman at Caltech. After university, he went to work at Los Alamos. By the way, brains apparently run in the family: Tsutomu's father won a Nobel Prize in chemistry.

Tsutomu earned a measure of fame when he helped track down the notorious hacker Kevin Mitnick. Mitnick had eluded the FBI for years by, among other things, cloning cell phones. But by comparing relevant metadata, Tsutomu was able to pinpoint Mitnick to his North Carolina apartment, where the FBI arrested him. Mitnick did five years in jail. The movie *Track Down* is based on the story.

I meet Tsutomu at a Berkeley organic restaurant where there's rhubarb juice on the menu but no Coke or Pepsi. It's unseasonably chilly, but Tsutomu is in shorts, hiking boots, and a T-shirt with an astral constellation print. He orders cauliflower soup.

I get right to it: Does data analytics work? Or are drones killing the wrong people?

Tsutomu's answer is as short as my question: "Correlation isn't guilt."

For the next twenty minutes, he gives me a riff on "high-yield data" and "extensible" databases. I understand maybe a third of it. What I do get, though, is that traffic analysis tells you only where to look for suspicious activity, but it never determines guilt or innocence.

"To establish guilt," Tsutomu says, "you need to dig a lot deeper, collect old-fashioned evidence admissible in a court of law."

To make his point, he tells me that while he was able to pinpoint the location of Mitnick's phone, the FBI ended up raiding the wrong apartment. Fortunately, their mistake was limited to pounding on the wrong door rather than sending a Hellfire missile through the wrong window.

The jury may still be out on drones, but shooting into the dark has never been anything other than an iffy proposition. Sooner rather than later you'll kill the wrong person and end up making more enemies than you eliminate. When you think about it, with the charges against drone victims irrefutable (at least from Washington's point of view), with body counts unverifiable, and with the definition of victory and defeat left to Washington politicians and bureaucrats who lie for a living, how could drone assassinations not have gone horribly wrong?

Drones are another reminder that scuttling an idiotic idea dressed up as a techno silver bullet is damn near impossible. Falling in dumb love with quants, algos, and their glittering promises, Washington was seduced by a quick, easy release from reality: war at a bargain, assassination without a downside. Extend the logic out far enough, and Washington will start to believe it can rule the world from a single thumb drive and a fleet of solar-powered drones armed with Hellfire missiles. It will have perfected murder, but it can't remember why.

While all along it remains that to win at any game that counts you have to have real skin in it, see things with your own flesh-and-blood eyes. Murder isn't some Shakespearean play where violence occurs offstage. Which means relearning quaint skills such as reading a map, getting your boots dirty, and summoning the guts to stick a dagger into the heart of an enemy. Like it or not, bare-knuckle reality will always trump an algorithm.

> **NOTE TO ASSASSINS:** As soon as the act starts to look like a robot assembly line, packaged and corporatized, you're heading down the wrong path.

NO DANCING WITH
THE FEATHERS

Since the act's objective isn't to catch up with an enemy, tweak divine justice, or divert attention from a political mess at home, there's no need to trumpet body counts, tally up scores, or, for that matter, do any crowing at all. A good kill will speak for itself.

USE THE MANY, PUNISH THE FEW

Equatorial Guinea has a reputation for swift and cruel justice. In 1975, the palace guard executed eighty coup plotters in the national sports stadium as a band played a shaky rendition of "Those Were the Days." Opponents of the currently sitting president accuse him of eating his enemies to "gain power."

It's not the normal trappings of state executions, but it's more evidence the state has an enduring interest in blending judicial murder with ceremony and show. Ancient Rome had its crucifixions, the Middle Ages its drawing and quarterings, and the emir of Bukhara his poisonous insect pits. The leader of North Korea reportedly threw his uncle to starving dogs.

I know it's a reductivist way of looking at things, but I'd say what's behind this is a belief that a vivid, excruciating death serves as a warning to any would-be miscreants. Or, who knows, maybe it has something to do with a revenge gene. The ceremonies of execution aren't something we in the West have exactly abandoned: Texas posts on the Internet the last testimony of the condemned.

Another thing the state sees in its interest is bringing to bear disproportional and irremediable force against any challenge to its authority and dignity. Cross one of its bright, shining lines, and a state will go out of its way to destroy you. You'll spend the rest of your life either sleeping on a cold concrete slab or receive a fatal jolt of electricity. American prisons—the guard towers, razor wire, and slit windows—are architectural statements to the notion that the state won't countenance slights to its authority or its dignity.

The assassin, on the other hand, doesn't have the leisure or resources to bother with ceremony or show. Political murder isn't political theater. Nor is it a moment of public vengeance or symbolic jackbooted intimidation. The assassin's not out to settle a grudge, right a historical wrong, or give someone a long-overdue public comeuppance. He banishes from his mind the notion of revenge, recognizing that it amounts to only an attempt to restore lost dignity. While the state is able to perform justice with the showmanship of a Super Bowl halftime show, the assassin has no choice but to cut to the chase. Efficiency and the preservation of force are always foremost in his mind.

The capable assassin is no Maori warrior making faces and stomping his feet on the ground to intimidate his enemies. He's not in it for the garlands, laurels, and gold medals. Nor does he care about the symbolism of it. What's the point in assassinating the queen of England, a person with no power? Or blowing up Shea Stadium?

The assassin also understands that if he's consumed by abstract obsessions such as the Clash of Civilizations, pogroms, ethnic cleansing, race purification, or any other fuzzy dogma, he's well down the path to defeat. He never forgets that ancient piece of Persian wisdom: You don't slap the king, you kill him.

Like many other true believers, Muslim jihadists are a set of people incapable of understanding the fine points of political murder. They've deluded themselves into believing that random butchery will somehow miraculously lead to the restoration of the caliphate. In 1997, Egyptian Islamic militants murdered sixty-two people near Luxor, mostly European tourists. It was a horrifying, headline-grabbing massacre, but it got them absolutely nothing. In fact, it only encouraged the Egyptian junta to step up its extermination of them.

At the turn of the twentieth century, another set of assassins, anarchists, also showed they didn't understand the instrumentalities of political violence. Not one of their spectacular assassinations got them anything other than a world determined to crush them. It was more murder without purpose, and in the end, the anarchists didn't leave as much as a welt on history.

No, the capable assassin understands that he must mete out death with a pair of fine tongs. It's always the man over the office and handmade violence over showy, elaborate productions. He's a literalist, a meticulous watchmaker tasked with repairing a delicate mechanism. No one's asked him to reinvent the watch or time. He knows the universe is too big and too complex for anyone to change it.

The assassin wants nothing to do with the monsters of history and their death cults—Hitler, Stalin, the Khmer Rouge, the Engineer. Or its saints. While the assassin obeys a higher law, he doesn't mistake himself for a prophet. No sermons, no glossy brochures, no Madison Avenue propaganda. He wants assassination to come off as the most austere of acts—narrow, precise, and effective. "Disinterested" isn't the exact word for it, but it comes close.

The assassin wants murder to be seen as a purely instrumental act—well thought-out, well executed, and with a closed end. In applying proportional force—a dagger over a surface-to-air missile, a quart of lethal antifreeze over a sniper's rifle—the assassin shows he's cautious of life. He's taken pains with the venue, ensuring that it results in the fewest collateral casualties. Hajj Radwan could have murdered Hariri that morning with a car bomb at parliament, but the random slaughter would have detracted from the act.

A couple of years ago an al-Qaeda suicide bomber attempted to kill a Saudi prince by stuffing plastique up his own butt and detonating it in the prince's proximity. The prince survived, but the point here is that al-Qaeda didn't care that it was an ignoble death for all. Its sole objective was to kill the prince rather than to create a made-for-TV event. The prince survived, but the Saudis nonetheless got the message that al-Qaeda had refined its tactics from producing mass casualties to something closer to a bullet with a man's name on it.

The assassin can never, of course, exhibit joy in the act. Nor can murder ever be an act of self-expression or validation. In 1971, immediately after murdering the Jordanian prime minister in Cairo, the assassin got on his knees and started to lick the man's blood off the floor. Instead of attempting to run away, he wanted to savor a moment of passion. He apparently didn't understand that ice-cold violence makes a much deeper impression on an enemy.

But it all comes back to the fact that the assassin wants nothing to do with anything that stinks of utopia or the apocalyptic, with all of its pointless symbolic murder. Or, for that matter, nothing to do with anything that stinks of belief in general. You don't murder Jesus Christ in the hopes of killing Christianity: His crucifixion had precisely the opposite effect. Joseph Stalin made the same mistake when he had an assassin drive an ice ax into Leon Trotsky's head: Trotskyism lived on just fine without its progenitor. And while Stalin was busy planning Trotsky's murder, Adolf Hitler was busy making preparations to invade Russia.

Of course, personal ambition should never drive the act. A genuine assassin isn't out to move up the ranks or make a packet in order to buy a villa on Spain's Costa del Crime. Nor is he out for a bigger cubicle or a better parking space. No, he's closer to a Cincinnatus figure. Having spared his country war, he's perfectly happy to retire to his farm to live out his life in anonymity.

The Venezuelan Communist turned Middle Eastern assassin Carlos the Jackal reduced his odds of survival to nothing by cultivating a celebrity and playboy persona. And indeed, two CIA people cruising around Khartoum recognized him at a stoplight, followed him home, and tipped off the French. Now rotting in a French jail, his celebrity is of no value.

When ego is allowed to consume the act, the audience becomes confused about the act's intent. Was it meant to improve the lot of man or the lot of the assassin? If Carlos thought he had a good reason for murdering the people he did, I for one don't remember what it was.

KEEPING A LID ON IT, OR
THE RECKONINGS OF THE STRONG

I often wonder why the Lebanese can't get along better. The way they're squeezed together between mountain and sea, you'd think they'd be forced to. Instead, it's been more of a case of the waves holding the shit (political nastiness) close to shore and everyone being forced to learn the finer points of political murder.

The way it usually works is that a tribe will cross a well-demarcated line and, in response, the wronged tribe will feel obliged to respond, often by lopping off the head of the offending tribe. But at the same time, the two tribes know better than to let their quarrel descend into a Hobbesian all-against-all fight. Okay, it didn't work so well in 1975 when the Lebanese civil war broke out and 120,000 people were killed. But this was the exception rather than the rule.

My hypothesis is that the Lebanese are able to contain violence because they don't thump their chests after the act. Take the September 14,

1982, assassination of the president-elect: No one ever claimed it. But then again, why would they? Its purpose was to eliminate a powerful, irreplaceable man rather than unnecessarily infuriate the president-elect's sect, the Maronite Christians.

I'd imagine the same consideration came into play with Hajj Radwan's 1989 assassination of the Lebanese president. (I'll get deeper into this one later.) Why pit his side, Hezbollah, against the state and the president's sect, the Maronite Christians? By leaving authorship vague, there was no general call to arms and no retaliatory killings. People might suspect Hezbollah, but without facts, they didn't feel compelled to act.

As I'll also get into in detail later, Hajj Radwan went to great lengths to disassociate himself from Hariri's murder because he saw no point in unnecessarily humiliating Hariri's sect, the Sunnis. He understood that people need a neat and clean motivation to go to war.

B eirut, Damascus, Amman, November 2009: The year after Hajj Radwan's assassination, I'm on my way to Damascus from Beirut in a shared taxi when Press TV in Tehran calls me on my cell to ask if I'd do a TV interview on the crisis du jour. I now can't remember what it was, but it probably had something to do with the fighting in Iraq. They ask to do the interview at the Iranian embassy.

I know it's not the best of ideas, considering the Syrians aren't exactly comfortable with an ex–CIA operative dropping in on them for an unexplained visit and popping off on TV about a conflict on their border. I agree though, if only to see where Hajj Radwan supposedly spent his final days.

An hour later, I'm out front of the new Four Seasons hotel, waiting for the Press TV van. The portico is jammed with elegantly dressed guests waiting for their chauffeur-driven cars. I think how this isn't the old Damascus I knew; it's more like its fin-de-siècle iteration. As I stand there, I wonder if Hajj Radwan had ever actually done a pickup here after he started posing as an Iranian embassy driver. Live your cover, as they say. Could he have not noticed how the Four Seasons was emblematic of the new moneyed Damascus, a world closer to Hariri's than the slum Hajj Radwan had grown up in?

I sit up front with the driver, a young bearded Iranian who speaks formal Arabic. He politely laughs at my Persian. He doesn't ask who I am or why his station would want to interview me. I think about asking him what Hajj Radwan was like, but of course I don't. Instead, we talk about the traffic and the weather.

The way the Iranian embassy sits off the main Mezzeh highway, with a sad walk of dusty trees out front and its neo-Stalinist architecture, it reminds me of an insurance company converted into a secret-police headquarters. The floodlights don't improve things.

A guard waves the van through. I follow the driver up a flight of stairs to a second-floor studio. He puts me at an empty desk to wait for Tehran to call. I wonder if Hajj Radwan once sat here, and then I think about the other threads of history connected to this place.

One building over is the main Iranian embassy, which in the eighties was the cockpit for Khomeini's revolution in Lebanon. It was here that Lebanese Shiite clerics and political figures first met after the 1982 Israeli invasion and then returned home to form Hezbollah. To this day, it's the main conduit for money and arms going to Hezbollah.

In 1984, there was an attempt on the Iranian ambassador in the same building. His would-be assassins sent him an explosives-strapped book. He survived but lost a hand. The Iraqis were no doubt behind it, apparently believing they could change their fortunes vis-à-vis Iran by murdering this man. The problem was that the ambassador was only a cog in Khomeini's revolution. And not to mention that the revolution was just picking up steam. I wonder if at that point in history even Khomeini's assassination would have changed things. Belief is a hard thing to kill.

But it's not as if the Iranians had mastered political murder. In April 1980 a group connected to Iran attempted to assassinate Saddam's foreign minister, Tariq Aziz. It's commonly believed that this event led Saddam to invade Iran. Causality is a tricky thing, but it's arguable this missed hit led to three disastrous wars—the Iran–Iraq War (1980–1988), the Gulf War (1990–1991), and the Iraq War (2003–2011). I doubt it's what the Iranians had planned. For the assassin, the law of unintended consequences is the sword of Damocles eternally hanging over his head.

But getting back to the attempt on the Iranian ambassador: It's now clear the Iraqis had gone after the wrong man. They incorrectly believed he was responsible for its problems in Lebanon, including the destruction of its embassy there in 1981. In fact, the best intelligence points at Hajj Radwan. Did the Iraqis not know who Hajj Radwan was or was it that they couldn't get to him? I don't know.

What I do know is that in the early years Hajj Radwan stayed away from the Iranian embassy in Damascus as if it carried the bubonic plague. He insisted that when Iranians came from Tehran they meet in Lebanon. He assured them it was the safest for all.

Hajj Radwan fully grasped that unyielding independence is what both kept him alive and allowed him to maneuver with the total freedom he needed. At one point, he even went out and made his own money. In 1985 he kidnapped four Russian diplomats in Beirut, killing one who happened to be a KGB officer. At their release, Hajj Radwan arranged to collect a $200,000 ransom. There was nothing the Iranians could do about it.

Over the years, we watched with curiosity as Tehran tirelessly tried to drag Hajj Radwan under its umbrella. It appointed him an official in the Amin al-Haras—the intelligence wing of the Iranian Revolutionary Guard Corps. But as I said, titles meant nothing to Hajj Radwan, who not only declined to don an Iranian uniform but also refused to participate in the ceremonies and mindless discipline that go hand in hand with an organized military. When relations between Iran and Hajj Radwan became strained, Hajj Radwan would disappear for months on end, ignoring Tehran's frantic appeals for a meeting.

Hajj Radwan despised the infighting in Tehran—the petty fights over status and money, the turf wars, the bureaucratic prevarications. When responsibility for being the liaison to him shifted from the Revolutionary Guard Corps to the Ministry of Intelligence, he stormed away, refusing to meet any Iranian official. He knew that petty bureaucratic rivalries can only undermine the mission.

Hajj Radwan would for years meet only Iranian officials he personally trusted. It was essential for him that his Iranian interlocutors understand Lebanon and its politics, as well as his views of the fine instrumentalities of political violence. Operating under an Iranian ignorant of Lebanon could only lead to disaster, drawing him into some ill-advised attack. Hajj Radwan had one confederate in Tehran he completely trusted, a man he called on every time there was a problem he needed sorted out. It provoked considerable jealousy in the Iranian leadership, especially as Hajj Radwan moved from one spectacular success to the next. Everyone wanted a piece of him to burnish his resistance credentials.

But at some point a shift occurred. This was at a time when Iran was losing its appetite for revolution. Among other things, it decided that the Western hostages Hajj Radwan had started taking in 1982 were more of a liability than an asset. Although he wasn't happy about it, Tehran overrode Hajj Radwan's objections and ordered their release. Hajj Radwan was being slowly sucked into Iran's ambit.

We also learned that in return for releasing the hostages Tehran gave Hajj Radwan a large one-time payment. But it was unclear whether he wanted the money for his organization or was lining his pockets. I wouldn't go so far as to say Hajj Radwan turned into a spoken-for, paid-up Iranian agent, but it was certainly starting to look like it. Was it about money or power? I don't know.

Hajj Radwan's brother-in-law was arrested by Kuwait in 1983 after blowing up the American and French embassies there, and he spent the next seven years in a Kuwaiti jail. When Iraq invaded and the prisons were emptied, he escaped and made his way back to Lebanon. As the brother-in-law told friends, he couldn't believe the change in Hajj Radwan's organization, how it had gone from a highly mobile, shadowy band of assassins to something closer to a bureaucracy, with all the attendant drag and bullshit. He was equally shocked by how so many of the operatives had settled for comfortable lives.

Somewhere along the line, the Syrians also seemed to get a piece of Hajj Radwan. When I heard from a businessman close to the Syrian president that Hajj Radwan regularly visited the presidential palace, I had a hard time believing him. But the businessman assured me that on a couple of occasions he'd seen Hajj Radwan cooling his heels, waiting to see the president. There was no reason the businessman would lie to me, but it wasn't the Hajj Radwan I knew.

Was the hot, blue flame of power too much for Hajj Radwan to resist? If so, it drew him away from the tight, spare tribal mind-set he'd grown up with in the southern suburbs, that impenetrable prophylactic that had kept him alive all of these years. Working at the Iranian embassy as a driver was okay as a cover, but as Hajj Radwan would find out too late, it wasn't foolproof.

He'd also apparently remarried, a girl from a good family. They settled down in a comfortable apartment in a quiet Damascus suburb. He received visitors at home and kept regular hours. Some sources have it that his professional life was limited to training Palestinian groups. He would go meet them in their offices.

When I look back at it now—Syria's and Iran's success in roping in Hajj Radwan, his settling down in Damascus, the apartment, the new wife—it's clear Hajj Radwan had let his standards slip. I'm not saying that Beirut would have forever remained the sanctuary it was in my days there, but it was definitely safer than Damascus.

By the way, the Press TV interview goes fine, the anchor impeccably polite and thoughtful.

Assassins, like politicians and journalists, are not attracted to losers.

—HUNTER S. THOMPSON

From Damascus I drop down to Amman by taxi. My intention is to see a retired Jordanian operative who'd once worked against Hezbollah. I catch him a couple of times on the phone, but he always has some excuse for not meeting me. By call number five I get the hint.

What I'm starting to figure out is that people want absolutely nothing to do with the tribunal. When I first started to work for it, I called a couple of my ex-colleagues who'd tracked Hezbollah over the years, but they only laughed at the proposition of helping. As for giving evidence at the trial, I didn't dare ask. (After Hezbollah ran its TV piece on me, I better understood the sentiment.)

With time on my hands, I call the widow of the Jordanian intelligence officer killed at Khost, a Jordanian prince by the name of Sharif Ali bin Zeid. I know she wants to ask me about her husband's death, as she's convinced she hasn't gotten the full story. I'm not sure why she thinks an ex–CIA agent will have a more authoritative version for her, but I agree to have coffee with her. We meet in the lobby of my hotel.

She starts by telling me how that morning, December 30, Sharif Ali texted her from Afghanistan that he'd been unable to get out of his mind that the only safe place in the world he could imagine was the small terrace of their house. He could picture it in its every detail, he wrote.

The two of them sitting there, their two dogs at their feet, the sun sinking into the Dead Sea.

She stops and worries her coffee with her spoon. "Do you think he had a premonition?"

In tight jeans and a cable-knit sweater, Sharif Ali's widow is pretty. Her English is nearly flawless, every word carefully articulated. Every once and a while she says something to remind me she's a Christian. It makes me wonder what she meant by premonition.

She tells me how Sharif Ali and she met when they were nineteen. It was an improbable match, he a prince and a descendant of the Prophet, and she the daughter of a Christian university professor. The king forbade their marrying, but Sharif Ali spent the next five years petitioning him to reconsider.

She says her husband was half American in the way he looked at the world. He'd fallen in love with the United States while studying at Boston College and later interning for Senator John Kerry. When they first started to date, he'd take her out on his motorboat in the Gulf of Aqaba, anchor it, and talk about his bright vision for Jordan, how with an open mind it could become the Hong Kong of the Middle East. Her husband, she says, was one of those rare people able to bridge the chasm between East and West.

In Joby Warrick's book about Khost, *The Triple Agent*, there's a picture of Sharif Ali posing on the running board of a Land Rover in the middle of a river in spate. A plump man, he's smiling, obviously thrilled to be on an adventure. I now try to picture Sharif Ali put down among the Pashtuns of Khost, a people as alien to him as they were to Jennifer Matthews. I can very well imagine him having a premonition that it was about to go bad.

The king finally relented to their marriage, but only under the condition that she convert to Islam. She agreed, and the two quickly married— six months before Sharif Ali went to Khost.

Starting to tear up, she changes the subject, saying she's about to lose her house. According to Jordanian law, she's obligated to give half of it to her husband's family. Without the money to buy them out, she now needs to look for a new place.

"It's the one place in the world he felt safe," she says again. "How can I let a stranger live there?"

She says that since she can't keep their house she wants to write a book about Sharif Ali, a love story. It would give purpose to his death. Could I look for an agent when I get back to the United States?

I look out the window at the blast walls, drop barriers, and armored personnel carriers surrounding the hotel. There are metal detectors at the entrance and a policeman with a machine gun. The hotel was turned into a fortress after suicide bombers struck Amman's hotels in 2005. I wonder if Sharif Ali confronted Jennifer Matthews about her decision not to run the doctor through a metal detector.

Sharif Ali's widow gets up to leave and then sits back down to ask one last question. "When you spend a life devoted to one thing like this, and it's taken away, there has to be a purpose. Right?"

It's a question I don't have a ready answer for; I'm not sure Zawahiri's assassination would have mattered. I keep coming back to the thought that al-Qaeda is only an idea—a notion that jihad must be pursued through violence. Even according to Zawahiri, any true believer can pick up a weapon and fight the unbelievers, with or without guidance. How do you kill a belief by killing one man? You don't. It's just as Saddam never stood a chance of killing Khomeini's revolution by assassinating his ambassador to Damascus. I keep it to myself, though. When is the truth ever a comfort in death? Instead, I mumble something about Zawahiri's being a mass murderer and, yes, his assassination would have mattered.

After Sharif Ali's widow leaves, I think how the Jordanians, or at least the rich ones, are so much like us—open, gentle, self-reflective. Although the Jordanians played their part in the attempt on Zawahiri and later on Hajj Radwan, they aren't a people who live off their murderous instincts.

That same night I drop by the apartment of a Jordanian prince. He's Sharif Ali's cousin. As soon as I bring up Khost, he becomes angry: "It was an unforgivable blunder."

He gets up to get his pipe and then sits back down with a sigh. Referring to the Palestinian doctor, he says, "You never throw a fish like that back into the pond. They turn on you in an instant. My cousin was a naïf."

The prince then redirects his anger to Jordan's intelligence chief, the man who sent Sharif Ali to Khost: "The man's a dull clerk. He rose far above his station. Worse, he's corrupt."

It turns out that around the time of Khost the Jordanian intelligence chief was deep into a crooked scheme to market stolen Iraqi oil. Apparently, he was too distracted about making money to think about the sort of danger he'd put Sharif Ali in. In February 2012, the chief would be indicted in Jordan for money laundering, embezzlement, and abuse of power. An added irony to the affair is that his partner in the oil scheme was an ex–CIA officer who'd once headed the hunt for bin Laden and Zawahiri.

But the prince's anger turns to puzzlement when he gets around to drone assassinations.

"In all seriousness, what's to be gotten? You don't seem to understand that you're only cutting away the fat for them."

For the next fifteen minutes he goes on a riff about how the demonstration of force isn't the same as the careful application of force. One's an ugly burlesque, the other a ballet. It's even worse when it's allowed to turn into a public spectacle. As British actress Mrs. Patrick Campbell put it, "Don't do it in the street and frighten the horses."

A SIN HALF CONCEALED IS HALF FORGOTTEN

It's never far from the assassin's mind that murder is a proscribed art, whatever the justification or motive. It's reason enough not to crow about it, to prance around, or even to acknowledge it with a wink and nod. In fact, the assassin should do his absolute best to bake into the act all the misdirection, lies, and water-muddying he can. Why gratuitously piss people off?

King Hassan II of Morocco went for the same polite-fiction approach when he decided to assassinate his security chief in January 1983. And today, more than three decades later, the official record is that Dlimi died in an auto accident. While most Moroccans suspect otherwise, without the ability to nail Hassan's lie, memories are so faded that it doesn't matter.

The Lao assassins never attempted to disguise their murders as something they weren't. But not one of them has ever stepped forward to claim authorship. Why put it in people's minds that you're an assassin? Assassination isn't a narcissistic act to be included on your résumé or what amounts to a medal to be pulled out on special occasions. Its sole purpose is to destroy a cancerous cell.

On the wrong side of the equation, the CIA's reported attempt on al-Qaeda's number two, Zawahiri, came off as something closer to political blustering than as a true reckoning of power. With all the embarrassing leaks, with the stupid cover-up, with a tell-all book, it left the curious like me to comb through facts that should never have seen the light of day—if for no other reason than that they make us look like a paper tiger.

Washington doesn't even make a good-faith effort to hide its hand in political murder, all but publicly embracing the two-thousand-plus people it's assassinated since 9/11. Some drone pilots have even gone public, airing their regrets and the mistakes. And so, with all the public hoo-ha and flailing around, drone assassinations aren't all that different from Equatorial Guinea's execution of the coup plotters in its national sports stadium. More show than efficient political murder.

I realize that both al-Qaeda and the Pakistanis know all about our drone assassinations. In fact, according to *The New York Times,* it was Pakistan that insisted on selecting the victim of the first CIA drone strike in the Pashtun tribal belt. But it was never part of the bargain for us to trumpet it around. I'd imagine the Pakistanis can only groan every morning they wake up to read another *Washington Post* exposé about a CIA assassination in their country.

George Bernard Shaw once famously said that if you can't get rid of the skeleton in your closet, you might as well teach it to dance. True enough, but I'm certain he never had assassination in mind. It's just one of those rare transgressions you never want to boast about.

With the Khost revelations, with Brennan's lie that drones have never caused the death of innocent victims, with all the hand-wringing and moralizing, could we not come off as rank amateurs in the business of political murder? We mostly do fine as human beings, but we're lousy assassins.

> **NOTE TO ASSASSINS:** Always the lie over the truth, no matter how implausible it may sound. Doubt is the truth's best corrosive. So make it as palatable as possible for everyone.

DON'T GET CAUGHT IN FLAGRANTE DELICTO

Keep your enemy in a state of ignorance and confusion. When you conceal even the most insignificant and benign details of your existence, your enemy will misjudge your abilities and strengths, and make commensurate mistakes. Just as a good conjurer never lets on how he's performed a trick, there's no point in your leaving behind a smoking gun.

YOU'RE A GHOST, INTIMATE WITH THE PLACE YOU HAUNT, BUT NEVER OF IT

Geneva, October 11, 1987: The chances are we'll never find out what really happened that night in room 317 of Geneva's elegant lakeside Beau-Rivage hotel. Its sole occupant was found dead in the bathtub, and whoever his visitors were from the night before haven't and aren't about to come forward. The mute facts of the case aren't particularly helpful either.

When the manager called the Geneva police about the dead guest in room 317, the hotel assumed it had a suicide on its hands. It's also what the cops thought when they first saw the handsome man floating in the bathtub. His name was Uwe Barschel; he was a German politician. He was forty-three years old.

The Geneva medical examiner's report is factual and dry. It notes Barschel was discovered at around one-thirty in the afternoon. The bathtub was full, but Barschel's head was above the waterline. He was fully clothed, his tie loose at the neck. The autopsy showed no water in Barschel's stomach or lungs: He hadn't drowned. The barbiturate lorazepam was found in his stomach, which supported the hypothesis of suicide. He'd also drunk a half bottle of wine.

What gave the police pause were the bruises and cuts on Barschel's corpse, signs of some sort of struggle. But it was impossible to determine whether they were connected to his death or not. The police also found it curious that the wine bottle couldn't be found. To add to the uncertainty of it, it couldn't be determined whether the quantity of lorazepam found in Barschel's stomach was sufficient to produce death.

Barschel's distraught wife immediately rejected the suicide hypothesis, convinced that her husband had been murdered. She told the story of how her husband had received a disturbing, mysterious call the month before he went to Geneva. "For the first time in my life, I am afraid," he told her afterward. He refused to explain to her who his caller was, or anything else for that matter. In spite of misgivings, Barschel met his mystery caller the day before he was found in the bathtub of room 317.

But what could the Geneva police do with thin, circumstantial evidence such as this? And not to mention that politics and suspicion of foul play are the perfect recipe for generating baseless conspiracy theories, especially in the minds of distraught spouses. And then, as these things so often go, things went from murky to murkier.

The former Mossad agent Victor Ostrovsky claimed it was Mossad that had assassinated Barschel. The motive? Barschel had surfaced as an obstacle to a secret arms deal between Iran and Israel. According to Ostrovsky's version, Israeli operatives lured Barschel into a meeting with a promise to help with some political problem. The Israeli operatives jumped Barschel as soon as the door closed behind him then killed him by forcing barbiturates and poison down his throat.

Israel denied murdering Barschel. But so what? skeptics asked. They argued Israel would have no interest in admitting to the murder of a German politician. Killing some Arab in Europe was one thing, but murdering a prominent European was something else. Good enough, but the truth remains there's no convincing proof Barschel was assassinated, let alone that Israel did it.

At this point, anyone serious threw up his hands and stopped paying attention, in particular serious journalists. When the facts become contradictory and confusing, people mindful of their reputations run from a difficult story. It's what happened with Iran and Pan Am 103. The way the press looks at it, everyone gets cut in a knife fight.

But it didn't deter the public prosecution department of Lübeck, Germany, which in June 2011 announced it would reopen the Barschel case. It promised that new scientific tools would clear things up. It's unclear why the Swiss, who have primary jurisdiction, weren't mentioned in the press report.

NEVER MAKE YOURSELF A TASTY DIGITAL MEAL

One ironic twist to the Barschel case is that the only other time the Beau-Rivage crossed paths with history had been the 1898 assassination of the empress of Austria. She was stabbed on the quay in front of the hotel and brought inside to die. Bystanders ran down her anarchist assassin and arrested him. Good old-fashioned vigilante justice.

The Swiss police took their time modernizing, but when they finally did, they did it with a vengeance. Incidentally, it was the Swiss who kindly introduced me to the brave new digital glue pot we all exist in today.

It happened on one glorious autumn drive to Zermatt. Unbeknownst to me, a police camera on the side of the road "flashed" me—caught me speeding. For a normal law-abiding person, it should have been a pretty much straight-up monetary atonement. When an overpriced ticket with a picture of your license plate and a notation of the excess speed arrives in the mail, you send back a check in the return mail. But genius that I am, I decided I could beat the Swiss criminal justice system. My thinking was that since the guilty car was a rental and not registered in Switzerland, they wouldn't bother about the ticket.

Two years later on a trip to Geneva, I arrived after midnight and went to bed, counting on sleeping in late. But at about five-thirty the next morning, the squawk of a walkie-talkie outside my door woke me up. There was a sharp knock. I opened it to find two starched and armed Swiss policemen. After they verified I was the person who'd checked into the room, they told me to get dressed and follow them to the police station to pay an outstanding speeding ticket.

As I was all but frog-marched through the lobby, I considered asking my escort whether their time wouldn't be better spent catching Barschel's assassins, but I was awake enough to know it wouldn't improve my situation. I paid the ticket and walked out of the police station vowing never again to commit a crime in Switzerland.

Very early on, the Swiss got the hang of the digital glue pot. For instance, in the early nineties they instituted a practice that when a visitor calls ahead to a Swiss airport to reserve a rental car the rental company will run an intrusive credit check on its new client. What it meant for spooks, criminals, and other scofflaws is no more alias passports or alias credit cards; a quick scroll down the page would instantly expose any villainy. Couple this with the advent of smartphones, the Internet, biometric chips embedded in passports, iris scans, and all the rest of the enemy-of-the-state snooping, and anyone with murder on his mind had better think twice about doing it in Switzerland.

BRIGHT FALSEHOODS TO BLIND THE EYE

As the story goes, one morning one of Hajj Radwan's gunmen needed to see him about an urgent piece of business. But without a phone number or an address, he wasn't sure where to start. He went around Beirut checking with Hajj Radwan's wolf pack. But no one knew where to find him. The man even dropped by the apartment of Hajj Radwan's wife. But she too didn't know; she hadn't seen him in six months.

Two months later, the man was talking to a friend in front of the Fransabank in the southern suburbs when they noticed a man on a wobbly motor scooter heading their way. Belching oily black smoke and stuttering like an old lawn mower, the scooter sounded as if it were about to cut out. Its rider was thickset, of middling height, and poorly dressed—soiled white shirt, cheap synthetic pants, scuffed shoes. Wrapped around his face was a kaffiyeh, a cotton scarf. On the rear rack was a burlap sack bound in twine holding some sort of cloth. He was a poor tailor maybe.

The scooter pulled up next to them, and the rider turned off the engine. They couldn't see the man's face because of the kaffiyeh. Caked in dust, he looked like he'd been traveling for a long distance on unpaved back roads. The rider said something they couldn't catch. He unwrapped the kaffiyeh from his face: It was the boss, Hajj Radwan. They all had a good laugh at Hajj Radwan's ability to conjure himself out of nowhere.

Who knows whether the story's apocryphal or not. But the point is that Hajj Radwan was the human variety of a *Gonepteryx rhamni*, a butterfly whose color and pattern is indistinguishable from the foliage around it. Operating out of the southern suburbs, and indifferent to the trappings of power, money, and celebrity, he knew how to disappear into the fabric of poverty and despair. And to be sure, he went out of his way never to subject himself to protofascist digital microscopes like Switzerland's.

If indeed Barschel was assassinated, I imagine his assassins pulled off their own *Gonepteryx* act. For a start, they left nothing behind for the police to work with—no weapon, no telephone or charge-card records, no CCTV images. In order to get past the Beau-Rivage's front desk, I imagine they dressed Swiss bourgeois chic—pricey tweed jackets, polished Bally shoes, Pringle cashmere sweaters. If they had gone with the scruffy look, they wouldn't have gotten as far as the elevator before the concierge stopped them. After the act, they would have immediately headed out of Geneva. I don't know this, of course, but it's just as Barschel's assassins would want it.

But as any able assassin will tell you, disappearing into dull obscurity isn't as easy as it would seem.

AND A FINE ART IT IS

Anyone in a dark profession who can't avail himself of a place like Ayn al-Hilweh had better learn the basics of garden-variety deception. In fact, every single moment of his life is best framed with an eye to concealing the most basic truths about his existence.

He will never want to volunteer anything anyone will remember him by. What's the point in advertising you have a demented mother-in-law or that you were second coxswain on the varsity rowing team? Or that you're a billionaire? Or that you're married to a former Miss America? Money and beauty are things that stick in people's minds.

The assassin always runs in the opposite direction from the limelight, away from places where people go to see and be seen—three-star Michelin restaurants, art openings, high-end dog shows. They're flytraps that come with attentive staffs, CCTV camera coverage, and private security people who watch everyone like a hawk. In other words, don't commit a murder in the Van Cleef & Arpels on Fifth Avenue.

If there's a choice between doing business at a Motel 6 in Hoboken, New Jersey, or the Plaza, take the Motel 6. Or if you really want to drop out of sight, take a Greyhound bus (pay for the ticket in cash) to an Indian reservation in northern Arizona and meet there. Good luck to the cops trying to reconstruct that trip.

The same sort of invisibility holds for couture. It's always Sears menswear over Brioni, Payless ShoeSource over John Lobb. And never wear anything memorable or that catches the eye—no nose rings, no T-shirts with trite messages, no fancy watches with altimeters. Always wear clunky and scratched eyeglasses; it's what people will remember rather than your eyes.

The assassin would as soon wear a ballerina's pink tutu as sport tattoos, mirrored Oakley wraparound sunglasses, and rippled muscles. Looking the part of a coiled and cold-blooded killer is something people will remember. And by the same token, the assassin studiously avoids giving off attitude—no impatient assurance or giving the impression he has the drop on anyone.

What he's after is a completely self-erasing manner. For instance, he will employ a disarming tic of cocking his head to one side and pointing an ear at his interlocutor, pretending he's riveted by every word coming out of the stupid bastard's mouth. Always lead with insecurity and deference; Mr. Magoo over Donald Trump.

While the assassin might selflessly pledge himself to action, he understands there's no point in flaunting his principles. He embraces the profoundly ordinary and ignorant, appearing to be a slave to every shallow convention, devoid of everything that makes a person stand out—the worship of money, overweening ambition, intellectual prescience. There's not a book in his house.

The assassin works hard at turning himself into a fire hose of public opinion and pedestrian convictions, giving off the hum of an empty mind. He clings to unsupported and wrong opinions as if his reputation depends on it. He unironically flies the flag on Independence Day and pastes a GO PACKERS! sticker on his bumper.

If the assassin's forced to talk politics, he recites unimportant, unrevealing, and reassuring facts. But in the end, he pleads that he can't make heads or tails out of politics. He doesn't sign petitions, write to his congressman, or keep a blog. If he posts pictures on Instagram, it's of his dog or Mount Rushmore . . . with nothing else in the frame. He's more than happy to let everyone know he thinks Nixon got a raw deal.

The assassin will want to make himself appear as jealous as a hunchback. While he'll shit all over the elite's pretensions—screening rooms, surfing in Bali, flying off to Europe on a private jet—and scoff at people with real intellectual lives, he'll never stop telling people he knows all about automobiles, from their prices to their performances.

Always working at dimming his shine, the assassin must never be caught coming up with a bright or original idea. He'll fight instead over the size of his cubicle or a better parking space. He embraces the stink of mediocrity and frivolity as if it's his cherished birthright.

By turning himself into a walking and talking purloined letter, by hiding in the open, the assassin will deceive people into believing that he's the least important person in the world, i.e., incapable of pulling off a perfect kill.

Life is a shitstorm, in which art is our only umbrella.

—MARIO VARGAS LLOSA

Dubai, January 19, 2010: The closed-circuit images instantly captivated the world's imagination, especially the one of the girl in the floppy hat and big sunglasses. Although the picture is pixelated and grainy, you can tell she's pretty. There's something about her—I don't know—a joie de vivre, a reassuring insouciance; maybe she'd be a fun date. As she checks in, she looks up at the camera above the reception desk and smiles: *Don't bother about me, guys, I'm just a happy-go-lucky tourist on holiday.*

There are more clips of her arriving at Dubai's airport, walking through passport control. And then back at the airport for her flight out. There are shots of her passing through a hotel lobby, wearing the same angelic smile. If she's performing for the cameras, I don't see it. What's obvious though is that there's never a clear shot of her face—always the glasses and the hat.

The Dubai police would never have thought twice about the girl had they not found a dead Palestinian in a hotel they'd caught her in on a CCTV camera feed. At first, it appeared as if he'd died of natural causes. He was tucked into bed, his clothes neatly draped over a chair, his room locked from the inside. But when it was found that he was traveling on a phony passport, that he was an arms dealer, and that he was on an Israeli hit list, there were too many coincidences for the Dubai police's liking. They opened a murder investigation.

The police were particularly intrigued by spots of blood found on the

Palestinian's pillow. There also were unexplained bruises on his face, nose, and neck. The headboard in his room was damaged. When the autopsy showed signs of an injection on his right hip, the possibility of murder was raised. It was confirmed when a drug that causes paralysis was discovered in his system.

The police's hypothesis was that the assassin or assassins forced their way into the man's room, subdued him long enough to administer a shot, and then neatly tidied up the room to make it appear the Palestinian had died in his sleep. Did the assassins climb out the window after locking the room from the inside? It was one question never answered.

By running an algorithm through Dubai airport's entry-and-departure records in the days in and around the Palestinian's murder, and by sifting through all potentially related cell phone calls and CCTV feeds, the police assembled what they believed was a convincing and coherent picture of the team that assassinated the Palestinian.

It appeared that most team members had arrived in Dubai early in the morning of January 18, 2010, and then left the next day—immediately after the assassination. There'd been two dozen of them, maybe more. With the exception of one, the assassins traveled to Dubai on forged passports. No one's explained why one assassin, who traveled under the alias Michael Bodenheimer, used a legitimate German passport.

The team paid for its hotel rooms either in cash or with prepaid credit cards, which were issued by a company named Payoneer. The team used prepaid cell phones that employed a "virtual call center" in Vienna. Based on records, some of the assassins had made preparatory trips to Dubai, no doubt to case locations.

From the CCTV images, it's clear the team always kept on their disguises, ducking into bathrooms to change wigs and dark glasses. Several put on baseball caps to break up their faces. Some even took pains to sit around the lobby with tennis rackets. It was a case of living your cover. It was all a nice performance considering the effort, but not good enough to fool Dubai's supercomputers and algorithms.

When the Dubai police made public the CCTV images and other details of the investigation, most people concluded the assassins had to have been Israelis. Israel had both opportunity and motivation to murder the Palestinian. But there was one question there's no good answer for: Aren't the Israelis better than this?

An Israeli journalist close to Mossad wrote for *GQ* that the Dubai job had been carried out by an ultrasecret Mossad assassination unit known as Caesarea. It's responsible for what the KGB used to call "active measures"—assassinations, break-ins, and sabotage.

All of Caesarea's operatives work under aliases and have no government connections, either by phone or e-mail. It's housed separately from Mossad, outside Tel Aviv. Its operatives are forbidden from discussing their work outside the Caesarea facility. In the espionage business, they're called "lily whites." But apparently the white of a lily isn't an easy color to match.

We all die with reasons.

—A DUBAI POLICE OFFICER TO ME

My first reaction to the Dubai job was that Mossad had gotten sloppy. What else could explain leaving a digital bread-crumb trail such as this? It definitely wasn't the same Mossad who'd murdered Atef and (maybe) Barschel. A couple of my former colleagues wondered if it wasn't a matter of Mossad's not caring whether it got caught or not. My question, though, is: Why did the team go to such pains to clean up the room and use a sophisticated drug unless their intention was to make the police believe he'd died of natural causes?

My hunch is that Mossad miscalculated Dubai's technical sophistication, failing to take into account its CCTV cameras, cell phone records, and advanced software. Maybe it was thanks to a stubborn bias that the

Gulf Arabs are Bedouin savages incapable of conducting a modern police investigation. If true, it meant that Mossad overlooked the blindingly obvious, like Dubai's ultramodern airport whose security and infrastructure is better than most in the West.

And let's not forget money. Anyone with deep pockets can purchase an Orwellian state apparatus to efficiently monitor every hotel, airport, and train station in the country. I once spent a day inspecting the London police unit responsible for the thousands of CCTV cameras monitoring that city. I walked away convinced London isn't the place you'd want to commit a high-level political murder. But neither is Dubai.

Not to mention that Dubai wasn't the first time Mossad botched an assassination. There was the failed attempt on the Red Prince in Lillehammer, Norway, in 1973. But equally sloppy was the Mossad attempt on a Hamas leader in Amman in September 1997. Two Mossad assassins were arrested, the victim survived, and a diplomatic blowup between Israel and Jordan nearly wrecked their relations. It seems that somewhere between Atef and Dubai, Mossad lost its way. Polite fictions are no longer in its bag of tricks.

I've often wondered if it doesn't have something to do with the Israelis' having gotten too comfortable with "targeted killings" in the West Bank and Gaza. Very much like the SAS in Northern Ireland, Israeli commandos enjoy a distinct home-turf advantage. With all Palestinian electronic communications and databases being monitored and a vast web of paid and vetted informants in place, the Palestinians live in a virtual high-security prison. Targeted killings are like spearing fish in a barrel.

Not long before Dubai, I happen to be visiting a West Bank refugee camp for a documentary and am able to walk the route taken by Israeli commandos on their way to assassinating a Palestinian militant. It winds its way through a maze of cramped alleys and open sewers, reminding me a lot of Ayn al-Hilweh. The Israeli team entered the camp in the middle of the night, I during the day.

The pathway between the makeshift houses narrows to the point I'm able to raise my arms and touch either side. There's no logic to the camp's layout, which means I keep getting lost and ending up in dead ends. Kids start to show up, and I soon have a pack of them following me, laughing at the stupid, lost foreigner. It's a mystery to me how Israeli commandos are capable of navigating a place such as this in the black of night, other than thanks to lots of practice.

The house where the assassination occurred looks like all the other houses around it—one story, cinder block, barred and shuttered windows, pebble-dash front door. A Palestinian tells me that after the Israelis crashed through the door it took them only seconds to find the false wall behind which the Palestinian was hiding. They shot him through the wall, only digging him out afterward to identify him. The commandos obviously had an informant close to the man.

I'm not saying Mossad would have covered its trail if it had tapped into Dubai's telephone system or something. And yes, the floppy hats and big dark glasses were a nice touch, but it remains that Mossad in the Gulf was a fish out of water. There just wasn't a way to hide two dozen Westerners up to something fishy. And not to mention that Mossad failed to build in misdirection, doing something such as—I don't know—leaving false clues pointing at the CIA.

A lie gets halfway around the world before the truth has a chance to get its pants on.

—WINSTON CHURCHILL

It's to the assassin's advantage never to forget that people prefer their myths and beautiful lies to facts. Only twenty-four percent of Americans accept the 1964 Warren Commission's conclusion that Lee Harvey Oswald acted alone. The rest believe JFK was murdered by, well, take your pick—the CIA, the mob, or the Trilateral Commission. Never mind that there's not an iota of evidence to support any one of those conspiracy theories. It's this sort of childlike credence that the assassin wants to leverage.

At every stage of the planning and execution, the assassin needs to build in misdirection. For instance, if a sniper rifle is to be used, he should steal it from, let's say, the mob, or anyone else who might plausibly engage in assassination. If a getaway car is needed, steal it from the FBI. The same goes for cell phones and computers.

There was misdirection built into the Hariri assassination at every step, which I'll get into later. But in the meantime, suffice it to say that a man's nose found at the bomb site still has investigators guessing. According to isotopic analysts, its onetime owner grew up along the Saudi–Yemeni border, which supported the initial suspicion that al-Qaeda was behind Hariri's murder. Did the assassins plant the nose to throw off the investigation? It's too conspiratorial to give it much thought.

It's just a fact that people get hung up on small, insignificant details and inconsistencies. With their abiding distrust of government, the facts surrounding an assassination are easily deflected, and then they quietly recede into infinite possibilities. On the other hand, when you leave a smoking gun as Mossad did in Dubai, you gratuitously cede that advantage.

A couple of years ago, a Miami-Dade homicide detective called me up to ask if the South Boston crime boss Whitey Bulger had been a CIA informant. I'm pretty sure he knew better, but some half-wit up the line no doubt needed to be reassured. (Bulger, in fact, had nothing to do with the CIA, which leaves me to wonder whether he hadn't been going around telling people he murdered on behalf of the CIA. He wouldn't have been the first criminal to do so.)

It all comes down to the fact that there's absolutely no reason to confess or in any way acknowledge the act. One day an enemy very well could turn into a friend. So why let a long-buried corpse with your knife in its back cast a shadow over a beautiful new friendship, especially when a little preventive fact-obscuring and fact-burying greatly improve amnesia? Iran might have been behind Pan Am 103, but now, with a diplomatic thaw in the air, it serves everyone's interest that Iran never owned up to it.

NOTE TO ASSASSINS: Ordinary life does not stop for a death, so don't give anyone a reason to decide otherwise. Find a way to avoid the digital flytraps. Ditch *all* phones, computers, and credit cards. Always use a public bus or taxi paid for in cash instead of a car. If a phone call is for some reason inevitable, use a burner phone and steal a Wi-Fi signal from outside a Starbucks. One call, one phone. Meetings are best set in advance, for instance, every second Saturday of the month, with an alternate twenty-four hours later. For other communications, use some sort of visual signal—move a flowerpot in the window or leave a chalk mark on the wall. In sum, never gratuitously give anyone a springboard into your life. Like ancient Scythian horsemen, give the bastards no center to counterattack.

DON'T MISS

It's better not to try rather than to try and miss. A failed attempt gives the victim an aura of invincibility, augmenting his power while diminishing yours. Like any business, reputation is everything.

God is not on the side of the big battalions, but on the side of those who shoot best.

—VOLTAIRE

Brighton, England, September 14, 1984: The Grand's front-desk receptionist, Trudy Groves, would afterward tell the police that she didn't remember much about the man who checked in that morning. The name he wrote down on the registration card, Roy Walsh, meant nothing to her either. Nor did his address: Braxfield Road, London.

Groves gave Walsh a key for room 629 because, as she said, "it was a nice room facing the sea." Walsh paid her in cash: £180 for three nights. She wished him a good stay and watched him head up to his room.

On September 15, Walsh and another man ate lunch in the dining room. They charged the meal to Walsh's room. As well as anyone could tell, the two spent the rest of the day in Walsh's room, a DO NOT DISTURB sign hanging on the door.

A waiter later would tell the police that Walsh seemed a pleasant enough man who liked to order his meals in the room. He remembered that on September 17, Walsh called room service for a pot of tea and turkey sandwiches. But when the floor waiter knocked on the door, a taller man answered the door, not Walsh. The waiter could hear someone in the bathroom. Later that evening, the two called down for a bottle of vodka and three Cokes. The waiter wondered if they weren't celebrating something.

No one remembers Walsh and his companion checking out on September 19. But there's no reason anyone would. He was just another tourist. In any case, the Grand's staff had other things to think about. In less than a month, the Conservative Party would hold its annual conference in the hotel, and the place would be mobbed. Prime Minister Margaret Thatcher herself would spend the night.

October 12: At exactly 2:54 a.m. a deafening roar convulsed the Grand. A center section of the old Victorian building rose in a fountain of black smoke and debris, held in the air for an instant, and then spilled out into the street. It was as if hell had taken a bite out of the hotel and spit it out. The only light came from small fires burning everywhere.

As the firemen arrived, it looked like guests had hung out their clothes to dry on the telephone lines and street lamps. It took them a moment to realize that it was curtains and bedding blown outward from the explosion.

One of the firemen who ran into the hotel met Thatcher calmly making her way down a blackened corridor, seemingly indifferent to the smoke and screams.

"Good morning," she said. "Thank you for coming."

F our guests died in the explosion, including a member of parliament. A woman later would die from her injuries. Thirty-eight others were injured. The press reported Thatcher survived only because she had stayed up into the early morning writing her speech for that day. Rather than in her bed, asleep, she was at a desk in the sitting room of her suite. But that was the press's version, which would turn out not to be exactly accurate.

Investigators estimated that it had been twenty to thirty pounds of gelignite explosives that had dislodged a large chimney and pulled down a center section of the hotel. On the basis of a pattern of shattered bathroom tile, it was quickly determined that room 629's bathroom had been packed with explosives.

The investigators discovered fragments of a video-recorder timer. The timer was set to go off in exactly twenty-four days, six hours, and thirty-five minutes—2:54 a.m., an hour when Thatcher, her cabinet, and the rest of the Grand's guests should have been in their rooms asleep.

From there it was a matter of investigators running down the names of guests who'd stayed in room 629 in the preceding weeks. There'd been couples from the United States, London, Hertfordshire, and a businessman from Mumbai. They could all be accounted for but one: Roy Walsh.

After Walsh's registration card was found, chemical and laser analysis picked up a fingerprint and a right palm print. Matching them to arrest records, it turned out that Roy Walsh was, in fact, Patrick Magee, a longtime operative of the Irish Republican Army.

Magee was arrested in 1985 in Glasgow, Scotland, while he was preparing a new bombing campaign. He was convicted a year later for the Grand's bombing, including the murder of five people and the attempted murder of Great Britain's prime minister and her cabinet. "Attempted" tells you all you need to know.

————

I t took me a while, but I think I finally figured out one of the elemen-tary rules that Hajj Radwan played by. It has to do with game theory, what I call the winning combination of the Prisoner's Dilemma. It's a lesson the IRA and Magee apparently missed.

The Prisoner's Dilemma basically goes like this: The police arrest you and your partner in a crime. Questioning you in separate cells, their objective is to send you both to jail for as long as possible. If you both refuse to cooperate, you each do one year in jail. But if your partner rats you out, he gets off, and you get ten years. If, on the other hand, you beat him to it, he gets the ten years. If you rat each other out, you each get five years. The choice then is you either "compete" against your partner in crime or "cooperate" with him.

The best course of action, of course, is to cooperate, neither of you confessing to the crime. You each do your year in jail, and that's it. But what keeps the game from descending into a free-for-all, the two of you falling for the police's game and turning on each other? Mathematicians played around with the possibilities for a long time and came up with the strategy that as soon as one of you starts to confess the other admin-isters a sharp reminder that the winning combination is to cooperate. Letting things slide and hoping for the best is the worst strategy, the only winner being the police.

But it doesn't mean that this is some tit-for-tat game of revenge. It's the police you want to beat rather than each other, i.e., the objective is to minimize your partner's pain as well as your own. It's a tricky strategy, but done right it avoids a mutually destructive escalation of violence.

Two years before Hajj Radwan's assassination I drove up into the Bekaa Valley to take a look at a burned-out and shrapnel-shredded black Mercedes. It had once belonged to the secretary-general of Hezbollah, the one before Nasrallah. He was riding in the car when it was struck by an Israeli guided missile. His wife, their five-year-old son, and four others were also killed. The attack occurred on February 16, 1992.

The Mercedes was still on the trailer it was hauled up to the Bekaa on and was now parked next to the town mosque. As I walked around it, a Shiite imam watched me, curious about a foreigner who'd come to see evidence of the man's martyrdom.

You could see where the Israeli missile came through the rear window and exploded in the backseat where he and his family had been sitting. I'd heard somewhere that the strike had been so precise that the driver survived. But right away I could see it wasn't possible: The Israelis had made certain no one walked out of that car alive.

I wondered why Hezbollah left the car out in the open like this. Why not put it in a museum? Did it have something to do with making death seem banal, reminding Muslims that it's a common destiny to die for the faith? Either way, the burned-out Mercedes is one more shrine to Hezbollah's bizarre death cult.

Israel's decision to assassinate Nasrallah's predecessor made sense. As a leader of the Islamic Resistance in the south, he was responsible for the deaths of hundreds of Israeli soldiers. With his departure, Israel's battlefield fortunes would improve. Cut off the head of the snake and the snake dies, right? But in fact, things went from bad to worse for the Israelis. Nasrallah proved to be a more intelligent and cunning enemy.

Israel also apparently didn't understand the inner workings of Hezbollah. While the public face of it consists of a dozen or so turbaned Shiite clerics, its true leaders are its invisible military commanders—people such as Hajj Radwan. As contacts would tell me, when a Hezbollah military commander enters a room, the turbans all stand and bow to him. No one observing this little rite has any doubt about the way Hezbollah's hierarchy of power works. In other words, in assassinating Hezbollah's secretary-general, Israel violated Law #2—Make It Count.

Israel, of course, had expected Hezbollah would retaliate for the assassination of the secretary-general and his family—it was a bright red line it couldn't ignore. But was Israel prepared for the way it came?

On March 17, 1992, one day and one month after the assassination, a suicide bomber blew up himself and his car in front of the Israeli embassy in Buenos Aires, killing twenty-nine and wounding more than two hundred. Two years later, in 1994, a second car bomb went off in the same city, this time destroying the Jewish community center and killing eighty-five. The evidence is fairly good that Hajj Radwan was involved in both attacks.

What the Argentine attacks show us is that Hajj Radwan was prepared to employ disproportionate force when provoked. In murdering the Hezbollah secretary-general and his family, Israel had violated the implicit rules: It had stopped "cooperating." Which makes the Argentina attacks an invitation to Israel to go back to "cooperating." Did Israel get the message? Apparently, as so far it's made no attempt on Nasrallah.

Something similar occurred when Hajj Radwan decided he needed to shut off the Hariri investigation. He struck fast, hard, and with precision—nearly a dozen assassinations and attempts. They were all against people who'd stopped "cooperating," in the sense that they were pushing for the investigation. As soon as the Lebanese shunned the investigation, the assassinations stopped.

The consensus inside the intelligence community, while not in the FBI, is that Iran (with or without Libyan help) destroyed Pan Am 103 as a direct response to the Navy's shooting down of an Iranian passenger Airbus over the Gulf. It was a reminder to the United States that civilian airliners are off-limits. Read: The United States had better go back to "cooperating." (Never mind that the USS *Vincennes* shot down the Iranian Airbus by accident; perception is what counts in assessing Iran's response.)

What the Argentina attacks and Pan Am 103 have in common is the understanding they couldn't result in misses. That would have been like sending no message at all.

"P" EQUALS PLENTY

Come, my dear, we are going home. They can't shoot straight.

—CHARLES DE GAULLE TO HIS WIFE AFTER
A 1962 ASSASSINATION ATTEMPT

I suspect Hajj Radwan would have sympathized with the IRA's attempt on Thatcher, but for the love of God, he must have asked, how could they get so close and then botch it? Like I just said, when you play the Prisoner's Dilemma, there's no tolerance for missing. Never slap the king, always kill him.

On August 22, 1962, French right-wing army officers made an attempt on President Charles de Gaulle as he drove from the Élysée Palace to Orly Airport. Although a dozen gunmen fired as many as 140 bullets at his convoy, they killed only two bodyguards. De Gaulle and his wife were untouched. It's what led de Gaulle to quip to his wife about his would-be assassins' bad shooting. But more to the point, the failed attempt politically bolstered de Gaulle while fatally demoralizing the rogue officers.

Let me go back to Hariri to put this in perspective. Hajj Radwan employed the equivalent of 2,500 kilos of TNT, enough to dig a six-foot-deep hole in the road. The investigators came to the chilling hypothesis that Hajj Radwan had arranged it so the van would intercept Hariri's armored Mercedes precisely as it passed between the St-Georges and the Phoenicia, the two tallest buildings on the Corniche. If Hariri somehow had survived the explosion, the reverberating blast effect would have microwaved him.

Finally, if it weren't already daunting enough a task, the van detonated in front of Hariri's Mercedes rather than behind it. The occupants of the car directly in front of Hariri's—only four feet ahead of Hariri's car—survived, thanks to the car's lifting up and allowing the undercarriage to take the brunt of the explosion.

In other words, there was no way to misinterpret the message: Hariri had to pay with his life for the wrongs he'd committed or was about to (whatever those were). The attack wasn't a shot over the bow, something that could have been safely ignored. Missing would have completely altered the message's content.

I suspect that one reason Hajj Radwan knew what he was doing was that he'd missed before and paid the penalty. In 1985 he made an attempt on the emir of Kuwait with a car bomb. Not only did the emir survive, but Hajj Radwan's brother-in-law, who had been arrested for the 1983 bombings of the French and American embassies there, was dropped even deeper down into the godforsaken Kuwaiti oubliette he was already in.

For seven years, Hajj Radwan did everything in his power to spring his brother-in-law from his Kuwaiti jail, kidnapping and murdering any Kuwaiti he could put his hands on. But nothing would move the Kuwaitis, and with each try, Hajj Radwan looked weaker and more impotent. In the emir of Kuwait's eyes, Hajj Radwan was not the stuff of nightmares.

I myself have a vague idea what it feels like to escape a near miss. It occurred in Central Asia not long after the breakup of the Soviet Union. I'd rented a small house to work out of, but apparently I'd chosen the wrong part of town. The first warning that I wasn't welcome came in the guise of a break-in. I then put up bars over the windows and posted an armed guard out front. That same night, I was across town when I heard a boom from the direction of my house. When I got back home, my guard was out front talking to the police, who were examining a hole in my front yard. The guard explained that he'd been in the living room when someone threw a grenade at the front window, clearly meaning for it to explode inside. It was only thanks to its bouncing off a bar that it didn't make it in. I never did find out whether the grenade was meant for the guard or me. But the point is that I chose not to take it personally—an assassination attempt. I took the precaution of moving out of the house, but otherwise kept doing what I was doing.

As is not the case in horseshoes, there are no points for coming close in assassination. It's something the IRA apparently didn't grasp.

NOTHING LIKE A PH.D. TO SCREW THE POOCH

Anyone who knew Magee wasn't surprised he tried to decapitate the British government. Anything to get the English to leave. The question was whether he was the right man for the job.

In Magee's favor, the tile work was good. Stuffing explosives into the bathroom wall of room 629 could only have been tedious work. The tiles needed to be put back just right and properly finished to conceal the fresh grout. It's no doubt why it took Magee and his nameless accomplice three days to do the job.

But anyone who's worked with explosives or tried to put together a complicated assassination like Thatcher's understands it was a matter of sheer luck that Magee came as close to murdering the woman as he did. The main problem was that he hadn't used enough explosives. In fact, the charge was so undersized that only one of the occupants of room 629 died and the other was only slightly injured. (Magee disputes the estimates of twenty to thirty pounds of explosives. There was five times that amount, he claims.)

The truth is that Magee ran up against the laws of physics—there's only so much space in the wall of a hotel bathroom. The alternative would have been to fill the basement with explosives or run "strip charges" along the supporting beams and main load-bearing walls of the Grand. But neither, of course, was feasible; someone would have noticed. Nor apparently was it possible to pinpoint Thatcher's room in advance to better position the explosives. While Hariri never stood a chance, Margaret Thatcher stood a very good one. But that wasn't the end of it.

Going light on explosives was a grave miscalculation, but other ones were just plain foolhardy. Take the name Magee used to check into the Grand, Roy Walsh. Walsh was a notorious IRA operative serving life for murder. All it would have taken was an alert desk clerk to recognize the name and bring it to the police's attention. Or if the police had done a thorough check of the guests who'd stayed at the Grand in the weeks before the conference, they very well might have stumbled onto the plot.

Magee also failed to take into account the possibility that the Conservatives would change hotels at the last minute. Or that Thatcher would come down from London for only the day of her speech rather than stay the night at the Grand. Magee should have taken the elementary precaution of including a mechanism to interrupt the timer. If the Conservatives had moved locations, inadvertently drawing the IRA into murdering only innocent guests, it would have been an even worse political catastrophe.

The crowning mistake came when Magee returned to England for the new round of bombings, freely and cheerfully flying back into the cage. He apparently hadn't grasped another elementary rule: An assassin never revisits the scene of the crime. And by the way, couldn't the IRA find a bomber without a criminal record, someone without fingerprints on file?

Like most IRA volunteers, Patrick Magee was born into economic and political blight—unemployment, prejudice, ignored grievances. He was two when his family moved from Belfast, Northern Ireland, to Norwich, England. Life was a little easier there, but not much. Norwich is where Magee acquired the accent that let him check into the Grand unremarked.

In 1969, Magee moved back to Belfast, not long after the Troubles started in Northern Ireland. He joined the IRA at eighteen and soon came to the attention of the police, earning a reputation as a bomber with a brain. He reportedly exercised it by doing the *Times* crossword puzzle.

Magee bounced in and out of the Castlereagh interrogation center like a yo-yo. The police tried every trick they knew to recruit him as an informer. A policeman who'd conducted one of Magee's interrogations had this to say about him: "He was a hard man, and we knew what he was like. We would have loved to have had him on our side." But Magee was cagey, neither agreeing nor saying no. He was smart enough back then never to leave evidence behind that the police could use to put him away.

It's unclear why Magee would make a clumsy mistake such as leaving a fingerprint on the registration card or failing to use enough explosives. But it didn't dent Magee's cocksure defiance as he was led from the court and addressed onlookers in Gaelic: "*Tiocfaidh ár lá.*" Our day will come.

There's an old saying that the only Catholics in Northern Ireland who get a good education get it in prison. It's true of Magee at least, who inside would earn a Ph.D. in literature by correspondence. (He also picked up a wife by correspondence, a novelist.)

It wasn't long after his release—thanks to the 1998 Good Friday Agreement—that he publicly tried to justify the attempt on Thatcher. So far, so familiar, but he could never stick to a single story or, for that matter, articulate why precisely the IRA needed to murder Thatcher. In one interview Magee said that "they" (presumably the IRA) wanted to murder Thatcher because "they" were frustrated with the war in Northern Ireland. "The obvious recourse was to take the war to England," he said.

As for targeting Thatcher instead of someone else, Magee said: "She was the leader of the British government, and she came into office determined to pursue a hard military line . . . You go up the chain of command and the buck stopped with her."

In another interview Magee said he'd accomplished what he'd intended to, namely push Britain into peace: "After Brighton, anything was possible, and the British for the first time began to look very differently at us."

In a third interview Magee pulled back, saying he was lucky to have missed Thatcher. "In fact, if half of the British government had been killed, it might have been impossible for a generation of the British establishment to come to terms with us."

It's all pure intellectual slop, of course. Just as the assassin knows the size of the charge it takes to do a job, he also knows exactly why he's picked his target. An assassin can never entertain second thoughts, never beg for understanding, and never let the faintest shadow of doubt cross his brow, either before or after the act. In an assassin's world, there is no tolerance for contrition or, for that matter, press interviews and Ph.D.'s.

Yes, the Brighton attack was spectacular, the kind of pyrotechnical display that got the IRA marquee billing. Arguably, it was the closest the IRA would ever come to making inroads into the consciousness of the wider British politic, which tended to look at the IRA as savages best kept in kraals. But in the end what did it really get out of it?

It comes down to this single truth: Either Margaret Thatcher deserved it or she didn't. And if she truly did, then the last thing the IRA should ever have let happen is the Iron Lady walking out of the smoke and debris of the Grand Hotel.

Almost as bad, the IRA senselessly frittered away what mystique it still possessed when it allowed Magee to put on display his small personal ambitions and frailties. Magee's sad public avowal will forever be a constant reminder that the IRA had tried and failed to murder Thatcher. Like an old fat man stripping down to nothing, the IRA turned itself into a thing of low contempt, the gang that can't shoot straight.

EVERY FAILURE AN OPPORTUNITY

As I said, Hajj Radwan made mistakes, as he did with the attempt on the emir of Kuwait. But what he did to mitigate them was to never confess to them. What's the point in acknowledging failure? It's not like it'll make things right with a would-be victim. In fact, it's better to do just the opposite, mislead people into believing you hit exactly what you were aiming at. Your objective is to leave the world in stupid dread rather than give it a ray of hope that you're not as formidable as first thought.

Let me go back to Hajj Radwan's car bombing of the American embassy annex in Beirut on September 20, 1984. (It occurred the day after Patrick Magee checked out of the Grand.) The best working hypothesis until now is that it was an attempt on the American and British ambassadors. If the British ambassador's security detail hadn't shot and killed the van's driver, thereby preventing him from making it into the garage, both ambassadors probably would have died. In short, Hajj Radwan missed. But try to prove it.

Hajj Radwan knew exactly what he was doing in arranging to leave absolutely no evidence at the site of the attack. The van was stolen, the explosives were untraceable, the suicide bomber unidentifiable, and all fingerprints burned off in the explosion. Like any good assassination, it came out of a clear blue sky and disappeared back into one.

Although the Islamic Jihad Organization—the same fictitious organization commonly associated with Hajj Radwan—would claim it, it never said what the target was other than the annex. It left a handful of people like me, with only fragmentary intelligence and contextualization, to hypothesize that it had been a failed attempt on the ambassadors. One opinion among many.

Somewhat in support of my argument, Hajj Radwan sharply altered his tactics after the attack on the annex, moving away from trying to murder a target by bringing down a building on top of him to murdering him in a moving car. To that end, he improved his odds by adopting sophisticated firing devices and shaped charges. As one day he would demonstrate, no one traveling in a car is safe.

Anyway, people remember the attack on the annex as a resounding success to this day—the van slipped through a tight cordon of security, the driver faithfully sacrificed himself, and the bomb went off as it was supposed to. As Hajj Radwan could have told us, seeming to get what you want is as important as getting what you want.

> **NOTE TO ASSASSINS:** An assassination is meant to preclude mean reversion. If it won't, go back to the drawing board.

LAW #16

IF YOU CAN'T CONTROL THE KILL, CONTROL THE AFTERMATH

A good, thorough cleanup is what really scares the shit out of people.

IN ORDER TO FULLY UNDERSTAND ANOTHER BEING, YOU HAVE TO WATCH IT DIE

Damascus, November 2009: Syria's a country in a hurry to slow down the future. It doesn't even bother to pretend it likes foreigners. And when it does grudgingly allow them inside its borders, it keeps them at arm's length. I'm not sure why I need another lesson in a truth so obvious, but apparently I do when I'm sent there by The Hague for the Hariri investigation. It's a year and a half before the Arab Spring.

I arrange through a friend to have a Syrian visa faxed to Syria's only border crossing with Jordan, where I'll cross by taxi. Having had my run-ins with Syrian officialdom, as I get ready to board the plane, I call my friend to make sure he's indeed faxed the visa. He tells me not to worry: A valid Syrian visa will be at the crossing.

As the Syrian border post looms into view, my taxi driver slows way down as if he's caught a bad case of cold feet and is about to turn around. Like all Jordanian taxi drivers who ply the road to Damascus, he is scared shitless by the Syrians. He fumbles with my passport with his free hand: "You're sure you don't have a visa?" I reassure him, no problemo.

He parks in front of the main building. We walk inside together. At the counter, there's a woman pleading with a surly border guard in a field-gray uniform who is sporting a twenty-four-hour stubble, his tie loose at the neck. He's a man who doesn't look happy to be at work.

He shuffles through a stack of papers in front of him and shakes his head. The woman keeps repeating she's sure a visa was faxed: It has to be somewhere there in his papers. He says something I can't hear, and she goes and sits down on a banquette against the wall. My heart reaches out to her.

When it comes my turn to belly up to the counter, I buoyantly tell the guard that, unlike the lady, I really do have a faxed visa waiting for me. The man's mood doesn't brighten an iota. But it doesn't stop me from grinning like an idiot, as if I'd driven all this way just to have a friendly chat with the bastard.

He grabs my passport without a word, sits down, and swivels his chair to face his computer screen. He punches in my name and passport number. After peering at the screen for about ten seconds, he swivels back and looks at me as if he's about to faint with excitement: "You came here as a journalist!"

Sadly, true. It was right before the Iraq War in 2003, for ABC News. I consider pointing out that it was six years ago, that I'm no longer a journalist, and that I never once filed a report on Syria. But I can tell it's a set of facts he won't give a fuck about.

Ever since my short stint as a journalist in Syria, it's as if a scarlet *A* were tattooed on my forehead. Some Syrian friends tried to have the journalist notation expunged from Syrian immigration computers. But neither cajoling nor bribes worked. Not that it truly surprised me. Police states such as Syria have a wondrous knack for discovering efficiency when it comes to keeping track of shifty foreigners.

As soon as I start to explain I'm no longer a journalist, he cuts me off with biblical finality: "You need a journalist's visa. Go back to Amman and apply for one."

I, of course, can't tell him the truth about being a consultant to the tribunal on my way to Damascus to snoop for evidence of Syrian complicity in the murder of Hariri. He would have trussed me up like a Christmas ham and delivered me to the *mukhabarat*—Syria's fingernail-pulling spooks.

"My very good friend in Damascus sent me a visa here," I wearily try a last time. "I'm sure of it."

He pats his stack of papers: "It's not here. No visa." He turns to a man standing just to my right, no doubt to tell him to bugger off too. Another burnt offering before a stone idol.

The guard stands up, walks across the office, and disappears through a door. The pirate posing as my taxi driver is now grinning like a drunken jackass, no doubt adding up in his head how much he'll overcharge me for the ride back to Amman.

I go sit down with the other doomed petitioners on the banquette, thinking about the time Mother beat the Syrian bureaucracy at its own game. It was when she first came to Syria on a month's visa but, fascinated with the country, wanted to stay longer. Try as hard as I could, I couldn't find anyone to help extend her visa.

So Mother took a taxi down to the Ministry of Interior, a place more feared than Count Dracula's castle, only to be informed a visa extension wouldn't be possible. Undeterred, she was back the next day, this time with a bagful of thick books. She took a seat and started to read. By closing time, the Syrians were in a panic. Who was this tenacious old lady? When she showed up the next morning with her books, it was clear this was a battle the great nation of Syria was destined to lose. She got her extension.

It's another twenty minutes before our tormentor is back. Everyone crowds the counter to renew their pleadings. When I finally nudge my way in, he looks at me as if he's seen me for the first time. But before I can even open my mouth, he says: "I told you there's no fax for you."

For a moment, I consider he might be after a bribe. But before I can make up my mind, a bright, malign bulb goes on in my head.

Before leaving on my trip, a friend suggested that I should take the occasion of my visit to Damascus to look up the *mukhabarat* chief, the same one who would pull my fingernails out if he were to find out I worked for the tribunal. He'd surely agree to have tea with me, the friend said. I had my doubts. The man was the Syrian president's most trusted henchman and had a reputation for brutality that made Syrians tremble at the mere mention of his name. Although there was no solid evidence for it, he was a suspect in Hariri's murder. But more to the point, why would he want to waste his time with an ex–CIA operative? But to make my friend feel better, I entered his name and phone number in my iPhone.

I lean far over the counter to get the border guard's attention. He looks up at me, now genuinely irritated.

"It's fine," I say. "Give me back my passport. I'll tell my friend in Damascus there's been a small error."

Detecting the faintest shadow of concern passing across his face, I press my advantage: "He works for the government. I'm sure he'll understand why you won't let me in your country."

I can tell he doesn't want to, but he can't resist: "Who?"

"You mean who do I have a meeting with?"

He searches my face, trying to decide the nature of the swindle afoot.

"Do you really want to know?" I ask. I may be wrong, but I sense the starch coming out of him.

I pull out my iPhone, hit Contacts, and find the *mukhabarat* chief's name. I turn it around for him to see.

"He's probably at lunch," I say. "We can call him at home."

A high, rattled laugh comes out from somewhere deep in the poor man's throat. He looks over his shoulder for salvation. Seeing none, he shoves back his chair and bolts across the office. He disappears into the same office he went into before.

It isn't a minute later when an older man with a lot of stars on his shoulder peeks out from behind the door. The guard whispers in his ear, pointing his chin toward me.

For the next ten minutes, I sit in the border chief's office, drinking sickly-sweet tea and eating soggy biscuits. No one says a word to me; people coming in and out avert their eyes. I feel like a leper with his bell clanging wildly.

After ten minutes, my passport is back with a meticulously centered and blotted visa. The border chief orders his adjutant to walk me through the rest of the formalities. I can see he wants to shake my hand; then he thinks better of it.

I wonder if anyone's ever passed through Syrian customs with such alacrity and deference. Or with a border guard carrying his suitcase. As we pull away for Damascus, my driver looks at me in the rearview mirror as if I were some kind of sorcerer.

I won't really understand it until the Arab Spring shows up in Syria, but what I just got was an aperçu into Syria's final days—the decline and fall of a police state once renowned for its brutal efficiency. It also helps me understand how Hajj Radwan's assassins managed to smuggle their explosives through this border crossing. For all I know, they did it by taxi . . . and no doubt without having to resort to an adolescent sleight of hand like mine.

As soon as I pass through the front door of Damascus's Four Seasons hotel, life gets a lot better very fast, the air-conditioning sucking the grit out of the air and offering back a gentle, cool breeze. The place is a celestial oasis.

Unlike my visa, my reservation is waiting for me, a suite overlooking the old city. Although I have only my small carry-on, the concierge insists a bellhop carry it up to the room. The elevator is a rocket, too fast to bother with music.

I kick off my shoes, settle back on the sofa, and flip on the giant flat-panel TV to CNN. I think about how there was a time when CNN was banned in Syria, like every other American news organization. Is Syrian censorship's ugly yoke finally about to come off?

I'm starting to doze off when there's a knock at the door. I think it's the maid to turn down the bed. I shout at the door no thank you. Instead of an answer, there's another knock, now more insistent. I start to panic: They've discovered my ruse at the border.

The more I think about it, the deeper my panic sets in. Maybe they've found out I'm here for The Hague. Since I'm not on a UN or diplomatic passport, I can see them cooking up some charge, throwing me in jail, and holding me for years. Or worse.

I open the door to find the assistant manager who just checked me in. "Your room's not quite ready," he says, craning his neck to get a look over my shoulder. Behind him stands the bellhop.

I look back at my room to see what the problem is. Nothing I can see—the bed's made, there's a stack of fresh towels in the bathroom, and a bowl of fresh fruit on the credenza. But of course there's nothing wrong with it! Someone's simply made the grave error of putting me in a room that isn't bugged.

I follow the assistant manager and the bellhop to the elevator, up four flights, and down the hall to my new room. It's identical to the one I just vacated—fruit, clean sheets, and all. The only difference is it has a better view of Damascus's old city.

That evening, a Syrian friend I'll call Dennis collects me to see a mutual friend, the same businessman who a couple of years before had told me he'd seen Hajj Radwan floating around the Syrian presidency waiting for a meeting. I hope now he'll throw me a scrap about Hariri.

It's not completely unreasonable. As Hariri's aides related the story, the businessman had showed up in Beirut a day before Hariri's assassination to warn him there was a plot against him. But like the other warnings, Hariri ignored it. I intend to ask the businessman point-blank what induced him to warn Hariri.

As we get out of the car in front of the businessman's office, Dennis catches my attention and draws an imaginary circle around his ear with his forefinger—a signal that the businessman's office is bugged. So much for bringing up Hariri or Hajj Radwan. Although both men are now cold in their graves, even gossiping about them is forbidden. I'll have to find a way to see the businessman later.

Although I've only been in town for a couple of hours now, blind paranoia has me around the throat like an enraged boa. The only appetite I have for this doomed investigation is to find a place not bugged and ask Dennis about Hariri and Hajj Radwan.

Over dinner at an outdoor restaurant, Dennis politely listens to my questions but keeps coming back to the argument it was Syria that paid in spades for Hariri's assassination. Getting kicked out of Lebanon has been a catastrophic defeat for it. The Syrian troops there were the only thing keeping a lid on the place. Why then would the Syrians—or, for that matter, Hezbollah—want to assassinate Hariri?

I think about pointing out that the worst way to assign blame for a political murder is to frame it in terms of cui bono—who benefits? By that measure, Lyndon Johnson murdered JFK. Or how about British intelligence arranging a phony attempt on Thatcher to justify cracking down on the IRA? But I don't say it, and by the end of dinner, I've gotten nothing out of Dennis.

I know this all sounds like a lot of belaboring of very thin leads, but in a murky affair such as Hariri's, where not a single witness has stepped forward to offer real evidence, thin is better than nothing. And I have nothing to lose. So I ask Dennis to drive me past the place where Hajj Radwan met his end.

The street we turn down could be any upscale suburb in any modern Arab city. There's a small grocery store still open, a man shopping. A couple is hurrying along, likely on their way home. Otherwise the sidewalks are rolled up for the night.

Dennis pulls over at the intersection and points in the direction of a hospital mid-block. It's in front of that hospital where he was killed, he says. I ask him if he saw the car.

Dennis says he was on his way home that evening when he was surprised to see the street taped off by police. But he couldn't get close enough to see what the problem was. He never saw Hajj Radwan's car.

A new Toyota Lexus is parked where Dennis pointed. Because the streetlights are dim, I can't see much else. There's nothing to mark the place. Then again, what am I expecting, the Syrians to put up a statue to Hajj Radwan? Unlike the Lebanese, they can't claim him as their own.

I wish Dennis would pull up closer so I can get a better look, but he wheels the car around to take me back to the Four Seasons.

"Who did it?" I ask.

"They're sure it was Palestinians. But working for Jordan and Israel. They have some names."

I keep coming back to my hunch that the soft pleasures of Damascus turned Hajj Radwan's head—the new wife, the French boutiques and patisseries, the fancy cars racing around Damascus. There's no solid evidence for it, but I've heard things, such as Hajj Radwan's son catting around Beirut in a new BMW like all the other spoiled Lebanese princelings. If true, it's a sign that Hajj Radwan succumbed to the temptation of money, letting discipline go. Did it also blind him to the fact that

Syria had slipped its totalitarian, police-state moorings, had become lazy and corrupt, and was no longer able to offer him the protective shield it once did?

When I'd heard the details of how Hajj Radwan had finally been run to ground, how the assassin had slipped through Syria's once-formidable security net, smuggled the explosives through the Jordanian border crossing, rigged Hajj Radwan's car with explosives in central Damascus, and even managed to avoid collateral victims, I better understood that the world had changed since my Beirut days.

But what am I missing? The first reports were that the headrest of Hajj Radwan's Pajero exploded, decapitating him. Later reports had it that a magnetic bomb, a "limpet," had been attached to the back of his car and detonated by a radio signal. A third version had it that the explosives were concealed in the car's spare tire.

What strikes me odd in all of this is the conflicting detail. In the West, we're accustomed to instantly learning the gory details surrounding a high-profile murder. It's as if we were entitled to them. We quickly found out about Swedish prime minister Olof Palme's assassination, including details about the police investigation. Anytime there's a noteworthy murder in the United States, a slew of gruesome pictures appear in the press. But then again, with the act completed, why not?

But none of this occurred after Hajj Radwan's murder—no photos, no police reports, no eyewitness statements. I'd eventually come across a blurry photo of his car taken from a camera phone, but it told me nothing. Hezbollah dealt with Hajj Radwan's murder by staging his blood-soaked clothing in his mausoleum. But as for the truly pertinent facts, its lips are sealed.

One thought I have: Hezbollah and the Syrians have every reason in the world to fake Hajj Radwan's death. Having been caught red-handed in Hariri's murder, he couldn't have been a particularly convenient personage walking around Damascus. Their letting people believe he'd been assassinated would make sense if he'd returned to the southern suburbs to wait for things to cool down. But this is just another baseless grassy knoll/black helicopter conspiracy theory.

What's apparent here is that Syria still has the capacity to obfuscate the truth, even the assassination of a prominent man in downtown Damascus. It still believes political murder is forbidden knowledge, never to be shared outside a tight, trusted circle. It's a consensus of silence we in the West can't begin to understand.

THE ROYAL ROAD TO DISCOVERY

Beirut, February 14, 2005, 12.54.00: The images from the CCTV camera mounted on the side of the HSBC bank building are grainy but good enough to see how the Mitsubishi van rides heavy on the shocks, carrying something heavy. The van hangs back, doing about eight or nine miles an hour. It hugs the right side of the road as traffic speeds by at forty miles an hour.

There's nothing erratic about the way the Mitsubishi's driver handles the road. Knowing what's about to come, you can't help but wonder what's going through his mind.

The van moves out of the camera's frame at 12.54.37, continuing along the seafront boulevard.

You can't tell it from the CCTV images, but Beirut woke up this morning to a light, fresh breeze off the Mediterranean. When the weather's nice like this, the Corniche is packed with walkers, well-heeled Beirutis in designer tracksuits and gold-foiled Nikes. They take their exercise seriously, scooting along at a half run, elbows churning. Older men stroll in twos and threes, gossiping, gesturing with fat cigars, mostly expensive Cubans. People sit on their balconies sipping their coffees without a care in the world.

It must feel like spring for Rafic Hariri too, a political spring to be precise. He's spent the morning at parliament, canvassing for the June elections, and now it's all but certain he'll be elected prime minister again. Sure, Hariri has his problems, not least among them the bruising fights with the Syrians. There have even been threats on his life. But it's something he's had to live with ever since he moved back to Lebanon in 1992. But as he's said often enough, they're the ambient noise every Lebanese politician learns to live with.

Hariri would never dare say it openly, but he's all the more optimistic about his political fortunes these days. He's counting on a certain give in the new Syrian president, Bashar al-Assad. A London-trained ophthalmologist, Bashar would flinch before committing violence. He wasn't the man of steel his father was, Hafez al-Assad, who died in 2000. Nor did Bashar seem to be a man to act on his grudges, the main gear that turns Middle East politics; he would flinch before committing violence. Not that he'd ever say it out loud. Hariri wouldn't be surprised if one day he woke up to the news that some Syrian general had overthrown Bashar. It would be a welcome plot turn that would give him even more room to maneuver politically.

After Hariri is through charming parliament, he walks over to the nearby Café de l'Étoile, his security entourage and aides struggling to keep up. This is Hariri's favorite part of Beirut, the old city, whose restoration he's personally overseen. Hariri handpicked the French architects, pored over their plans, and personally arranged for the loans to finance it all. He even put in his own money.

As he walks around the Étoile, you can see from the TV images how Hariri loves the game, the way he moves from table to table, shaking hands, hugging old friends. The smiles flashed back in return say it all— Hariri the rock star, Mr. Lebanon.

But it's not power alone that propels Hariri. Or money, the billions and billions he made loyally serving the Saudi royal family. It's something much more vital, primeval even—a deep tribal loyalty to Lebanon's Sunni Muslims. As I said, the Arabic word is *asabiyyah*. Tribal solidarity. No matter how rich or celebrated he became, Hariri never betrayed his roots.

Hariri's status as the leader of Lebanon's Sunnis was undisputed. It may add up to nothing more than dumb blood loyalty and influence peddling, but what the Sunnis saw in Hariri was both their anchor and beacon—a man who would better their lives, put them back on the pedestal they thought they deserved to be on. Without Hariri, they would be a people diminished and weak.

You also have to wonder whether class had something to do with what's about to happen. Every time Hariri drove from the airport to his mansion on the hill, and passed through the southern suburbs where the poor Shiites live, he thanked his lucky stars he'd clawed his way out of poverty. Did he think that the Shiites deserved to live in squalor, to wallow in their sectarian impurities? No, but some of his fellow Sunnis didn't always share the same sentiment.

As he walks around the Étoile that morning, it must seem to him like the future's all coming together nicely. He's succeeded in restoring Lebanon to its rightful position in the Middle East's firmament. And to crown it all, the Sunnis would be at the helm. Would that young punk in Damascus dare to try to stop him?

As Hariri climbs behind the wheel of his Mercedes 600 to drive home for lunch, he says something to the man in the passenger seat next to him, a parliamentary deputy. No one will find out what it was. But they both laugh. Hariri loves his jokes.

The next we see of Hariri is his six-car convoy entering the frame of the CCTV camera on the HSBC wall at 12.56.17. The last car exits the frame at 12.56.25. Later, it's calculated from the camera that the convoy was doing just under forty.

A split second later, the camera starts to shake, and a ghostly wave passes across the images. The camera's blown about wildly and hurled off the wall. Dangling by a cable, it watches through a haze of dust the people pouring out of the building's door, covering their mouths, choking.

Seven minutes later, there's a new optic, one too horrifying to show the public. A man on a motor scooter with a high-definition video camera arrives at the scene. The images he records are horrific. Hariri is burning by the side of the car, bystanders trying to put him out. His friend, the parliamentary deputy, is on fire, clawing to get out the door.

L et's be clear, Hariri had made his mistakes. The worst of them was to misjudge the Syrians and Hezbollah. He didn't understand how they looked at him as a threat. Whether witting or unwitting, he was a bullhorn of resurgent Sunni Islam. Nor did Hariri truly grasp that democracy and the rule of law are a sham in Lebanon, how the state's monopoly on the means of violence was never truly restored, and how Hezbollah called every important shot related to national security . . . and how, in extremis, it wouldn't hesitate to eliminate anyone who got in its way.

In Hajj Radwan's eyes, Hariri was a political poseur. He might be a fabulously rich, well-connected oligarch, but his pretensions to power didn't match reality. He had some armed people under him, but nothing like Hezbollah's military. Couple that with the perception that Hariri intended to turn back history to a mythical Sunni past, and the only possible resolution to the conflict was a bloody one.

Hariri apparently also missed how jumpy the Shiite offshoot regime in Damascus was. In neighboring Iraq, the Sunni revolt was in full flower against the Shiites. Could it be long before it slopped over the border into Syria? In Syria's world, you cut the head off a baby snake before it becomes a full-grown serpent.

These are easy conclusions to come by, but it's unarguable that Hariri somehow overplayed his hand. He wasn't a complete innocent in his own murder.

IS ASSASSINATION A LOST ART?

From a technical standpoint, Hajj Radwan nearly carried off the perfect kill. He put his best people on the job, figured out a way to cover all three of Hariri's possible routes home that day, and made sure the van intersected his car and exploded at exactly the right moment. He brought to bear everything he'd learned over the last twenty-five years.

Hajj Radwan also went to great lengths to hide his hand. The team covering Hariri that day purchased prepaid cell phones under false names. Since everyone in Lebanon and his dog has a cell phone, and because the Lebanese are a garrulous people who make hundreds of thousands of calls every hour, he must have calculated that tying to-gether these phones would be impossible.

A taped confession of a faux suicide bomber was a nice piece of mis-direction. On the face of it, the young bearded man declaiming in Salafi gibberish about why he needed to murder Hariri (and himself) was con-vincing. Throwing it over the wall of the Salafi-loving TV channel Al Jazeera was another nice touch. On the face of it, it was entirely plausible that a fanatic would sacrifice his life to eliminate a pawn of the Saudi royal family. (Not to mention that the tape served as a sort of bill of indictment, reminding the Lebanese that Hariri was a corrupted Saudi stooge.)

And finally, there was the Yemeni-Saudi nose I wrote about. It jibed nicely with the Saudi Salafi angle. It made no difference that no one could say who the nose belonged to, the point being that outsiders mur-dered Hariri. Whoever thought that one up on Hajj Radwan's team was a true genius.

But like so much else with political murder, appearances often don't hold up.

---

ajj Radwan may have invented modern political murder, but he was no Moses. He'd often enough lose a step, as he did with the attempt on the emir of Kuwait. Or maybe it's just that technology finally caught up with him. Either way, his Hariri assassination went off the tracks in a big way.

Let me start with whether Hariri deserved it or not, Law #1. I can see why Hariri's dumping money into Sunni causes, maybe militant ones, along with his making noises about disarming Hezbollah, caused Hajj Radwan (and his sponsors) heartburn. But did it really add up to a death sentence?

Taking Saudi money didn't make Hariri a foreign invader. He never invited in foreign troops, and he wasn't actively trying to destroy Hajj Radwan or Hezbollah. In short, while it must have been tempting to label Hariri a traitor, it's not completely convincing to frame his murder as an act of self-defense à la Laos, kill or perish. Maybe Hariri could have later turned into a genuine threat, but he wasn't one the day he was murdered.

I suspect Hajj Radwan was horrified as he watched the Lebanese pour out into the streets to protest Hariri's assassination and demand Syria's withdrawal from Lebanon. And when the Syrians did, he must have pinched himself to make sure it wasn't a nightmare. Syria was his rear base and logistics lifeline. Would Damascus cut off his supply lines?

Things must have looked all the more ominous when the Lebanese police grew a backbone and started to seriously investigate Hariri's murder and, even worse, when they brought to bear the latest tools of modern police work, including data analytics. With the telephone companies readily turning over their records to the police, Hajj Radwan must have felt the net start to draw around him.

It all quickly unraveled. An algorithm tied together the eight falsely purchased prepaid cell phones. According to GPS tracking, all eight cell phones, in one way or another, were along Hariri's route from his house to parliament that morning. For the police, it was proof the phones had been used to coordinate his assassination.

But the real nugget came the morning of Hariri's assassination when a call from one of the prepaid cells to a residential landline was discovered. The recipient of the call, a young lady, told the police her boyfriend had called her the morning of Hariri's murder. It became even more interesting when she said he worked for Hezbollah. She didn't know anything about his calling from a prepaid cell, but the police concluded that he must have violated his team's protocol by calling outside what the police dubbed "the first circle of hell"—the eight prepaid cell phones. Allowing the police to put a name to one of Hariri's watchers that morning was never supposed to happen.

It didn't take long for data analytics to connect the young man to Hajj Radwan and the rest of the Ayn al-Dilbah Gang. When Hajj Radwan realized what was happening, he no doubt recognized it as the smoking gun he'd tried so hard never to leave behind. And that's exactly what that one two-minute call was.

Was Hajj Radwan surprised by the ensuing international investigation? He shouldn't have been. The West looked at Hariri as the Good Arab, a reasonable, cultivated man you could do business with. Moreover, he'd showered a lot of money on the powerful, from French presidents to Washington's favorite charities. Which added up to his murder being an unforgivable snub to the West, making a UN investigation all but inevitable.

A guess is always a guess, but mine is that Hajj Radwan was dumbfounded by how fast things turned to shit. Who would ever have thought an Arab dictatorship such as Syria would be forced to do anything under pressure from the street, not to mention be destabilized by it? Not everyone will agree, but some mark Hariri's assassination as the beginning of the Arab Spring. If true, Hariri's murder led to the wider conflict he had tried so hard to avoid. It's a 180-degree opposite of what the act was designed to do.

With Hariri's murder starting to look a lot like a rogue drone missile circling around and ready to blow half way up his ass, Hajj Radwan had no choice but to clean up.

MAY YOUR WORDS TASTE YOUR BLOOD

Beirut, October 19, 2012: Two years after Hariri's assassination, my eldest daughter, Justine, moved to Beirut to study for a master's degree and improve her Arabic. The day after Hezbollah took its shot at me on TV for helping the tribunal, I call her to suggest it might be a good time to give Lebanon a break. She laughs, asking me how could I possibly contribute to the Hariri investigation. After all, I hadn't lived in Lebanon in years. When I tell her that in order to live you have to walk backward, she doesn't get it. I tell her about my three-by-five cards, how Hariri's murder was rooted in the eighties when I was assigned to Beirut. She doesn't say anything, but then assures me she'll be fine.

A little more than a year later, Justine is at home in her apartment in Ashrafiyah when a terrible explosion nearby shakes the foundation of her building. She doesn't need anyone to tell her it was a car bomb. Her only question is who the target was.

The man assassinated was the police general in charge of the Hariri investigation. Seven other people were killed in the explosion. A Sunni and a Hariri loyalist, the general was the driving force behind the investigation, never letting up on the Hezbollah angle. He gave the tribunal every piece of intelligence he could put his hands on.

Although Hajj Radwan was nearly five years into the grave, his signature was all over the general's assassination—a car passing through a narrow defile. The general had returned to Beirut only the day before, an indication that his assassins' intelligence must have been very good. As for the motivation, everyone assumed it was to put the final nail in the Hariri investigation. And with no witness daring to travel to The Hague to give evidence before the court, it looks like it worked.

The first unmistakable sign Hariri's assassins were serious about shutting down the investigation came in the guise of another car bomb. It went off on January 25, 2008, killing the police officers involved in identifying the eight prepaid cell phones. Other murders followed in quick succession—the boy who sold the prepaid cell phones to Hajj Radwan's people died in a highly suspicious car accident; the team member who'd made the phone call to his girlfriend that morning reportedly was found on the side of a hill, dismembered; a Syrian general close to Hajj Radwan was found in his office shot six times. In all, there were a dozen or more murders related to the investigation. It was as if Al Capone had assassinated J. Edgar Hoover and then worked his way down the FBI's hierarchy, only stopping when the FBI raised a white flag.

Hajj Radwan's people also got into Lebanon's official databases and erased every immigration record, police file, intelligence file, phone record, and birth and death certificate that possibly could be used against Hajj Radwan. It reminded me of when Hajj Radwan had his passport records stolen.

In the end, the Lebanese got the message: "Competing" against Hajj Radwan was tantamount to a death sentence. He and his apparatus had turned on its head Stalin's dictum about the state being an instrument owned by the ruling class to break the resistance to that class. In their version, they broke the state's resistance.

MORE ABOUT PETARDS BLOWING UP IN YOUR OWN FACE

Hajj Radwan died a hero to his cause. The way his face stares down from placards along the airport road, you'd think he'd been beatified. But in that same spirit, no one's about to point out the fact that he'd dug his own grave.

I can understand the "campaign desk" on display in his mausoleum and his special pencil box, but come on: a cell phone? Even Nasrallah knew better than to carry one. An aide carried his, always at a distance well out of a drone missile's kill radius.

The easiest explanation is that when you're a player in the imperial center (Damascus) you don't have a choice. You can never know when you might get a call from the palace and be asked to pop up for a cup of tea and a chat with the president. The old Hajj Radwan, who once disappeared for months at a time, ignoring his paymasters, had finally been sucked into the machine.

The picture of Hajj Radwan that Hezbollah put up around Lebanon also surprised me. He's in a starched uniform, his beard stylishly trimmed, and he's wearing expensive designer glasses. He was no longer the humble tailor putting around on an old motor scooter. The only thing he's missing in the pictures is a rack of medals.

For me, it's more evidence that Hajj Radwan had been co-opted into the establishment, both in Damascus and Tehran. With all their petty ambitions, pretensions, and unfounded certitudes, those two capitals were the equivalent of Louis XVI's Versailles—an allure for the elite but poison for what the French call an *homme de terrain*, an operator. The pressure on Hajj Radwan to become a company man on company business must have been irresistible.

The other thing that spun out of Hajj Radwan's control were the crosscurrents of history. Well, actually, the Arab Spring turned out to be more like a lethal wind shear. He, like so many others, miscalculated the street, how easily the Sunnis were tipped into revolt, and how they were about to turn his ideas about political violence on their head. But it wasn't the first time he'd been caught crosswise of history. I'd seen it with my own eyes in Beirut, and in fact, it was that occasion that would give me my first and only clean shot I got at the bastard.

NOTE TO ASSASSINS: It's all in the timing.

HE WHO LAUGHS LAST SHOOTS FIRST

You're the enemy within, which means there's never a moment they're not trying to hunt you down to exterminate you. Hit before it's too late.

ALWAYS FLATTER THE GUY WITH A GUN IN HIS HAND, RIGHT UP UNTIL IT'S TIME TO ACT

Beirut, November 22, 1989: The Lebanese had had it with their civil war. Well into its fourteenth year, the war had killed nearly 120,000 people and there was absolutely nothing to show for it. Only the most bloody-minded didn't want the Lebanese government back, warts and all. And indeed, the violence did seem to be ebbing, but not even the sunniest optimist thought the calm would hold.

When the time arrived for parliament to elect a new president, the delegates met at a remote military base, helicopters buzzing overhead and tanks prowling the perimeter. But the day passed as quiet as the grave. A lot of people thought it was thanks to Syria and the United

States compromising on a single candidate. Some even predicted he'd be the man to finally stand Lebanon back up on its own two feet.

In the name of caution, the newly elected president rarely left his palace. When he did, his motorcade routes were cleared of parked cars to prevent an assassin from turning one of them into a bomb. This offered the added advantage of allowing his motorcade to move at high speed. To prevent an inside job, his personal security people were all related by blood, cousins and second cousins. But what no one could do anything about was the official functions that the president felt obligated to preside at. It offered any would-be assassin a fixed place and time.

By Lebanese Independence Day—just seventeen days after the election—the president was a bit more at ease. The evening before, the Syrian intelligence chief had told him Syria wouldn't tolerate an attempt on his life. Anyone who posed a potential threat had been rounded up, he said. Considering that Syria occupied about a third of Lebanon, the Syrian intelligence chief's assurances carried a lot of weight in the president's mind. Who'd want a Syrian armored division bent on retribution coming down on his head? As the Syrian was about to leave, he proposed that one of his men accompany the president's convoy, both to the ceremony and then back to the palace.

It rained the night before, offering up a crystalline morning and a rich, benevolent sky. The snow-dusted mountains and the silver-flecked turquoise sea were a spectacular amphitheater for it all. When the band started to play the national anthem, the president had to hold back a tear. Afterward, he stopped to talk to old friends. Aides had to hurry him along, ushering him into a black Mercedes. He sat in the backseat.

The lead police car pulled away with a screech of tires and sirens wailing. The convoy moved through the cleared streets at a brisk fifty miles an hour, spreading out across two blocks. People tried to get a glimpse of their new president, but with the convoy's speed and nearly identical cars with smoked windows, it was impossible to tell whose car was whose.

Just as the president's convoy started up a hill into Beirut's commercial center, there was a flash and a terrible trembling of the earth. It felt like a 747 had crashed somewhere nearby. At first, the only thing certain was that the convoy had been right in the middle of whatever it was.

As the smoke drifted off, it now was clear there had been an explosion. Several cars in the convoy were on fire. What was left of the president's security detail jumped out to check on the president, only to find his Mercedes gone. Vanished. They thought at first that the driver had taken advantage of the confusion to get away. But then someone noticed what was left of the Mercedes. It had been ripped in half, the pieces blown hundreds of feet away. The rear right door had taken the brunt of the explosion, exactly where the president had been sitting. A tank's armor wouldn't have saved him.

It turned out that an abandoned candy shop along the route had been packed with explosives, about a ton. But in order to concentrate the force into something like the size of a dinner plate, the assassins had molded the explosives into a conical hollow, a so-called shaped charge. Its force was such that it passed through one interior wall and then an exterior wall. But other than that, the investigators had nothing to go on. The firing device had been obliterated in the explosion. There were no fingerprints, no witnesses, no claims. Motive and intent were also a mystery.

The only thing clear was that it took talent to hit a car moving at fifty miles an hour, not to mention driving the explosion's force through two walls. The assassins clearly had had some sort of advanced military training. That and a lot of practice. But the real mystery stood: Who were these people capable of carrying off the assassination of a head of state in seventeen days?

———

Although no one dared put it to paper, a few investigators thought they recognized the work of Hajj Radwan. By 1989 he'd mastered the art of shaped charges, thanks to experimenting with them on the Israeli army. He could hit any moving vehicle no matter the speed. He'd also picked up the technique of "enhancing" a charge by mixing heat-generating aluminum powder in with the explosives.

Years later, a high-ranking Lebanese intelligence officer would tell me he'd come across some chatter that put Hajj Radwan in the middle of the president's assassination. When I asked him why it had never come out in an official report, there was no mistaking the incredulity in his voice: "Don't you understand what these people are capable of?"

I tried to persuade him to give me more, but he wouldn't budge. In fact, he cautioned me not to write anything about Hajj Radwan—it could get me killed. When I asked him whether it might be worth calling the president's widow to get her opinion, he said he'd advise her not to talk to me.

I tried a couple of other people but had no luck. Most didn't even know who Hajj Radwan was, and they were content to blame Syria for the president's murder. Being a distant and clumsy enemy, Syria was a ready-made scapegoat. Who knows, there's always the possibility it was the Syrians who commissioned Hajj Radwan to do the job. Just as I suspect they'd done with Hariri.

It left me to speculate why Hajj Radwan—or whoever it was—would want to murder the president of Lebanon in the middle of a touch-and-go war with Israel. You'd think he'd have more important things to attend to than assassinating a man of little political significance. Why not finish off the Israelis first and then put Lebanon's house in order?

What I'm pretty sure was at play is the principle that assassination is an instrument that serves the powerful whose power goes unrecognized rather than the merely powerless. If I'm right about Hajj Radwan's part in it, he murdered the Lebanese president to put the Lebanese statists on notice that they could forget about their fantasies of getting their state back. He and Hezbollah were in charge now, and no one was going to revive Lebanon with some silly parliamentary vote, especially a vote by parliamentarians who possess no power. The new president could go on all he liked about restoring the state's sovereign authority and standing Lebanon up out of the ashes, but the truth was that Lebanese sovereignty was a fiction.

Indeed, Hezbollah was pretty much the de facto Lebanese state. By the president's assassination in 1989, it had subverted much of the army, large parts of the security services, and the police. It effectively ran Beirut's only airport and its main seaport. In other words, Hezbollah was in a position to destroy any fool who wouldn't recognize reality for what it was.

Consider Hajj Radwan's point of view: With the new president proclaiming that he was determined to revive the state, could Hajj Radwan afford to sit on his hands while he tried? Wouldn't the first thing on the president's agenda be to exterminate Hajj Radwan and his coven of assassins? Hajj Radwan then saw no choice other than to put the state in its place.

There are a lot of parallels with the Hariri assassination. With his personal fortune and unreserved backing in Washington, Paris, and Riyadh, Hariri had started to labor under the delusion that he was the state. How long would it be before he deluded himself into trying to disarm Hezbollah? I imagine Hezbollah decided it couldn't wait around to find out. (See Law #21—Get to It Quickly.)

Every country has its own constitution; ours is absolutism moderated by assassination.

—AN ANONYMOUS RUSSIAN

Assassinating people with hollow pretensions to power isn't peculiar to Lebanon. Whether Benazir Bhutto was murdered by the Taliban, the Pakistani government, or a group we've never heard of, her loud and empty claims to power condemned her. She was tragically deceived into believing power in Pakistan is won at the ballot box.

Even in countries where the rule of law is given passing respect, the state at times will find it in its interest to murder upstarts who don't seem to understand the way things really work. What's sometimes called the "deep state"—secret units in the intelligence services or hired assassins—is called in to give the slow-to-comprehend a not so friendly reminder.

Between 1988 and 1998, Iranian intelligence operatives assassinated more than eighty dissident intellectuals. What the victims shared in common was a delusion that the mullahs' power was on the wane and a political space was about to open up. Dubbed the "Chain Murders," the assassins seemed to know what they were doing, never missing or murdering the wrong person. In many cases, they attempted to conceal that a murder had been committed at all. Some deaths occurred by injections of potassium chloride to induce a heart attack, others by fake car crashes.

A lot of people suspected that Iranian intelligence was behind the murders, and as the bodies started to pile up, even the regime recognized it looked silly trying to deny it. Its default defense was to point the finger at "rogue elements" of Iranian intelligence, conveniently naming an operative who himself may have been assassinated. Whether or not the assassination orders went all the way to the top or not, I doubt we'll ever find out. But the point is that the assassins got what they were after: drowning the budding Iranian Spring in blood.

Just as Vladimir Putin was coming to power in 1999, a wave of assassinations hit Russia's shores with a ferocity that surprised even the most cynical. No one seemed to be immune—big-name journalists, senior army officers, billionaire oligarchs, and even humble book-keepers. One victim of assassination may have been Putin's old boss, the ex-mayor of Saint Petersburg. According to a couple of reputable Russian journalists—a dying breed, to be sure—he was murdered by a poisoned lightbulb. The way it worked was the assassins coated the bulb of the ex-mayor's bedside table with a toxic substance that atomizes with heat. A little late-night reading, and that was it for him.

Then, of course, there was the 2006 celebrated assassination of ex–Russian intelligence officer turned Putin critic Alexander Litvinenko. A minute but deadly dose of the isotope polonium-210 killed him. It's almost certain that the assassins had expected the poisoning would go undetected. But when British police officials did discover traces of it, they concluded with near certainty that it was the Russian state that had assassinated Litvinenko.

(One of the small ironies in the Litvinenko assassination is that he may very well have signed his own execution order by openly accusing Putin of murdering a prominent journalist, who herself may have been assassinated because she'd accused Putin of assassinating a Russian general serving in Chechnya. I suppose if there's a lesson to be had, it's that it doesn't pay to call an assassin by his name.)

But it's not that regime assassinations are without risk. Again, it's all in the timing. Too early and you get a reputation for unnecessary brutality, too late and you're in trouble. The KGB must have often regretted not early on assassinating Lech Walesa, the Polish labor leader credited with opening the first crack in the Soviet bloc.

While there's no way of getting the timing exactly right, Machiavelli advises a prince to undertake extrajudicial executions (read: assassinations) at regular intervals.

"For one should not wish ten years at most to pass from one to another of such executions; for when this time is past men begin to vary in their customs and to transgress the laws."

Or as the old Chinese proverb goes, "If you want to scare the monkeys, kill the chicken."

All armed prophets succeed, whereas unarmed ones fail.

—NICCOLÒ MACHIAVELLI, *THE PRINCE*

Montreal, January 20, 2004: A young Canadian man I knew called me one morning to ask if I'd come up to Montreal. He wanted to introduce me to a man he was thinking about doing some business with. I'll call my friend Marc.

Marc had just opened a nightclub in downtown Montreal. Although only in his late twenties, he was determined to make serious money. I was more than happy to help him if I could, but I was tied up with a new book and asked if I could put the trip off for a couple months.

"Are you sure?" Marc asked. "It's very important to me."

He told me how his would-be business partner had read my memoir and genuinely wanted to meet me. If only I could fly up for dinner, or even lunch.

I didn't know what to say. There wasn't a shred of practical business advice in any of my books. I left it with a vague promise that I'd do my best to make some time for a trip.

Two days later, Marc's father, an old friend, called me. He was a man who spoke deliberately and with a gravelly voice you had to take seriously. "You really must meet my son's friend," he said. "He's a good family man. The two of you have a lot in common."

I wondered what was going on with the two of them pressing me like this, and I decided I'd better go up to Montreal sooner rather than later. But before I could make reservations, Marc called the next morning: "Now it's urgent. My friend's been arrested."

"Arrested?"

"Some bullshit charge. Please come up and talk to his son. He'll explain everything."

Before I got off the phone, I made Marc tell me the father's name.

"Vito Rizzuto," he said. Other than I knew it was Italian, it meant nothing to me. I wrote it down to Google later.

I drew in a deep breath as I read about the notorious Canadian Mafia boss named Vito Rizzuto. A capo in the Bonanno family who more or less monopolized North American heroin smuggling, he was one of the most powerful gangsters in the world. The Canadian press dubbed him the "Teflon Don." He was memorialized in the film *Donnie Brasco*, where in a true-to-life scene his character jumps out of a broom closet, a pistol blazing, cutting down three Bonanno family rivals. A classic *regolamento di conti*. A settling of scores.

Rizzuto had just been indicted in New York for those murders and racketeering, and the United States was now asking Canada to extradite him to stand trial. Rizzuto's arrest in Montreal on January 20, 2004, was the first step in the process of extradition.

Now I was definitely interested. I didn't care so much about the mob as I did about Rizzuto's connections to the Lebanese heroin trade, which were supposedly tight. Taking into consideration the rumors that Hajj Radwan might have been dealing in the stuff to support himself, I wondered if there wasn't something to be done with it. I'd come right out and ask the Rizzutos about him.

Marc was curbside at Montreal's airport, behind the wheel of a new black Porsche Cayenne. With his angular face, slicked-back hair, and Hugo Boss suit, he easily could have passed as a made man.

"You want something to eat?" Marc asked as I climbed in. "Or maybe go to the hotel and take a rest?" He didn't wait for an answer: "Let's go grab a drink." Marc accelerated fast, nearly clipping a bus pulling away from the curb.

Marc caught me looking at the patchy snow along the skirt of the highway: "Welcome to Montreal, dude. More on the way tonight, a big dump." You couldn't tell it from the sky. It was patchy too, thin blades of sun slicing through it.

When Marc pulled up in front of his club, the lights were off, but a tall, slouchy blonde with high cheekbones and a short tube dress stepped out of the doorway. Her accent was Russian. We got out, and she took the Cayenne's keys from Marc.

As Marc pushed through the front door, I asked him where he'd found the Russian. He didn't answer. I followed him up a flight of stairs, two steps at a time, and then through two doorways with bead curtains. We came to a room with a proper door. He closed it behind us, turning on the lights. It was a private dining room, a dozen erotic Japanese gouache drawings lining the walls.

A second girl, as beautiful as the first, came in with two glasses of white wine on a tray. It wasn't even noon, but I took one. Marc motioned for her to put his glass on the table. He told me he needed to step out to make a call.

Fifteen minutes later, Marc was back with a slender man in a tan cashmere overcoat and turtleneck. I stood up to shake hands. "Delighted to meet you," he said. "I'm Leo Rizzuto."

Marc pulled up a chair next to mine so Leo could sit next to me. Marc called into the darkness of the hallway: "Please bring us a bottle of red. A decent Bordeaux."

"Do you smoke?" Leo asked, holding open a slim gold cigarette case. When I said no, he put it away without taking a cigarette.

"My father had so wanted to meet you," Leo said. "It's too bad you were busy."

Marc had told me on the drive in from the airport that Leo was a lawyer with a good, legitimate practice. Now meeting Leo, I believed him. He seemed uncomfortable speaking with an ex–CIA agent on behalf of his Mafia father. But as Marc's father told me, the Rizzutos were a tight family, which meant Leo had no choice in the matter.

Marc walked over to the window and pulled back the curtain, flushing the room with light. As he'd promised, it was snowing—small, dry flakes. It must have turned cold very fast, I thought.

Marc turned to me. "I have something to do. I'll leave you two alone."

He closed the door behind him as he left. I noticed that Leo hadn't touched his wine.

"I don't want my father extradited to the United States," Leo said. "He could spend the rest of his life in jail."

"I'm not a lawyer, and I'm not sure how I can help."

I considered asking him if his father really was in on killing the three men in Queens. But it would have been an unwelcome, not to mention pointless, question—the facts had been established long ago. A better question would have been whether it was the murder of his three rivals that had propelled Vito to the head of the Bonanno family. But I wasn't going to ask that one either.

Leo went on: "My father knows a lot of people . . . a lot of things about them that aren't well-known . . . about heads of state in Africa, South America, and the Middle East. He knows who's selling what to whom, who's on whose payroll. He has people everywhere. He knows people and can get things done you can't imagine."

I now finally understood what Vito Rizzuto wanted from me: a channel to American intelligence, the CIA. He'd probably tried but failed to reach a deal through the Department of Justice, and now he was looking for a back door. I couldn't come up with another explanation.

"Was your father well connected in Lebanon?"

"I believe he was. But he'd have to give you the details."

I had to laugh to myself when I pictured my returning to Washington and calling up the CIA to let them know that, after all these years of missteps and failure, I had finally found the perfect assassin to take care of Hajj Radwan. All I'd need is their help springing him out of a Canadian jail and the clutches of the Department of Justice. The telephone would have melted in my hand before I could get halfway through my pitch.

That night Leo and Marc took me to an Italian restaurant for drinks. They drifted off to talk to friends, leaving me to talk to a squat man united with a Roman nose. He never took off his fedora as he told me how tough things were in the wholesale fish business.

After round three of grappa, he asked me if he could trust me. When I said yes, he told me that, the night before, his car had been fire-bombed and burned to the rims. It was over a contract dispute.

"They'll pay," he said. "Don't you worry about that."

I changed the subject: "I have to go to Lebanon next month. [It was a lie.] Ever been there?"

"No."

"No Lebanese business contacts?"

"No."

I looked out the window at the snow; it was now a driving blizzard.

Somewhere between the Italian restaurant and a nightclub, Leo disappeared. As Marc drove me back to my hotel, breaking through a wall of falling snow, I thought about Leo's offer, or at least the one I thought he'd made. It intrigued me; I could only guess what sort of people the Rizzutos keep on their speed dials, no doubt among them the heroin dealers in Hajj Radwan's backyard, the Bekaa Valley.

But I didn't think anything was really lost. The American Mafia may have a long history of settling disputes in blood, but they're loath to do it for outsiders, especially governments. Maybe in Italy, but not on this side of the Atlantic. (At this point, some fool's going to raise his hand to ask if the CIA didn't try to recruit the Mafia during the Kennedy administration to assassinate Castro. It did, but it never got off another fool's drawing board.)

None of this is meant to imply that the Mafia doesn't know what it's doing when it comes to murder. They know who their enemies are, who deserves it, and who doesn't. They know to strike early, before the victim gets the same idea. The three Bonanno captains Vito murdered in the Queens social club would have done the same to him had they known about his ambitions. Murder is a two-way street.

In December 2009, Vito's son—not Leo, but rather his heir apparent—would be assassinated in a Montreal suburb. Nearly a year later Vito's father, the Rizzuto patriarch, would meet the same fate when a single sniper's bullet punched through the double-paned patio doors of his house, killing him instantly. As for Vito, he was jailed for five years at the supermax prison in Florence, Colorado. He was paroled early, but died of cancer on December 23, 2013. I imagine this was the end to the Rizzutos' reign, the complete destruction of its *tabula patronatus*.

> **NOTE TO ASSASSINS:** It works best inside the family.

LIKE A BOLT OF LIGHTNING OUT OF A CLEAR BLUE SKY

Speed, secrecy, and surprise are your best allies. When they are applied in proper doses, the target will not have time to even cower. As for the survivors, they'll live in grim dread that their turn is next.

One more pothole, one less asshole.

—ANONYMOUS

Madrid, December 20, 1973: Franco's new prime minister was a creature of habit. For as long as anyone could remember, at nine sharp every morning Admiral Luis Carrero Blanco would emerge from his apartment building, climb into a waiting car, and take a short ride to San Francisco de Borja church to attend daily mass. His schedule and route never varied; his neighbors joked that they could set their watches by it. In fact, it would be Carrero Blanco's habitual observances that would contribute to his undoing.

By the early seventies, the Basque separatist movement ETA decided it was high time to knock a tooth out of the mouth of the doddering Franco regime, hoping to nudge it down the road to the realization that it wasn't worth holding on to the Basques. Among ETA's calculations: Franco's health was bad; there was no real dauphin; the left wing of the Catholic Church had broken from the ultraconservatives, a serious blow to Franco; many Spaniards born after the civil war (1936–1939) didn't think Spain needed a strongman to hold the country together. In short, with the consensus frayed, one high-profile murder would be a game changer.

ETA also decided it needed a spectacular display of violence to put itself on the map, to give it the voice that Franco had denied it all these years. As one ETA assassin put it in a long, taped confession to Blanco's "execution": "Spaniards have an enormous incapacity to understand the Euskadi [the Basque nation] is a country."

ETA apparently didn't share George Bernard Shaw's opinion that assassination is the extreme form of censorship. For them, it was a means to uncensor themselves.

In those days, Spain was an overconfident police state, and all that ETA had to do to find Carrero Blanco's apartment was look it up in the telephone book: Calle de los Hermanos Bécquer, 6. ETA members located it on a subway map. In the following days, they watched his apartment, which soon confirmed a tip about the prime minister's daily trip to San Francisco de Borja.

The church was open to the public, which allowed the assassins to study its layout and workings at their leisure. The very first day, they caught Carrero Blanco leaving mass. The next day, they got there early enough to see him arrive and attend mass. Only one bodyguard accompanied Carrero Blanco inside the church.

Every day an ETA assassin waited at the church for Carrero Blanco to arrive. At one point one of them tested the reaction of Carrero Blanco's bodyguard by kneeling on the prie-dieu next to him. Although he was only a foot or so from Carrero Blanco, the bodyguard did nothing.

It was then that ETA understood just how vulnerable Carrero Blanco was. At first, they had considered kidnapping him, but when he was appointed prime minister he was assigned too many bodyguards to make it feasible.

In the meantime, the assassins did their best to go about life as inconspicuously as possible. But it wasn't all that easy in Madrid, a city that ran on the rhythm of a dull estuary. Young men without jobs, who spent their days and nights sitting in parks and cafés, weren't exactly invisible. On top of it, there was no way to hide their Basque accents.

Since none of the assassins had lived in Madrid long enough to become completely familiar with the city, everything was hard, from finding an apartment to renting a car. They didn't have a good network of friends and contacts to rely on. Nor did they have a safe way to communicate other than with face-to-face meetings. The one thing they did have going for them was Spanish lassitude—and the fortune that Spain's secret police weren't particularly efficient.

The Basque assassins twice accidentally fired off rounds in their apartments. It was sheer luck that neighbors didn't call the police. And in what can only be described as a rash act, they stole a machine gun from a sleeping sentry at Spain's military headquarters. What did ETA have to do to get noticed? Apparently nothing, and with each day, ETA's confidence in its ability to assassinate Carrero Blanco grew. In spite of the mistakes, its members still retained the element of surprise.

On the morning of December 20, Carrero Blanco emerged from his apartment building at five after nine. His bodyguard and driver were waiting by his new Dodge 3700 GT, as was the rest of his security detail.

No one has ever come forward to say they'd noticed anything out of place that morning. To be sure, no one noticed a chalk mark on Calle de Claudio Coello, a street behind Francisco de Borja. The unsteady vertical line on the wall looked like a child's thoughtless scrawl. But in the high-end-murder business it's called a "timing line"—a mark to help clock the speed of a moving car.

Another thing no one noticed that morning was the ETA assassins who'd been posing as sculptors. Two months before, they'd rented a basement studio on Calle de Claudio Coello. This time of the morning they'd normally be making a racket, chipping away at their blocks of marble and carrying out heavy bags of something. Marble chips, the neighbors assumed. No one, of course, had a clue they'd been tunneling under the street. But not a peep out of them now.

No, to all appearances it was a typical morning, the usual people on their way to work, the same early shoppers. The only thing unusual was that the U.S. secretary of state, Henry Kissinger, had been in Madrid on a visit and had stopped by the American embassy, which was only a couple blocks from San Francisco de Borja.

Carrero Blanco stepped out of the church at about half past nine, the driver holding open the Dodge's rear door for him. Carrero Blanco took his usual seat. His bodyguards looked up and down the street, searching for anything out of place. The two chase cars of his security detail were double-parked behind Carrero Blanco's Dodge, idling. Everyone started off at once.

The convoy took its usual route south on Calle de Serrano, a one-way street, and then a left on Calle de Juan Bravo, another one-way street. It made an immediate left on Calle de Claudio Coello. It would have been a straight shot down Calle de Claudio Coello. But mid-block there was a double-parked car. No one was in it. But so what? This was Madrid, and Blanco's driver thought nothing about it. He slowed down to maneuver around it.

Carrero Blanco's Dodge had barely passed the double-parked car when the street heaved and exploded in flying debris and concrete. Where the Dodge had been, there now was only an enormous crater, quickly filling with water and sewage.

Carrero Blanco's dazed detail had no idea what had happened to him or his Dodge. It was as if he'd been plucked from the earth by an unworldly force. They wouldn't know where he was until people came running out of San Francisco de Borja to tell them that the car had landed on a second-floor terrace on the other side of the five-story church. Carrero Blanco immediately survived the blast, but he died afterward in the hospital. His driver and bodyguard also died.

Franco would be dead less than two years later. But Spain went after ETA and Carrero Blanco's assassins the best it could. In 1978 one of them was himself assassinated in France by a car bomb. A few others were hauled in, or drifted off to other occupations. One became a successful filmmaker. ETA never got its own country. Whether or not Carrero Blanco's assassination hastened the end of Spanish fascism is a matter of interpretation.

ALWAYS APPEAR TO BE DULL AND UNIMPORTANT, DISTRACTED BY THE FLEETING BUSINESS OF LIFE

Beirut, July 11, 1987: The Victorians would have called it Eastern licentiousness, but the way I looked at it at the time was that the Lebanese are a people who know how to throw a rollicking birthday party. It was my thirty-fifth birthday, and one I'll never forget.

A new friend of mine, whom I'll call Colette, put it together. She was a smart, sweet girl and, as the Italians say, *un bel pezzo di figa*. She picked an outdoor restaurant just downhill from a mountain village called Faraya.

Right away, I liked the feng shui of the place, how the restaurant was carved into the limestone hillside, its terrace thrown open to a spectacular set of seashell-pink Roman ruins and, beyond the ruins, the inevitable Mediterranean framed by a spotless blue-lacquered sky.

I thought it would be only four of us, but more people kept showing up, about a dozen in the end. The more the merrier, I thought. These days I was doing my best to pass myself off as a foreign roué come to Lebanon to party. Which was only partially true.

The more pressing truth was that I was now as paranoid as Chuck. I could feel Hajj Radwan's hot breath hard on the back of my neck. There was nothing specific other than the slow accumulation of evidence that he had free run of the Christian enclave. The French assassinations and a lot of recent really good chatter were proof enough for me.

But it wouldn't be until the Hariri investigation that I fully understood just how right I was. As I wrote before, Hajj Radwan's brother-in-law—the on-the-ground coordinator for Hariri's assassination—had set himself up on the Christian side of Beirut posing as an Armenian jeweler. If he could embed himself in the Christian enclave so easily, it must have been all the easier for Hajj Radwan's less prominent operatives. Hell, for all I knew, my downstairs neighbors worked for him.

It all meant that a Carrero Blanco–like assassination would have been a cup of tea for Hajj Radwan. Which left me the choice of either hiding in our fortress, counting the days until it was time to leave Beirut, or going out among the Lebanese and pretending to be something I wasn't. If I could have, I would have posed as a priest or something, but it never would have worked. So, I was left with the womanizing act.

The party started with about fifty plates of Lebanese mezze—hummus, tabbouleh, fresh vegetables—and an enormous bottle of home-made arak. It's the Lebanese version of Greek ouzo. It disappeared faster than I thought possible.

I wished the hard drinking hadn't started so early; these people were interesting. Mostly Greek Orthodox, they were in their twenties and hip. Their politics were open-minded and ecumenical; of all the Lebanese Christians, they were the closest to the Muslims. It also wasn't far from my mind that one of the assassins of the Maronite president-elect in September 1982 was Greek Orthodox. It was a long shot, but I was hoping one of my fellow partyers might know a way into Hajj Radwan's world.

All too soon things started to get watery, the conversation descending into giggling and professions of eternal love between America and Lebanon. Mercifully, someone stood up on a chair to recite a poem—in Greek. At the end of it, even though I understood nothing, I downed my arak with the best of them. The next bard jumped up on the table and stomped his foot in cadence with his delivery. We emptied our glasses again, only this time smashing them on the floor. All of the dishes on the table soon met the same fate; the owner stood in the door, smiling at us.

I suspected lunch was over when my fellow revelers got up, staggered to their cars, and came back with their assault rifles. Each couplet now was punctuated by the rat-tat-tat of firing into the air. I watched as the tracer rounds arced over the Roman ruins toward the sea. We were on borrowed light by the time we finally left.

That night I couldn't sleep, thinking how I'd been caught up in the lunacy of this country, falling for its charms like so many other expat saps. Or maybe harder than most did. I was always after that anonymous moment when some fact or tidbit of information would clear up some burning question or explain the byways of political violence that govern these people.

Not long after my birthday party, I took over a source who had some good inroads into Fatah. He soon got into trouble though, obligating me to put him up in one of my apartments to wait for things to cool down. One night over a whiskey, he asked me if he could trust me. It's a question I always have a pat answer for: Yes, absolutely.

After a lot of hemming and hawing, he said that Fatah had been behind the 1982 assassination of the Lebanese president-elect. There's too much detail to get into here, but the upshot was that it had been Yasser Arafat who'd personally given the orders. Arafat decided the president-elect was a dire threat to the Palestinians and that he had no choice other than to murder him. But it didn't mean that Arafat could afford to claim it or, for that matter, even use his own people. It's the reason he enlisted a breakaway faction of the predominantly Greek Orthodox Syrian Social Nationalist Party to do the job. If my source hadn't been able to provide chapter and verse, I would have dismissed his story out of hand.

The story became even more interesting when the source told me one of Hajj Radwan's gunmen might have been connected to the president's assassination. When I asked him whether Hajj Radwan was in on it, he said he didn't think so. When I asked him if there was a way to check, he shot back that he wouldn't ask.

The deeper I waded into Lebanon's swamp, the murkier it seemed to get. There were layers upon layers of hidden relations I couldn't make sense of, entire worlds closed to me. At times it seemed as if there were a caste of assassins who hired out their services. Hajj Radwan first murdered for the Palestinians and later for the Iranians and the Syrians. The fact that it wasn't always about politics added to the complexity. Hajj Radwan spent seven years trying to free his brother-in-law from his Kuwaiti prison. But there was no way for me to tie it all up in a pink bow. I did have my little consolations, though. If ETA could bumble around Madrid and not tip its hand, so could I.

Death is not an artist.

—JULES RENARD

There was one girl from my birthday party who'd caught my attention. She had a voice that could drive the birds from the sky, but a sixth sense told me she was a good connector. I called her to ask her out for drinks.

We met in a noisy bar near the Green Line, a place called the Beirut Cellar. I'd heard that you'd have to dodge the snipers if you left the place too late. By the time I started to frequent the club, there was always the racket of gunfire from the Green Line, but a sniper never took a shot at me, either arriving or leaving.

The night's crowd was noisy. The girl led me by the hand and sat me down next to a smallish, half-bald man in a suit and tie. "My good friend," she said, introducing me. "He's a journalist." After a little chit-chat, she wandered off to say hello to a friend.

The journalist was from Tyre, but he had come up to Beirut to attend university and then stayed on to work in journalism. When the civil war started, he moved over to the Christian enclave. It worked because his wife was Christian.

But it was the mention of Tyre that interested me. Hajj Radwan traced his origins to a village close by. I was doubtful, but I wondered if the journalist might have run across him. I resisted asking, though; a curiosity in Hajj Radwan isn't the best calling card.

I got up and went to the bar for two beers. "How about taking me to Tyre to show me the sights?" I asked as I sat back down.

He took his beer, searching my face to see if I was serious or not. When he decided I was, he said: "We—I mean you—would be taken right away. It's not safe."

I knew that, of course. A couple of months before, Hajj Radwan had kidnapped an American colonel working for the UN in southern Lebanon. He would later execute him.

But my motto is to always lead with innocence: "Oh, come on, who would notice us?"

He gave me a harassed smile: "Surely, sir, you have a family to think about."

"Don't you know someone in Tyre who'd be willing to show me around?"

He thought for a moment. "Listen, I have a colleague who covers Tyre. When he's next here, I'll introduce you."

BEWARE OF THE UNINVITED

From downstairs came the shriek of a door opening on rusted hinges. I wondered when the last time the apartment's heavy iron front doors were both opened at the same time. Probably at the start of the civil war when the building's inhabitants were desperately fleeing the fighting, piling their crap on the tops of their cars and heading up into the mountains.

From the stairwell came grunting, men hoisting something very heavy up the stairs: "Put him down . . . Let's take a breather . . . No, wait till the landing."

It was Ali and his men. I pictured them in the gloomy dark of the stairwell, throwing their backs into hoisting Ali and his wheelchair up the stairs, sweating, terrified they'd drop him.

I'd met Ali through the journalist from the Beirut Cellar. His colleague from Tyre had refused to meet me, and as a consolation, he had introduced me to Ali. Up until a sniper's bullet paralyzed Ali, he had been a militia commander in the southern suburbs. Out of the action and broke, he was happy to take the CIA's money in exchange for his "explaining Lebanon" to me.

I'd now been meeting Ali for two months, but I had never got around to asking him how he managed to cross the Green Line without a problem. I guessed it had something to do with his being wheelchair bound. Or maybe he had some Christian connection who helped. Lebanon is all about the right connections.

An unsteady light leaked under the door, a flashlight, then a knock. When I opened the door, Ali rolled himself into the apartment. In the dark, I could make out three men in the hall. I consoled them with a smile and closed the door. I went into the kitchen to make coffee on a Bunsen burner.

As soon as I sat down, Ali yelled at the door for someone to bring in the package. A man let himself in, carrying something neatly wrapped in cloth. Ali took it and handed it to me. It was heavy. I unwrapped it to find a submachine gun with the dimensions of a large pistol. There were also two long magazines held together by a rubber band.

"Beautiful, isn't it?" Ali said. "A PM-63."

A PM-63 is a Polish-made submachine gun favored by tank crews and Middle Eastern thugs, mainly thanks to its handy size. A rare weapon, it was a thing of real value in Beirut.

Ali said he'd personally taken this one and a dozen others from Arafat's security detail when Arafat was run out of Beirut in 1982.

I wasn't a gun collector, and I had no idea what I was going to do with it. But the point is that Ali had given it to me as a token of trust. I got up and gave him a hug.

I didn't have a gun to give Ali. But what I did have for him was my version of a token of trust—a thick plastic-wrapped stack of "sterile" hundred-dollar bills. (Out of delicacy, I'd put it in a plain white envelope.) I handed it to Ali, who, without saying a word, put it in an inner pocket.

About five blocks away, toward the Green Line, there was the burr of a large machine gun. Ali and I stopped to listen. When we didn't hear an answer to it, we both relaxed.

What interested me was Ali's past: The Shiite militia he'd once headed was based in the southern suburbs next to the airport. He knew all the fighters there, from the lowliest gunsels to the commanders. He knew their origins, who lived where, who controlled which street. It seemed there wasn't a name he couldn't run down for me. A lot of it I was able to confirm from chatter.

An ironic man with a good sense of humor, Ali understood just how pointless the fighting had all been and that one day the Lebanese would have to go back to living like normal people. Like the colonel who'd wanted no part of my plans to assassinate Hajj Radwan, Ali wanted to immigrate to the United States and open a convenience store in Detroit.

It took me half a dozen meetings before I felt confident enough to test him on the subject of Hajj Radwan. I eased into it by asking questions about Hajj Radwan's neighborhood, Ayn al-Dilbah. Ali said he knew it well, pretty much house by house. Not wanting to raise his suspicions right at the start, I left it there.

At the following meeting, I brought up the TWA 847 hijacking—the one that earned Hajj Radwan a sealed arrest warrant for the murder of a Navy diver. I said almost in passing that there was a theory that some of the hijackers were from Ayn al-Dilbah. Again, I intentionally didn't mention Hajj Radwan's name.

Without missing a beat, Ali said he knew exactly who the hijackers were. He offered me three names. I'd heard them before, but only in the press.

Now I started to worry. I knew for a fact that the three had nothing to do with TWA 847. Chatter had put them in the Bekaa at the time. Was Ali fishing for a bonus? Or was it something more sinister?

Ali then compounded the error by saying he'd seen the three with his own eyes exiting and entering the plane. He'd grown up with them, he said, and there was no doubt about it; they were like his brothers. I told him we'd talk more about it at the next meeting.

I stood in the window, watching Ali's men hoist him into the back of his old van, still stumped if Ali was lying about TWA 847 to get a bonus or to cover for someone.

At the next meeting, Ali rolled into my apartment with a big smile plastered across his face: "You know what a Stechkin is?"

I did: It's a small Russian fully automatic pistol.

"Well, I think I got you one, and it's a very special one. At one time it belonged to a KGB officer."

Ali didn't need to tell me he was referring to the 1985 kidnapping of three Russian diplomats and a KGB officer. The KGB officer was wounded in the attack and died. His Stechkin was taken from him. As I wrote before, we knew that Hajj Radwan had organized the attack, taking a $200,000 ransom.

Paranoia is a wonderful astringent, not to mention a wonderful way to tune up your senses. Right now they were screaming at me that the missing KGB pistol was a big, juicy piece of bait—and at the other end of the line was Hajj Radwan. Offering me the pistol was sort of like telling a concert violinist that you've just found an old violin in your attic, made by some Italian named Stradi-somebody. My only question was what was next.

At the next meeting, Ali showed up with the serial number for the Stechkin. When I unfolded the torn-off piece of paper and read the numbers, my heart turned to water. They were correct.

"The man who has it is ready to meet," Ali said.

As I listened to Ali offer the outlines of the deal, I could only wonder what Act III would be. A burlap bag over my head and a quick ride across the Green Line? Or maybe, more efficient, two bullets in the back of the head.

My mind started racing, trying to figure out how to retake lost ground. What I knew was that for a start I had to make Ali believe I'd taken the bait. I shook Ali's hand: "Fine work." I folded up the paper with the serial number and put it in my jeans pocket. I said I needed to check on something before we could proceed.

After Ali was out the door, I went to the window to check the street. Other than Ali's van, there wasn't a car in sight. But so what? It's not like kidnappers would be so stupid as to park out front.

I cursed myself for the idiotic daisy chain I'd started down—the birthday party, casual friends, the journalist. It's a spy's version of dumpster diving, all so goddamned haphazard and lazy. Not even Carrero Blanco's assassins would have set a trap for themselves like this.

IT'S HARD CLEANING UP OLD WHORES

These days it's almost impossible to shed your past, especially if it's in any way shady—an old DUI arrest, bad credit, flunking out of junior college. It's like carrying around a dead fish in your pocket. Margaret Thatcher's would-be assassin, Patrick Magee, was caught thanks to the police having his fingerprints on file. It's one reason, I suppose, that assassination is a young man's game.

Call them naïfs, lily-whites, cleanskins, or anything you like, but the point is that people without a blemish on their record are your ideal recruits. As pure as a pink chrysanthemum, they can slip into most anywhere without coming to anyone's attention. People such as retiring librarians, octogenarian spinsters, and friars work okay, but it's the young and seemingly innocent you really want.

Hajj Radwan understood the principle as well as anyone. The young man he chose to fire the opening shot in the war on Israel wasn't even a mote of dust on Israel's radar. Only seventeen years old, and with no radical ties, he could have been raised by wolves on the steppe as far as the Israelis were concerned.

Years later, I'd meet his family, who lived in a small village above Tyre. Who knows for sure, but they convinced me that they had no idea what the boy was about to do. But of course, why would he tell them? It's all about the need to know.

As best as could be determined, it was shortly after the 1982 Israeli invasion that Hajj Radwan approached the boy to enlist him as a suicide bomber. Had someone else spotted the boy beforehand, gauged his readiness for martyrdom? Or was he a longtime acquaintance of Hajj Radwan's? We don't know. But the upshot was that the boy agreed to sacrifice his life in order to end the foreign occupation of his country.

In the days after their invasion of Lebanon, the Israelis genuinely believed that the Lebanese were grateful they'd given the Palestinians a good dusting. In fact, they were so confident of it that Israeli tour groups started to organize visits to south Lebanon. El Al, the Israeli state airline, opened an office in Sidon. Scantily clad Israeli tourists even took to sunbathing on Lebanese beaches.

Early on November 11, 1982—less than six months after the invasion—Hajj Radwan's young recruit drove his old, explosive-packed Peugeot through the front door of the seven-story building. The truck detonated, bringing down the building. It killed seventy-five Israeli soldiers and some two dozen Lebanese and Palestinian prisoners.

For the first time, the Israelis got a glimpse into the Lebanese hell they'd thoughtlessly wandered into. Hajj Radwan clearly had done a good job of casing the place. He'd gotten the timing of the attack exactly right, coinciding with the return of the night patrols and before the morning patrols left. Heavy rain that morning had driven more soldiers inside. Had he planned it around the weather? Unlikely, but who knows?

I don't know when Israel discovered that Hajj Radwan was behind the attack or even whether, in fact, he was. What is certain is that the attackers were in an entirely different class from Carrero Blanco's. Not only did no one from his side shoot a gun into a ceiling, they also didn't offer a long and detailed admission to explain themselves. The act was meant to speak for itself.

And just as Hajj Radwan wanted, there were more questions than answers. For instance, how had he managed to enlist his lily-white suicide bomber, and even more remarkable, how could he be so sure that the boy would take his own life? As it turned out, Hajj Radwan had on the bench scores of lily-whites just like him, but not one of them was on an Israeli suspect list. For that matter, the Israelis didn't even know who Hajj Radwan was until very late in the game.

Although Ali didn't work out, the reason for my sifting through my new Greek Orthodox friends was to find a lily-white of my own, someone who could naturally insinuate himself into Hajj Radwan's circle. But as I was reminded again and again, the membrane between Christian and Muslim Beirut went pretty much one way.

SILENT PRAYERS FOR A DEAF GOD

I've always been good at is turning failure into opportunity. I counted on it now with Ali as I tried to find a way to string him along with some bullshit story, buy myself some time. Hajj Radwan was good, but it didn't mean that he was immune to red herrings.

Systemic misdirection used to be a standard practice for CIA officers in Moscow. As soon as one of them arrived in town, he'd make as much smoke as possible. He'd strike up a conversation with an unsuspecting passenger on the subway, slipping him his calling card. His KGB tail would have no choice but to haul the poor bastard in and sweat him. Or he'd walk into a police station to file a complaint about someone parking too close to his car, the idea being to force his KGB tail to ask the cops why he'd paid them a visit. Swarming the KGB with false leads such as these tied them up in knots and wore out its surveillance teams.

At my next meeting with Ali, I showed him a picture of a bearded man sitting behind the wheel of a car. He's grinning at the camera, a front tooth missing. I told Ali we'd recently discovered he'd played a role in bombing the Marine barracks in October 1983. (It was a lie cut from whole cloth, but there was no way for Ali to know that.)

Ali studied the picture, put it back on the coffee table between us. He said he didn't know the man but would find him for me. I now pulled out a picture of an apartment building. There was an address written on the back.

"Would you be able to have someone watch it?" I asked.

"The building?"

"The man in the picture visits here. Yes."

For the next half hour we haggled over money, what it would cost for

Ali's people to watch the apartment around the clock and, eventually, the man himself.

When we finished, I said who could know whether one day we might decide to grab him. Ali reached over and shook my hand: "Brother, it would be an honor to bring this man to justice."

Did I think I could beat Hajj Radwan with bullshit like this? No. But I counted on it buying me time.

NOTE TO ASSASSINS: Always be ready with a clever lie or two to confuse the curious.

ALWAYS HAVE
AN ENCORE
IN YOUR POCKET

Power is the ability to hurt something over and over again. One-offs get you nothing or less than nothing.

WHEN THE ASSASSIN SPEAKS, LET NO DOG BARK

Beirut, January 1988: Many a morning I woke up trying to gauge the weight of the courtiers, eunuchs, and imbeciles who occupy Washington like an alien army. But I would quickly remind myself it was a wasted thought: Their deliberations were as opaque to me as a Pashtun *loya jirga*.

By my first cup of coffee I'd generously decide that Washington's bureaucrats weren't so much imbeciles as they were people who genuinely believe they were born to walk within the lines drawn for them. But did they never stop to think it might have been imbeciles who drew the lines in the first place?

The point here is that I made Langley nervous. Whenever I'd propose something dicey, the only thing I'd hear back was the scampering of cold feet. No one wanted to risk his career for uncertain gain on a dim, distant battlefield, especially with me in the middle of it. It meant that I spent more time than I needed to trying to figure out how to get around Langley's human weather vanes.

I'd also learned from hard experience that it was impossible to get Langley interested in what made Lebanon tick. For a while, I sent in long, thoughtful pieces about how the various Shiite personalities, families, and clans fit in, but I couldn't even get a yawn out of Langley. And forget making them understand how Hajj Radwan's *Machtpolitik* worked, all the ins and outs that explained the man. They couldn't have cared less that Hajj Radwan had first been recruited into Fatah by a Christian Palestinian who had converted to Islam and that Hajj Radwan was consequently infected by a convert's uncompromising beliefs. When I tried to fill in the details about his involvement in the first embassy bombing in April 1983, Langley wrote back that it was ancient history and that I needed to give it a break.

Were they distracted by off-sites and campfires on the Pecos River? No doubt. But what really was at the center of it was that Langley was unfamiliar with the ways of political violence. My bosses didn't even want to consider the possibility that it might come with a set of rules and logic. They were more than happy to wallow in the prejudice that the barbarians kill one another and us for no good reason.

One man I answered to had recently come back from an important Arab posting. As the story went, when things started to heat up in the middle of his tour, he ordered a .12-gauge shotgun. Shotguns are of no use when you want to kill at a distance, but they do okay when you are trying to hold back the mob from overrunning the premises.

When the gun arrived, he was as excited as a five-year-old on Christmas morning. He found a box of shells, loaded the shotgun, and pumped a shell into the chamber. BANG! Having no idea it was a police riot gun that chambers and fires a round in the same action, he stared at the gun in disbelief. Too shaken to realize what he was doing, he chambered a second round. BANG! Terrified, he threw the gun across the office, where it came to a stop under a cabinet. It would stay there for months, no one willing to pick up the thing.

The story only gets better: When his deputy came back to the office and saw the hole in the wall over his desk, he decided that the chief, whom he'd never gotten along with, had sent him a not so subtle warning. He forthwith resigned from the CIA to marry a fabulously wealthy heiress.

Act two: When the station's administrative officer finally summoned the nerve to retrieve the gun from under the chief's cabinet, he took it back to his office and couldn't resist working the action to determine what the problem was. BANG! The casualty of the third and last accidental discharge was the office refrigerator.

Act three: A bomb tech from Langley finally gave the shotgun a decent burial in the desert.

I may not have got this sequence exactly right—isn't that always the case when it comes to office lore?—but the point remains that, contrary to popular opinion, the CIA isn't a pack of cold-blooded assassins. Like me, they're mostly feckless liberal arts majors who learn on the fly. I suppose it's one good reason Americans are always reading about their fumbling spooks in the newspapers.

What made it worse was when Ronald Reagan decided it would be a good idea to outsource national security. The CIA was cheerfully sucked into that great deceit, contracting out all sorts of its core functions. We felt it in the field. While the bosses at Langley were schmoozing the Northrops and Boeings of the world, our raison d'être was reduced to not rocking the boat. And God forbid if anyone took the mission seriously. But it got even worse when Langley started to meddle in operations to further someone's political or financial interests back home.

At one point, the DEA handed off to the CIA one of its confidential informants, a small-time Lebanese drug dealer. The only thing to recommend the man was eleven outstanding arrest warrants—all garden-variety murders. His last was for blowing his sister's head off with a shotgun. She'd apparently dated the wrong guy. Or maybe it was his sister-in-law. Does it matter? The point is that he wasn't exactly the most trustworthy proxy.

But it didn't stop my boss at Langley, the one with the accidental discharge under his belt, from employing him to kidnap the hijacker of a Jordanian airliner. Indeed, the sister-murdering drug dealer did arrange for bikini-clad FBI agents to arrest the hijacker on a pleasure boat sitting off Cyprus. The hijacker was brought back to the United States for trial and received a life sentence. Justice served, Americans could now go back to a good night's sleep.

But at no point did anyone ask what message this little stunt sent to Hajj Radwan. Could he not have asked himself why we would bother with someone who wasn't a true threat to the United States? After all, the hijacker hadn't hijacked an American airliner or even killed an American. Yes, the arrest may have gone down smoothly, not a shot fired and no one breaking a fingernail, but in the end, what good did it do? Hajj Radwan would have wisely ignored the man and moved on to more worthwhile prey.

It didn't help that the rest of our foreign policy only strengthened Hajj Radwan's disregard for us, from the invasion of tiny Grenada to the Iran-Contra swindle. It all played right into his prejudice that Washington plays to the stands and special interests. For someone with a ruthless construct on life, we looked soft at the core—an open invitation to hit us all the harder.

Let me go back to Iran-Contra in order to remind you that it was Hajj Radwan who was holding the hostages Reagan wanted back—he was at the pointed end of the deal. So when Oliver North showed one of Hajj Radwan's Iranian sponsors—the so-called Second Channel—around the White House, Radwan must have wondered whether we'd completely lost our minds. It was sort of as if the president had shown the Khmer Rouge leader Pol Pot around Disneyland, hoping to soften him up. It wasn't only Langley that didn't understand that there are such things as hidden levers of power. After I left the CIA, I wrote a book in which I tried to make sense of Iran's two-decade detour through political violence. In one chapter I recount a short visit to Iran to make a documentary film on suicide bombers. Among the people we interviewed was the family of the Hezbollah secretary-general assassinated in 1992. (It was the assassination that provoked Hajj Radwan to attack two Jewish/Israeli targets in Buenos Aires.)

I was intrigued by the fact that the daughter of the assassinated Hezbollah secretary-general had married into the family of Iran's first modern suicide bomber, a boy of thirteen who sacrificed himself in order to destroy an Iraqi tank. To me, the marriage seemed like a bizarre iteration of the Order of Assassins, the twelfth-century Persian group that invented political murder. But it turned out my obsessive fascination with political murder wasn't shared by all. One eminent critic of my book reacted with disbelief, horror, and shock when I wrote that our documentary crew couldn't find a decent restaurant in Tehran. If we couldn't sniff out Tehran's hip nouvelle cuisine, how could we possibly understand the real Iran?

She might have a point. There's a good argument to be made that political murder is only a footnote to Persian history. The Order of Assassins didn't change much of anything, either for the better or for the worse. And I have no doubt that people will argue with me over whether Hajj Radwan's assassinations changed history in any lasting and significant way. Was I making the mistake of confusing the obscure with the important? Maybe.

I need to add that it's not as if the American government embraced my point of view. In Beirut, I'd always start my day off reading State Department telexes dealing with Lebanon. They'd drone on about what the Lebanese president was doing or what some parliamentary deputy was saying. Even back then Hariri was taken by Washington as an authoritative source on Lebanon. But in none of it did the name Hajj

Radwan appear or, for that matter, the notion that there might be a ghost calling the shots.

The same goes for Pan Am 103. I recently started e-mailing one of the FBI's lead investigators in that attack. I raised my suspicions about the chatter, how it implicated Iran. He wrote me back that he hadn't looked at the chatter related to Pan Am but that "they [the National Security Agency] opened their files to one of our agents who pored through everything they [allegedly] had." But he hadn't read the intelligence himself! In other words, he and I were singing off two completely different sheets of music.

MORE STRAY CATS

It had been easy enough to persuade Chuck to help me look around for new sources, and it wasn't long before he fished up a shady Christian businessman who claimed he could get to anyone in Lebanon. I'd heard that one before, but I decided to give Chuck's new source the benefit of the doubt.

About a month after meeting the Christian, Chuck came into the office waving a crisp new hundred-dollar bill in my face: "A supernote, Bobby boy. My guy [the shady Christian] just bought it for me."

A "supernote" is a counterfeit U.S. hundred-dollar bill designed to withstand serious scrutiny. Like a real hundred, it's printed on cotton rag paper. The plates used to print them are engraved with a geometric lathe, a very rare piece of equipment. Supernotes are of such high quality that the counterfeiters include in them tiny mistakes so as not to be deceived into taking back their own product.

I asked Chuck how much his source wanted for it.

"One-twenty."

I looked at Chuck, waiting for the punch line. He saw where I was going. "Fuck, I don't know. That's what he paid for it."

Was Chuck's source's plan to entice us into the counterfeiting business? If so, the economics obviously didn't make sense.

All things being equal, I'd have encouraged Chuck to drop the guy. But we were drawing a complete blank trying to find someone to get inside Hajj Radwan's world. I recognize that keeping Chuck's businessman on the books amounts to trolling in a bus station, but even a rotten piece of bait can catch a fish, right?

Which brings me back to Jennifer Matthews and the Jordanian doctor who murdered her. It took me a while, but I finally came to the conclusion that the main reason political murder is so difficult for us is that we don't have at our disposal a ready, committed pool of proxies. The Communist Third International had all the true believers it could use, as does al-Qaeda today. But what do we have to draw a committed following? While everyone in the world is ready to immigrate to the United States or take a free trip to Disneyland, it doesn't mean they're prepared to murder for us. It's a problem I was reminded of every day, and when on the rare occasion some true believer did manage to find his way to me, he inevitably turned out to be as crazy as a tree full of owls.

Not long after Ali dished up that suspicious story about the TWA hijacking, I ran into a former Christian warlord who couldn't care less about money but wanted to kill Muslims. He in turn introduced me to two Christian military officers who'd on their own taken to ambushing Syrian army patrols. They in turn introduced me to a master car-bomb maker who'd once simultaneously set off eleven car bombs. A Shiite from the southern suburbs, he had a virtual laissez-passer to enter Hajj Radwan's neighborhood.

When I showed the bomber the picture of a place I thought Hajj Radwan frequented, he immediately offered to flatten it with a pair of gargantuan car bombs the moment Hajj Radwan showed up. The man's bomb-making skill had a certain appeal to me, as did the redundancy of the charge, but I demurred. My intent wasn't to cause mass casualties, à la the attempt on the Lebanese ayatollah in 1985. And, on top of it, how could two car bombs ever be construed back at the Department of Justice as an arrest gone wrong?

No, I'd have to keep looking for the real thing, someone who could put himself within the blast range of Hajj Radwan and not take a city block with him.

READING BIRD ENTRAILS

One Saturday morning, three of us were waiting at the helicopter landing pad to catch a ride over to Cyprus on a pair of Black Hawks. I definitely needed to get away. A moldy sky had been holding over the city, neither rain nor sun. With the state of my hunt for Hajj Radwan at a frustrating standstill, a couple of days with the family in Cyprus could only do me good.

There also seemed to be a lot of unsettling stuff happening on the other side of the Green Line. While I was dancing around with Ali, and Chuck with the Christian businessman, we'd found out that Hajj Radwan had started to solicit the services of various Palestinian groups, buying up both their technology and experts. He was after it all too, from infrared triggering devices to command detonators. But what concerned us most was Hajj Radwan's interest in bombs designed to bring down airliners.

Over the last decade, the Palestinians had perfected suitcase bombs to the point they could be smuggled through any airport security regime in the world, even the most up-to-date. It was all the more ominous when Hajj Radwan brought under one roof bomb makers from two different groups. Combining their skills, they were capable of building the perfect airplane bomb.

Having started out his professional life with the Palestinians, it made sense that Hajj Radwan would now turn to them to catch up on technology. Incidentally, we were pretty certain it was the Palestinians who'd first put him on the path of combining shaped charges and sophisticated electronics to accurately clock and destroy an automobile traveling at high speed. So why not airplanes?

It all fit in nicely with Hajj Radwan's evolving tactics, how he kept striving to more narrowly channel violence, how he'd gone from destroying buildings to destroying cars. While buildings are fixed in space, cars come with enough predictability (traveling along fixed roads) that they too are extremely vulnerable. Sitting ducks pretty much.

Always trying to extend his range, Hajj Radwan also started to experiment with "belly charges." He tested them against the Israelis in southern Lebanon, proving that with enough explosives buried under a road, no vehicle, including a heavy tank, is safe. By the way, they're another one of the Secret Service's darkest nightmares.

Another thing that worried me about Hajj Radwan was that he was intent on projecting power across the globe, applying tactics and technology he'd learned in Lebanon. Like a shark, he felt he had to keep moving to stay alive. Clearly, his plan was to be able to hit us from all sides, a redundancy of a sort.

Hajj Radwan kept in play overlapping cells. For instance, when he was tasked with assassinating Saudi diplomats but things were too hot in France, he switched the job to a cell in Bangkok. When in 1992 he was tasked with hitting the Israelis and things were too hot in London, he switched to a cell in Buenos Aires.

But there were certain countries that worried us more than others, particularly West Germany. Overlapping police jurisdictions there, a weak national police, and a large immigrant community offered Hajj Radwan another happy hunting ground. Although he wasn't involved, we saw proof of it in 1992 when a Hezbollah-connected group murdered an Iranian Kurdish dissident in a Berlin café. Or when the Iranians decided to hit in Paris, they used Hajj Radwan's networks in West Germany as a transit route.

But it wasn't until the Pan Am investigation that we found out just how extensive Hajj Radwan's German networks were. They seemed to be everywhere, from Hamburg to Frankfurt, from Berlin to Strasbourg in France. Burrowed deep into local Lebanese communities, they were indistinguishable from law-abiding Lebanese. They operated with the same discipline as his Lebanese organization: no business over the phone, no contact with Hezbollah party offices or mosques, no gunplay, no beards, no attending pep rallies, no meetings in mosques or Islamic centers. They could strike without warning.

In the early part of the Pan Am investigation (before it was switched to Libya), a cell answering to Hajj Radwan was discovered in Dortmund. Its head was connected to a hijacking in Africa. What particularly intrigued the German police was that a young Lebanese passenger on Pan Am 103 had stayed with the cell's Dortmund chief and then later at another Hajj Radwan–connected apartment in Frankfurt. Did the Lebanese passenger have something to do with Pan Am 103, or was it just another coincidence like the ambassador being booked on the plane?

With all the unexplored German connections, with the calls into the Beirut embassy, with Chuck being on the airplane, with Hajj Radwan's pointed interest in bringing down civilian airliners, there'll always exist in my mind the suspicion that Hajj Radwan had something to do with Pan Am 103. Maybe it was as simple as the Libyans going to him for technical assistance. I know the FBI will dismiss this as pointless speculation, but they'll have to do a lot better to convince me a lone Libyan was behind this atrocity.

I was searching the Mediterranean for our two Black Hawks when I caught sight of Chuck coming down the hill toward me with his bearish gait and his wrecking-ball head. He'd forgotten his assault rifle; something was up.

"You gotta hear this," he said, walking up to me with his Mona Lisa shit-eating grin. "I just saw my buddy."

I didn't like the sound of anything that had to do with his shady Christian businessman.

"He can get me Buckley's radio."

When Hajj Radwan's people kidnapped Bill Buckley, they also carried off his briefcase and Motorola radio.

"Bullshit," I said. "Haven't you ever heard of the why-am-I-so-lucky principle?"

"If he says he can get it, he can."

Chuck and I at the same time caught sight of the two Black Hawks approaching the shore. They reminded me of malevolent wasps as they flew low and fast over the water. The guards on top of the shell of the old annex fed ammunition belts into their machine guns.

I'd already made up my mind that Chuck's shady Christian businessman was an inveterate swindler who couldn't be trusted with anything. So what exactly is his angle now? I wondered.

Chuck smiled to let me know he wasn't done: "He gave me the serial number."

Chuck handed me a piece of paper with a string of numbers on it.

I didn't need Chuck to tell me they matched the serial number on Buckley's Motorola, but I asked anyhow.

"You got it," he said.

We were both startled when the two Black Hawks popped out from a ravine and sidled over to the helicopter pad, throwing up dust and small stones. The noise was deafening. They swayed in their own backwash like a fat man trying to mambo, then settled down on the pad. They kept their engines revved in case they had to take off on short notice.

I bent half over and ran over to the loadmaster. I shouted into his helmet: "Scratch me off. Baer. I don't feel well. Baer's the name." I didn't wait for his answer.

I ran back and grabbed my bag and Chuck. He didn't say anything as I walked him behind a squat building to get away from the noise.

"You know what's happening? The fucker's setting us up."

I now was sure of it. First Ali's offer of the KGB Stechkin, then Buckley's radio—two bright, shiny baubles for the two CIA dupes.

"Go see him to say we want the radio," I said. "We'll pay one hundred thousand for it. Ten down now."

No one was going to authorize me to buy back Buckley's radio, and I wasn't going to ask. But I did have ten thousand dollars in the safe, enough to make Hajj Radwan believe we'd taken his bait. I'd figure out later what to do with it.

My palpable fear now was that Hajj Radwan was coming at us from two different directions, Ali and Chuck's businessman. But why should I be surprised? Hajj Radwan had in his possession a large killing machine on both sides of the Green Line. He could target us from anywhere he liked and whenever he liked. He'd built both depth and redundancy into his machine.

I may be guilty of ascribing superhuman abilities to the fucker. But it's a fact that he did things in pairs or multiples. When he hit the French, it wasn't a one-off—first the military attaché, then the intelligence officer, then the gendarmes. He did the same to the Israelis, the first attack in Tyre, in November 1982, and then again there the following year. On October 23, 1983, he hit both the French and the Marines. With Hariri, he closed down the investigation thanks to nearly a dozen quick and dirty assassinations.

Which brings me back to the Israelis and the Red Prince. After the Red Prince's assassination in 1979, the Israelis set about assassinating one senior Palestinian official after the other. Atef was only one among them. They may even have murdered Arafat in 2004. Although a postmortem wasn't conducted right after his death, Swiss forensic scientists did conduct one in 2012. They found traces of polonium-210 in his clothing and personal items, opening up the possibility he'd been assassinated. Arafat's list of enemies was long, but at the top was Israel.

Whether the Israelis murdered Arafat or not, it remains that over the last fifty years Israel carved out the heart of the core Palestinian resistance thanks to one considered assassination after another. Like Hajj Radwan, they knew that a one-off wouldn't take them to where they wanted to go. It's always a spate rather than a drop.

What I'm saying is that it was completely plausible, if not predictable, that Hajj Radwan would line the two of us by running Ali and Chuck's shady businessman into us. What better way to find out what we were up to?

As we walked back to the office, I stopped Chuck so he wouldn't misunderstand what I had to say. "If we don't start moving a lot faster, he's going to get us first." Chuck didn't say anything, leading me to wonder if he believed me.

NEVER EXPECT TO BRING DOWN THE EDIFICE IN ONE GO

Paris, May 14, 1610: It's hard to imagine, but there was a time when Paris's traffic was worse than it is today. Medieval Paris still stood then, its winding alleys cramped, store displays spilling out into the street, and people jostling one another to get by. Your own two feet got you across town faster than a horse, and certainly faster than a carriage.

That morning King Henri IV decided he needed to see his finance minister, the Duc de Sully. But the duke was sick in bed, which meant the king had to drive across Paris to see him. The king took an entourage of only three in a carriage drawn by six very large horses. His route passed through some of the worst parts of town, including Les Halles, where itinerant workers, prostitutes, smugglers, thieves, and cutthroats roamed its narrow streets looking for opportunity and trouble.

On Rue de la Ferronnerie something ahead brought the king's carriage to a stop. A footman jumped down and ran to see what the holdup was. At that moment a tall man with red hair jumped onto the side of the carriage, filling the window. He reached through it with a knife and stabbed the king twice, severing his aorta and puncturing his lung. King Henri was rushed back to the Louvre, where he died.

The assassin, a Catholic fanatic, apparently acted alone. Not surprising, the king's murder didn't improve French Catholicism's fortunes. But what his assassin did get right was to trap Henri in his carriage. A vehicle may be a wonderful convenience, but for the victim it's too often a coffin on wheels.

NOTE TO ASSASSINS: Treat failure as an opportunity, every exit as an entry, and every success as an invitation to the next.

NOTHING WOUNDED MOVES UPHILL

When things become precarious and chaotic for your enemy, there will be unforeseen opportunities.

EVERYBODY WHO'S MARKED FOR DEATH MUST DIE

Kawkaba, Lebanon, February 28, 1999: Was there a hint of what was about to happen? An ominous piece of chatter? An unexplained broken-down car on the side of the road? As with Carrero Blanco's assassination, there was nothing that anyone has ever come forward and admitted to. It was just another shitty day in the little slice of Lebanese hell Israel still held on to, the so-called security strip.

The strip traces its origin to Israel's 1978 invasion of Lebanon. It entered Lebanon to stop cross-border Palestinian attacks, but instead of pulling back, Israel ended up creating a semipermanent buffer zone in southern Lebanon. The assumption was that the north of Israel would be vulnerable to attacks without it.

The strip may have looked good on paper, but it soon turned into a death trap of its own. Sparsely populated and broken up with bald, jagged limestone hills, southern Lebanon normally shouldn't have been particularly good guerrilla country. But the Muslim guerrillas who started to infest it in the eighties proved to be inventive and resilient. They stayed off cell phones and radios, never carried weapons in the open, and operated out of caves.

What the Israelis had going for them was technology—new sophisticated ground sensors, *Star Wars*–like fortresses, and drones. The guerrillas couldn't move in groups without being immediately detected and destroyed. But the lynchpin in Israel's strategy was to turn the strip into a "killing box"—shooting at anything that moved. The guerrillas would be pretty much left out in the open after everyone with any sense was driven out. Or at least that was the theory.

On the morning of February 28, 1999, the Israeli commander of the strip, General Erez Gerstein, and a reporter from Israel Radio climbed into an armored Mercedes for a quick trip into the strip. The stated purpose was to attend the funeral of a local Lebanese militia commander who'd died fighting for Israel, but Gerstein's ulterior motive was to show the reporter that a drive up into the strip was as safe as a drive around Tel Aviv on the Sabbath—i.e., to prove that all the money and blood Israel had put into the strip was worth it. The journalist could put it on the radio when he got back.

Although Gerstein's Mercedes was armored and souped up, on the outside it was old and beat-up—indistinguishable from the old beat-up Mercedes the Lebanese drive. It bore Lebanese plates and tinted windows, making it impossible to tell that the occupants were Israeli military. The trip wasn't advertised. Couple that with the fact that Gerstein and the reporter would be in and out of Lebanon in less than two hours, and no one, no matter how good, would have the time to put together an ambush. A proper assassination, as Gerstein well knew, depends on good preparation. But so does avoiding one.

Chiseled and fit, and with a well-deserved reputation for bravery and toughness, Gerstein was a soldier's soldier. One story has it that when he commanded the elite Golani Brigade he'd demonstrate the mushroom-like kill zone of a hand grenade by lying down next to one and pulling the pin. He would jump up out of the smoke and dust, untouched and with an I-told-you-so grin.

Gerstein had campaigned (and been wounded) in Lebanon for more years than he cared to remember, and he knew the country as well as his own. When he was offered command of the strip, he had no illusions about what he was up against. The equally tough problem, though, was to convince his fellow generals that holding on to the strip was worth it. He'd have to do the same with a skeptical Israeli public and press. Thus the decision to take a journalist to the funeral.

As soon as Gerstein and the journalist's convoy crossed the border into Lebanon, it hit speeds of up to eighty miles an hour. Anyone standing by the road saw only a screaming blur of metal heading for who knows where. Even if a guerrilla partisan alerted the command up the line, what could they do about it?

The funeral went fine. The handshaking and hugs over, Gerstein and the reporter jumped back in his Mercedes for the return ride home. Just as on the trip up, the road was clear of traffic, letting the four Mercedes move at breakneck speed.

As Gerstein's convoy breasted an incline in the road, a terrific blinding explosion spewed rock and dirt in all directions. But the main force of it hit Gerstein's Mercedes dead center, lifting it off the road and down into a ravine. At the bottom, it burst into a ball of flames, instantly killing Gerstein, the journalist, and two soldiers. The rest of the convoy made it through.

The reaction in Israel to the news of Gerstein's assassination was instantaneous. One anonymous Israeli soldier wrote to a newspaper: "Reality has thrown us a slap in the face."

It was the same pretty much across Israel: Don't waste another drop of Israeli blood trying to hold even a square inch of that cursed country. The politicians also got the message. Ehud Barak, at the time the head of the opposition Labor Party and himself a former general, announced that if elected he would pull the Israeli army out of Lebanon.

Three months later, Barak was elected prime minister, and a little more than a year later ordered Israel's troops out of the strip, abandoning it to the Islamic guerrillas. It was the bitter end of a twenty-two-year struggle to tame Lebanon.

As for Israeli intelligence, it settled down to figuring out how Hajj Radwan—could it have been anyone else?—had pulled it off. The shaped charge had his signature all over it. As did the clear-cut motives: Gerstein's murder tipped the scales, breaking the gossamer thread holding together the frayed Israeli consensus to stay in Lebanon. But without Hezbollah offering any details other than claiming the assassination, Hajj Radwan's precise role is stuck in the realm of speculation.

HIT A SITTING DUCK WHILE IT'S STILL SITTING, AND EVEN BETTER WHEN IT'S SITTING AND WINGED

One Thanksgiving, Mother showed up in Washington, insisting on seeing our provincial aristocracy in its natural habitat. The Four Seasons wasn't yet built, so I offered her the staid downtown Madison for lunch. Only a couple of blocks from the White House, it was opened by John F. Kennedy in 1963. My wife, nine months pregnant with our first child, tagged along. It was 1984.

We arrived early; only one other table was occupied. Knowing that our fellow diners would immediately spot us as interlopers, I asked the maître d' to put us at an out-of-the-way table in the back. What's the point in unnecessarily ruffling feathers? And indeed, it wasn't long before Nixon's former counsel John Ehrlichman showed up with two other people. (For his part in Watergate, Ehrlichman went to prison for conspiracy, obstruction of justice, and perjury.)

The maître d' sat Ehrlichman and his guests at a table in the center of the dining room, the best perch to see and be seen. Do people never learn?

Throughout lunch, Mother impaled Ehrlichman with a stare. I had a premonition she wasn't going to let the moment pass, and when the bill had been paid, I mumbled something about needing to go to the bathroom. I scurried across the dining room at a good clip, catching out of the corner of my eye Ben Bradlee, the legendary executive editor of *The Washington Post*. More than anyone he was the man who brought down Nixon, along with Ehrlichman.

Against all my innate cowardly instincts, I stopped just outside the entry to watch as Mother made a beeline for Ehrlichman's table, my waddling wife in tow. Sensing trouble, Ehrlichman looked up at her and then at my pregnant wife. Did this improbable pair disarm him even for a moment?

Mother fumbled for something in her purse, finally fishing out her checkbook. She thrust it toward Ehrlichman, along with a pen.

"Sir," she said in a voice that carried across the Madison's dining room and sounded like a crystal bell dripping with ironic sarcasm. "You are a great American hero. What a great service you've done for our country! My grandbaby would be so proud to have your autograph." She patted my wife's belly.

Not knowing what else to do, Ehrlichman signed the back of her checkbook. His guests were searching the ground for a hole to crawl into. Bradlee put his napkin up to his mouth to hide his giggling.

OF PEELING THE VENEER OFF THE LIE
AND OTHER UNYIELDING DEEDS

A successful assassination depends on terrain and surprise. But its chances are improved when the victim feels safe and at ease. It's a basic truth that when people are absorbed with their comforts and habits they're inattentive and predictable, unintentionally offering inroads into their lives. What Mother had going for her was the Madison's ritually observed etiquette: Don't bother the other guests. I imagine the last thing Ehrlichman was expecting was another diner pouncing on him.

Mother's other advantage was that with Ehrlichman's indictment he was a winged bird. If she'd gone after Bradlee about some dumb *Washington Post* article, she would have been a lot less successful. The point is that when a target is on the run, making one stupid mistake after another, he's easier to take down. Gaddafi running out of a culvert into the hands of a mob comes to mind.

It's common sense that when the enemy's weak, disoriented, his consensus frayed, and he's indecisive about fighting or fleeing, there stands a much better chance that political murder will work. Wehrmacht officers turned on Hitler after it was clear that he'd lost the war. Saddam's clan turned on him after he'd lost the war. The Russian aristocracy gave up on royalty after the murder of Czar Nicholas II in 1918.

Only months after the 1982 Israeli invasion, Hajj Radwan set about methodically unstitching the Israeli consensus for staying in Lebanon, launching one devastating attack after the next. His way of measuring progress was to draw on a Hezbollah unit responsible for monitoring the Israeli press. It was devoted to looking for rents in the Israeli body politic. I don't know whether Hajj Radwan had predicted Israel would pull out of Lebanon after Gerstein, but I suspect he had a good idea it would. Israeli tolerance for wars in Lebanon isn't without limits.

Neither Chuck nor I was so deluded as to believe we were in Hajj Radwan's league. While he moved from success to success, we were still futzing around with radioactive dross like Ali and the Christian businessman. But it didn't stop us from blindly soldiering on. Or, as they say, when you roll into hell, keep going; there is no reverse.

It wasn't all stubborn bravado, though. I'd recently recruited a young man who could get within spitting distance of Hajj Radwan. For obvious reasons, I can't name or describe him other than to say he was my first real breakthrough. While he couldn't tell me in advance where Hajj Radwan would be, I was confident I could come up with a use for him.

As for Ali, nothing came of my red herring that I'd put in Hajj Radwan's path. Did it fool him, put him on the wrong scent? I don't know. My best guess, though, is that I was only burning up more CIA money . . . while all along Hajj Radwan was tightening the noose around our necks.

A new obstacle Chuck and I ran into was a new chief, an ex-Marine. He reminded me of a squat volcano that from time to time would erupt for no good reason at all. Worse, he was a smart son of a bitch, meaning it was only a matter of time before he caught on to our chasing after a ghost.

Then, as these things so often go, opportunity landed on our laps with a loud thud. It was about four a.m. when what sounded like a lunatic throwing himself at the glass doors of my balcony woke me up. I was about to jump out of bed to see, but then there was a series of bright flashes in my window followed by a dozen booms. Doing exactly what they tell you not to do, I got up on my knees to look out the window. The hill below me was on fire. It looked like we'd just been hit by a barrage from a Stalin organ—a 132mm Katyusha multiple rocket launcher. They're not accurate, but they do get one's attention.

I thought about the "Welcome to Beirut" kit I'd found in my apartment when I first moved in. Among other helpful hints for coping with their fair city, it recommended crawling to the center of your apartment during a shelling. I thought about doing it, but it was now dead quiet. With the shelling apparently over, I went back to bed.

As I found out later, the people at the other end of the Stalin organ belonged to a Shiite militia that had just made the mistake of going to war with Hezbollah. In some contorted, make-your-hair-hurt Oriental machination, they thought that if they could start a war with the Christians they'd somehow divert Hezbollah's attention. It was as if the United States had decided to bomb Mexico to keep the Japanese from attacking Pearl Harbor. And indeed, it made not the slightest difference; the fighting only picked up and spread.

To make a long story short, Hajj Radwan was sucked into it, taking over a unit fighting south of Beirut. But much more important for our plans, Hezbollah enlisted him to secretly procure emergency supplies of weapons and ammunition from an old contact, a Christian warlord. (Although it was all very hush-hush, the Christians were more than happy to help the Muslims kill one another.)

As we started to pick up details about these transfers from chatter, it occurred to me that Hajj Radwan had just been offered up to me on a silver platter. Who would have ever thought a Christian warlord would be his soft underbelly? I felt like the Israelis must have when they found out about the Red Prince's visit to his mother or the IRA when they found out about Thatcher's Brighton speech.

For a while, I considered approaching the Christian warlord to ask him to do the job, but then I thought better of it. A wise man knows better than to come between a beast and his red meat, namely all the money the Christian warlord stood to make from Hajj Radwan. No, I'd have to do the hard work myself.

It took about a month, but I finally caught one of Hajj Radwan's people in a walkie-talkie discussion of a specific arms transfer that would be staged from a particular house on the Muslim side of the Green Line. I knew the house.

So here's what I needed to do: Nail down the specific time of a transfer, persuade my new source to rig the building with explosives and, most important, make sure Hajj Radwan was there in the house for the transfer. If I could pinpoint the room he'd be in, a small shaped charge through the wall would do the job. As for finding explosives and a house opposite Hajj Radwan's transfer house, it was a lead-pipe cinch.

Here I need to remind the reader that I've been obliged to fudge some of the names and details of this story, as well as fall back on secondary narratives—and omit the central plot against Hajj Radwan. But, again, let's not forget this is a personal journey through political violence rather than history. What's absolutely true, though, is that Chuck took an instant dislike to the house I picked to stage Hajj Radwan's murder. Except for a couple of skeletal dead trees out front, there was an unobstructed field of fire from the other side of the Green Line—nothing to stop a sniper from sending a bullet through our house's front windows. When I told him we didn't have time to find a better place, he shrugged his shoulders. "I suppose we could sandbag the shit out of it."

Frankly, I was worried about Chuck these days. He was itching to get something going. But the Lebanese were driving him crazy. They have this annoying habit of racing up behind a car and flashing their lights to let the other driver know he had better speed up or get out of the way. I'm not sure what he hoped to accomplish, but Chuck asked our tech to help him bore a small hole in his trunk from where he could shoot out the front lights of the bastards flashing him. (He planned to use a pellet gun.) The tech—an easygoing Texan with the radio call sign Garfield— talked Chuck out of it.

The rest of the house was equally unappealing—a decade of ruin and filth. There was a coppery smell of urine in the back bedrooms. The mattresses were gone from their frames, and trash was piled everywhere. There were bookshelves on one wall but no books, only a couple of faded magazines covered in an inch of dust and plaster.

There was a good view of the southern suburbs from the roof, including the house where Hajj Radwan staged the transfers. There was no sign of life now, but since the transfers went on at night, I wasn't surprised.

Directly behind the house loomed the Ministry of Defense. My hope was that this would dissuade the local Christian warlord—Hajj Radwan's arms dealer—from deciding to police us up. It also helped that with most of the houses reduced to piles of rubble there weren't many neighbors. In fact, no one in their right mind hung on here.

There was a knock at the door—two gray old ladies leopard-spotted with age and all in black. By the looks of them, I guessed they were the owners, who, I imagined, wanted to see the idiot foreigners their nephew had swindled into renting their place.

We all sat down as if we were at pink tea at the Dorchester. Courtesies over, they asked if we would agree to pay the entire year's rent in advance. Since it was only twenty dollars a month, I said fine. I pulled out of my wallet two crisp one-hundred-dollar bills. I got Chuck to give me two twenties.

The one with the densest liver spots coughed in her sleeve and then asked where we might be from. I said we were Hungarian engineers. I kept my fingers crossed she wouldn't now ask for a lease after all. The only Hungarian word I knew was *"Magyar."*

The two women looked at each and spoke rapidly in Arabic. I caught one saying it was a good sign Hungarians were moving in. Was it a harbinger that the civil war was finally coming to a close?

FROM FLASH TO BANG

In Beirut in those days, putting your hands on things such as explosives, detonators, and radio-controlled firing devices was as easy as buying a bottle of Johnnie Walker Red. And I mean everything from tanks to heavy artillery. It was only a question of money and knowing the right person.

It took one of my arms dealers less than twenty-four hours to find me two out-of-the-box American-made LAWs. A LAW is a single-use disposable rocket and rocket launcher. We made the transfer in the parking lot of a posh restaurant, no one paying us the least attention. It was fifty dollars a LAW.

Another arms dealer was a young American Armenian who knew his way around more exotic instruments of murder. I'd first gotten in touch with him to see if he could build a replica of a Samsonite airplane bomb.

He was supposedly very good at it. My objective was to show Langley how easily and expertly these things could be constructed.

The Armenian's workshop was deep in an Armenian neighborhood called Bourj Hammoud. As it was in Hajj Radwan's neighborhood, the unbidden didn't dare set foot in it. According to one story, a local Christian militia sent a team in to arrest someone, but before making it ten feet in, they were all mowed down in a blaze of gunfire. I'll call my Armenian arms dealer Joe.

The day my replica airplane bomb was ready for pickup, Joe met me on the road that skirts Bourj Hammoud. We drove about a hundred feet down a street so narrow that I was sure the side mirrors would snap off. We pulled up in front of what looked like a junk shop.

It was pitch-black inside. Something with a pair of menacing red eyes was curled up in a blanket on a sofa. It reminded me of an alert reticulated python.

I sat down at a workbench. Joe went in the back and brought out a new, ash-gray Samsonite suitcase.

"Open it," he said. "You can't even smell the glue."

Joe turned on a Coleman camping lantern and hung it over the suitcase.

The work looked good to me. There was no sign the interior lining had been replaced by mock plasticized and rolled penthrite explosives—PETN. I picked it up; the weight felt right too.

Joe: "Let 'em X-ray it. They won't see a damn thing. Fuck, Samsonite couldn't tell the difference."

From upstairs came the crying of a child, which gave me an opening for a new piece of business. I pulled out a picture of a baby's bassinet: "Could you work with one of these, turn it into a bomb?"

"Of course."

"With PETN? I need it to cut through a wall. A shaped charge."

Joe smiled: "Does the pope shit in the woods?"

"And hook it up to an infrared trigger, at about a mile distance?"

"You got it."

Joe fished around in a drawer until he found a double-sided circuit board with filaments of wire and diodes attached to it. "It's a light-sensitive trigger switch," he said, handing it to me to look at.

"More faithful than Old Faithful. When 8,192 counts have been received, the generator is turned off, the light-sensor circuit is enabled, then the relay driver is enabled. Got it?"

I vaguely knew that he was talking about a wiring scheme that would make this thing foolproof, but other than that, I just had to trust him.

"You see what's cool about this is that the device has no memory effect." He looked at me and no doubt saw I didn't have a clue what he was talking about.

"Let me try again. Any exposure to light during the safe/arm delay time will have no effect. It's only the illumination right after the safe/arm delay that triggers this baby."

He was starting to warm up to the subject. "You'll love this feature. A red-light-emitting diode monitors the state of the output. If the output is energized, the LED glows."

I asked him where he'd gone to school. "Brigham Young," he said.

By the time I walked out of Joe's cabinet of wonders, I'd put in an order for a device that closed the detonating circuit after 8,192 counts, an infrared relay, and a PETN-rigged bassinet (multiprimed).

As I started to accumulate my arsenal, the problem was to make sure it worked. Fortunately, we had our very talented tech Garfield, the good old boy from Texas who had talked Chuck out of shooting out the lights of cars pissing him off.

Garfield could turn anything into a bomb, even a jar of Maxim instant coffee. (Maxim is a wonderful oxidizer.) He also could make old crappy Soviet weaponry work. Once, in order to check out a batch of Soviet surface-to-air missiles, he fooled the missiles by hanging a lighted cigar from a string and swinging it back and forth. The missiles' "gimlet" followed the cigar like a hound dog on a wild pig's scent. Garfield also was a genius with video. A couple of months before, he'd rigged up a camera on a warehouse associated with Hajj Radwan, allowing us to record the comings and goings.

Garfield put all of the weapons in good working order. But there was a problem with Joe's infrared device. While the IR link worked fine, the reception at our end was bad.

Garfield listened for a minute. "Bud, your UPS is giving you AC but chopping off the signal."

UPS stands for "uninterrupted power supply," and AC is "alternating current." It took Garfield about a day to fix it.

By the way, the deeper I got into the mechanics of murder, the easier it seemed it would be to cross the tropic of murder. I'd already absorbed the zeitgeist of this place, along with the Lebanese way of looking at the instrumentalities of political violence. I'd lost all perspective on the rights and wrongs of it, other than thinking I was on the right side. The kill-or-be-killed thing wasn't some abstract notion I'd read about in a book; it was all around me. So rather than sit around parsing the morality of the act, I was single-mindedly focused on making it work.

In training, they'd taught us how it's possible to cut through the strap muscle and sever a man's carotid artery with a razor-sharpened karambit (an Indonesian claw-shaped knife) wielded with sufficient force. The instructor said it was a matter of concentrating on a man's anatomy and nothing else. It's the way I now started to frame things in my mind.

LITTLE WARNINGS THAT FALL ON DULL, COLD EARS

Hajj Radwan apparently wasn't distracted enough by the intra-Shiite fighting to entirely forget about us. We'd picked up bits and pieces of intelligence that he was planning an attempt on the ambassador—the same ambassador who'd told us to get serious about bringing Hajj Radwan to justice. The ambassador's security detail was beefed up, and the hunt for Hajj Radwan's mole inside the embassy was intensified. State Department investigators had narrowed it down to a single man, but they were struggling to come up with enough evidence to do something about him.

One morning the ambassador was on his way back to the embassy from an appointment when two cars straddling the road blocked his convoy. When the gunmen leaned over the hoods of their cars and pointed their automatic rifles at the convoy, the Delta Force gunner behind the .50-caliber machine gun in the turret of the lead Suburban opened fire. The gunmen fled, but then gunmen from across a field bordering the road opened fire on the convoy. The .50-caliber returned fire, and the convoy made good its escape.

If it was an attempt on the ambassador, it was a clumsy one. And no one thought Hajj Radwan was behind it. He was better than that. Anyhow, he would never have risked a classic ambush in the Christian enclave. But it didn't lessen our fear that Hajj Radwan had something up his sleeve. I needed to speed things up.

A dirty, complicit moon hung over the cluster of shabby apartments. Colette, the girl who hosted my birthday party, was sitting on her balcony, wrapped in a blanket. She waved to me to come up. The telephone was on the table in front of her. She was looking at it as if it were dead. I apologized for not calling.

The day before, we'd eaten lunch at a restaurant in a little mountain town called Brummana. Untouched by the fighting, it was picture-postcard beautiful. We took a table out on the polished limestone terrace, a Prussian-blue-and-white-striped umbrella shading us from the midday heat. I ordered water pipes and arak.

We watched in silence as the waiter went through the ritual of preparing two glasses for us: the arak was always poured first, then the water, then the ice. Colette said she wanted my help in getting out of Lebanon. Anything had to be better than here—the hate, the war, and now the Christian warlords were getting ready for their own little in-house fight.

Colette's family was from the south, Hezbollah country, which meant they weren't going home anytime soon. They'd be permanent refugees in their own country for who knows how long. But my mind was else-where. It sounds like the flattest of clichés, but hunting another man concentrates your senses, makes you feel—I don't know—more vital. Never mind that I had nagging doubts about whether I could go through with it.

We were the last to leave. When I dropped her off that afternoon, I told her I'd pass by the next night after dinner with some sort of plan to help her get out. And now I was back, sans plan.

Colette pulled the blanket up around her neck, then laughed as if she were scaring away some unwanted thought. Abruptly, she unwrapped herself from the blanket, went inside, and came back with a bottle of wine and two glasses. She poured me a glass but left hers empty. I drank mine and filled it back up. I was drinking a lot these days. For the sugar boost, I told myself.

I didn't have the nerve to tell her I was leaving in less than a month. My replacement had already come and gone on a quick familiarization trip.

Colette again brought up the coming fight between the Christians: "It's coming, right?"

I nodded. Who hadn't predicted it?

There was a streak of lightning over the port. We'd been promised rain, and now I believed it.

I hated the ugly clarity of my thoughts. But in the Lebanon I'd gotten used to, there's a transactional side to every relationship, use and be used. Colette wanted to leverage our friendship into a ticket out; I'd used her to meet Ali. It was the same thing as my trying to use the Colonel to murder Hajj Radwan in return for my help in settling him in the United States.

I stood up and said I had to leave. We'd get back together tomorrow, I said.

As soon as I pulled away from Colette's apartment, the rain started. A hundred feet farther down the hill, I noticed a pair of headlights behind me. Strange, I thought, someone else out on the road at this time of the morning. Then again, there are a lot of Lebanese who live by night. I decided not to worry about it.

The rain started to really come down, sheets of water rolling across the road. I slowed down, and so did the car behind me, holding back maybe two hundred feet.

Rather than the direct route home, I took the Beit Mery road. Beit Mery was sound asleep, not a light on anywhere. When I came around a bend at the edge of town with a particularly good view of Muslim Beirut, I slowed down long enough to see an exchange of tracer rounds from the southern suburbs. *Keep it up, you bastards,* I thought. *At least another week.* The car behind me slowed down too.

Somewhere between Beit Mery and Monteverdi, the car dropped off, leaving me to wonder why I wasn't more tired. I'd been up at five this morning for tennis, lunch at Kaslik, dinner, a nightcap, and now Colette's. I had apparently caught whatever manic pestilence afflicted the Lebanese. Was it the reason I'd decided to settle things with Hajj Radwan with a shaped charge?

I wasn't more than half a mile below Monteverdi when I noticed the same pair of lights behind me. It has to be my imagination, I thought. Or maybe it's another car. In my two years here, I'd never once caught surveillance. So why now? It didn't matter; I'd outrun him and think about it later.

I was doing more than forty when my BMW lost its footing on a switchback, sliding sideways on the wet pavement. When it slowed enough, I yanked it out of the oncoming lane. I checked my rearview mirror. The car was there, stopped above me.

At the flats now it was a straight run from Mkalles to Jdeideh, nothing but pavement dimpled with rain. In an instant, the BMW got up to a full gallop. The engine was at a high-pitched whine. I didn't look, but knew I was doing more than a hundred. The way the water gunneled on either side, I felt as if I were in a speedboat. No way anyone could keep up with me now.

And then out of nowhere a pair of car lights shot diagonally across the road about a quarter mile ahead. I was going too fast to tell if the car was even moving. But then it definitely started across the road, oblivious to the two tons of metal hurtling down on it. It was way too late, but I slammed on the brakes.

Instead of skidding as I thought it would, the BMW spun in circles, a dizzying waltz, faster and faster. It felt as if I were on a fixed axis, but the view kept changing as I headed for the other car. The thing I noticed was the silence. Had I stopped hearing myself living?

I wondered why it was taking so long to hit the fucker. For some inane reason, I tried to remember how old I was, but I couldn't. It occurred to me that it didn't matter, not now or on the other side of life. It was some idiot fatalism, or maybe it's just that I'd had too much to drink. I closed my eyes.

I only opened them again when I realized the BMW wasn't moving. It was in the middle of the road, staring into a darkened clothing store. A pair of surprised mannequins in the window looked back at me. The hood of the BMW was steaming in the rain, the engine stalled. I noticed my heart wasn't racing. Fuck, these damned people really have infected me with all their bullshit about how death finds you when it's good and ready. Life beyond consequence, I guess. If I didn't get out of this country fast, I'd be a paid-up member of their idiotic death cult.

I got out of my car to see what happened to the poor bastard I'd almost taken into the black abyss with me. But the car was gone. Then I noticed it fifty feet down the cross street. Its lights were off, but it was in the middle of the road. The driver's door was open. I walked down to take a look.

It was an old Peugeot—dented, cracked windshield, tattered upholstery. A stack of flat bread wrapped in plastic was on the backseat. There was the smell of fresh cigarette smoke. Was he parked along the side of the road, smoking while he waited for me to come along? It was one more wasted thought, one I decided to kill in the cradle.

I also decided that there'd be no point in searching for the registration. Car registrations don't mean anything in this country. The real owner's never on it, or just as often, the car's stolen. It didn't matter; I'd take it as an omen. Get the fuck out of this place.

NOTE TO ASSASSINS: The frightened bird strives for light. Figure out what looks like light to him and wait for him there.

GET TO IT QUICKLY

Don't wait until the enemy is too deeply ensconced in power or too inured to violence before acting. He'll easily shrug off the act and then come after you with a meat cleaver.

WHEN YOU DON'T KNOW WHO THE MARK IS, IT'S YOU. EVEN WHEN YOU THINK YOU KNOW WHO THE MARK IS, IT'S STILL YOU

The morning started out above suspicion, a few sleek clouds scooting across an opulent sky. There was only the faintest of breezes. It was Sunday, and standing out on my balcony, I could see there was already traffic heading for the beaches. A couple of sailboats were out. More rain was promised, but you could've fooled me.

I went out on the balcony to listen to the Green Line. There were a couple of muted booms. *Good,* I thought, *the Shiites are still at one another's throats.* Which meant that Hajj Radwan was even shorter on ammunition and would be back knocking on the Christian's door, asking for more. But it wouldn't last forever.

There was no doubt in anyone's mind that Hezbollah would prevail in the end—if for no other reason than that they had belief on their side and a lot of practice at war. When that day came, my little causeway into Hajj Radwan's world would shut down. Like all soft underbellies, this one wouldn't be around forever.

Missing the worst traffic, I got to Byblos early for lunch and wandered around streets unchanged since Phoenician times. After twenty minutes, I went to the restaurant to wait. I sipped a glass of wine as I watched a sailboat tack into port. A young girl was at the helm, mom and dad taking down the sails.

The Christian politician who joined me for lunch wanted to talk only about the upcoming elections and how the army commander intended to steal them by force. The Christian militias wouldn't stand for it, he said. The fighting would be bad. He offered names, the usual suspects of Christian bigotry. Every once in a while, he'd say that the United States needed to do something to stop it. He kept coming back to our "great betrayal" of the Christians and how we shouldn't have sent the Marines if we hadn't intended to finish the job.

When I brought up the Shiite civil war, he looked at me blankly. It could have been occurring on the other side of the world as far as he was concerned. If I'd suggested that there was such a person as Hajj Radwan who one day would be calling the shots in the Christian enclave, he wouldn't have believed me.

I got away about two, the return beach traffic still light. Before I got to Halat, there was a boom. It had to be close for me to hear it over the radio. Oddly, though, I couldn't see any smoke. Maybe it was a nearby quarry I didn't know about. But why would they be working on Sunday?

The road took a tight turn around a finger of rock that jutted out into the sea. Just as I came around it, there was a thundering explosion a few hundred feet in front of me, rock spewing out into the road. I thought that it had to have been a large-caliber artillery round. A bank of gray smoke and dust drifted up the side of the cliff.

There was an old Mercedes on the other side of the road, its nose into the rock, the windows spidered by shrapnel. The driver's door opened. A man got out. He was holding his head, blood running down his face. He moved quickly and opened the back door. I slowed down, looking for a place to pull over. I watched him as he pulled a small girl from the backseat, cradling her in his arms. Her left leg from right below the hip was shredded, gushing blood.

There was static from my Motorola, then someone keying it. "Maverick, Maverick."

Maverick was my radio call sign. I picked up the radio and yelled into it. "What!"

"Sorry to disturb you whatever you're in between." It was Chuck.

"Fuck off."

There was nothing I could do for the girl bleeding to death not twenty feet away, but I put down the radio and started to get out of the car.

The radio was insistent now. "Maverick, don't forget we got a meet at seventeen hundred."

It was our private code that there was movement at Hajj Radwan's transfer house—and that we should meet up at ours.

There were people piling out of cars now. A man had the little girl on the ground on a coat. He was tying a tourniquet around her leg. It wasn't going to work; she would die. I wasn't going to watch.

I expected that traffic would be backed up along the coast road, but it wasn't. It was as if there'd been no shelling at all. I wondered about the Lebanese's capacity to shrug off violence, whether they were just numbed by it or if it was a case of sheer defiance.

I had no idea what the shelling had been about. But what I did know was that Muslim Beirut wasn't in range; it had to have been from a Christian position. Was this the start of it, the Christian civil war? Fuck these people and their shitty little blood feuds.

Instead of the direct route to our house, I continued along the coast road toward the port. Before I got there, I cut east through Sin el Fil. I stopped and turned the engine off to listen to the Green Line. There was some gunfire, the usual stuff for this time of day.

I stopped at a fork below the Ministry of Defense. It had a good view of the southern suburbs. No sign of fighting. I got out with a pair of binoculars. Our house looked as abandoned and forlorn as ever. I couldn't see Chuck's car, and there was no sign of movement at Hajj Radwan's transfer house. What was Chuck talking about?

I eased down the hill, still listening for any uptick of fighting. I called Chuck on the Motorola, but I was now out of repeater range. It was probably just as well; no doubt the chief had his radio on and was listening to us.

I walked around the house, checking to see if anything was out of place. I looked into the window and saw the Coke can on the coffee table that I'd left there on my last visit.

I opened the old padlock to the front door. It had taken Garfield two weeks to find an old rusted combination lock that still worked. I checked the untamperable plastic-encased counter above the door. Its purpose was to number each opening and closing of the door. It was at thirty-eight. The last time I'd been here, I closed the door at thirty-four. Had Chuck let himself in since we were last here? I'd have to wait until he showed up to ask.

I tried Chuck on the radio again, but there still wasn't a ping off the repeater. I went into the kitchen and pulled the dead refrigerator from the wall. I pulled off the back panel. The IR receiver was there. But there was no way to tell whether anyone had gotten to it.

A rocket's scream. The impact was maybe half a mile away, in the middle of the no-man's-land between the house and the southern suburbs. Where had it come from? I pushed the refrigerator back against the wall. There was a distant pop of a mortar launch and then another.

Death was now diving around the house, at least a half-dozen explosions. I crawled to the back bedroom, the one that smelled like piss. Too bad there was nothing to pull over me. I squatted in the corner. There were several more impacts and then silence. It was time to leave.

Thank God the car started right away. I peeled away and headed up the hill, the car fishtailing with every rock and hole I hit. At an intersection I slowed down to get a look behind me. The Green Line was dead quiet. Had it been some dumb bastard on the other side unburdening himself of old mortar shells?

Then a new mortar round landed somewhere above me. I floored the car. By the time I got to the main road, two more fell in quick succession. They'd fallen so close together that I knew they'd been fired from separate tubes.

I didn't slow down at the intersection with the main road and only saw the van when it darkened the right side of my car. I don't remember the crash or anything else that happened in the next few minutes.

I looked up to see a craggy old woman in black looking down at me. I thought for a moment she was one of my landladies come to ask what I'd done to her house. The woman said something I couldn't hear.

I was curious how the world had gone liquid and blurry, and then noticed the van was implanted in the side of my car, water from its radiator splashed into and across the wreck of my new car. I wondered what had happened to its driver.

I felt around on the passenger floor for my Motorola. It wasn't there. Someone had reached in and grabbed it, I thought. Why hadn't they also taken my Kalashnikov and my 9mm Browning, which were still on the floor? There were more people now gathered around the car. Someone opened the door for me and reached in to pull me out. As I started to get out, I felt something under my foot: my Motorola. I picked it up and keyed it. "This is Maverick. Anyone near the MOD? I need a ride."

Garfield came up: "What's the problem, Maverick? Forget where you parked your car?"

That night Chuck didn't help clear things up when he told me that he'd seen where the mortars were fired from. It wasn't from the southern suburbs, but from our side, a Christian position. And it wasn't far from where he and the tech had been arrested six months before.

I felt as if ice water were coursing through me. Had Hajj Radwan's arms supplier found out about us and mortared our house as an invitation for us to kindly get the fuck out of his business? Or maybe Hajj Radwan himself was somehow behind it, letting us know he knew all about our plans. For all I knew, my two landladies worked for Hajj Radwan and told him about us. Not a shred of evidence for it, of course. I was worse off than Chuck with his Claymore mines and pellet gun.

I also never did find out who shelled the Byblos road. Maybe it had something to do with the upcoming presidential elections, not that that made any sense either. While I'm at it, I still don't understand exactly why the Colonel wouldn't help his natural ally, the United States, go after our common enemy, Hajj Radwan. The truth is that I wasn't anywhere near understanding this country.

But what I was certain of was that it was time to get out. Our house was compromised. If the Christian warlord hadn't noticed us before, he did now. I told Chuck he should leave too, but he told me he wasn't ready to get out of the game. Who knows, maybe he thought my replacement would know what he was doing.

Society attacks early when the individual is helpless.

—B. F. SKINNER

To this day, I have no idea whether Hajj Radwan even knew who I was, let alone plotted my murder. I recently had a chance to ask Garfield about it. "Don't know, bud," he said. "What I do know is that a couple of mortars were enough to make you turn tail and run away like a three-legged jackrabbit."

I also don't know whether Law #2—Make It Count—applied by the time I got around to planning Hajj Radwan's murder. Would it have made a difference by 1988? Would it have prevented Pan Am 103 and Chuck's murder? I doubt it. By then, someone else would have instantly filled Hajj Radwan's shoes.

What did I really know about Hajj Radwan? He supposedly had bottle green eyes, a color you don't easily forget. But without a good picture, it wasn't something I could ever pin down. It was the same thing later when I couldn't determine whether his new wife was Lebanese or Syrian. Who cares? No one. But the point is that if you can't tell whether a man has hazel or blue eyes, how can you even begin to get at the harder question about determining the value of his blood?

Like the Pashtun tribal belt, Lebanon is a horrendously byzantine place, and I mean byzantine in the sense that the country is incomprehensible to outsiders. Its hidden mechanisms of power, secret alliances, and opaque interests are forever out of our reach. My three-by-five cards might get me in the door, but they're not even close to a road map for political murder.

In other words, the chance of our following Law #21—Get to It Quickly—wasn't in the cards. By the time we figured out who he was, it was three years too late. He'd already driven us out of Lebanon, created a guerrilla force capable of beating any conventional force, and terrified the Lebanese to the point no one in his right mind dared defy him.

If there's anything I learned over the years about political murder, it's that you have to know your enemies as well as you know your own country. It's the only possible way to meet and destroy a rising threat. The French should have done something about Ho Chi Minh when he was a sous chef at the Ritz in Paris. The Saudis should have taken care of Osama bin Laden in the mid-nineties, long before he gave substance to smoke.

When you decide to swim in the deep end of Vietnam, Saudi Arabia, or any other foreign land, you'd better know exactly what's in the water swimming with you. Both the British Raj and the United States failed in

Pakistan's tribal belt because they didn't have a clue about the enemy they were fighting.

It's no consolation, but the American government isn't alone in being out of touch. On December 3, 2013, a senior member of Hezbollah was shot dead just after midnight near his home in the southern suburbs, not very far from Hajj Radwan's transfer house on the Green Line. A professional job, he was hit at close range and the assassin or assassins got cleanly away.

The New York Times described the victim as a "major player," and the BBC called him a Hezbollah "commander." What neither apparently knew was that he was the right-hand man of Hajj Radwan, approximately number three in the Islamic Jihad Organization. He'd been instrumental in the attacks on the Marines and the two attempts on the American ambassadors. If indeed Hajj Radwan was involved in Pan Am 103, I suspect that this man also played a role.

Two weeks later, a pro-Hariri former finance minister was blown up by a car bomb as he traveled through Beirut. When someone asked me "why him" and "why now," I could only offer that the man was an active backer of the tribunal. So maybe it was a matter of more cleaning up— Law #16. Or he might have been selected to pay down the debt of the murder of the Hezbollah "major player" from two weeks before.

This may all sound like too much grainy detail and a lot of pointless barbarian bloodletting—and it is for those who've made up their mind that political murder is an anachronism—but the point here is that these murders were well planned and undertaken with a well-defined purpose in mind: Preserve force and head off war. They were a stand-in for an all-out Shiite-Sunni civil war.

Which brings me back to the central question of whether Hajj Radwan's assassination in 2008 truly counted. Did it make us safer? The answer quickly dissolves into a lot of hypotheticals that will never be answered. But my take is that the melee of assassins Hajj Radwan bequeathed to Lebanon is still out there, very much active. Hajj Radwan's brother-in-law fit nicely into his shoes. He knows how to make the perfect shaped charge and hit a car on the move. In short, the Islamic Jihad Organization, or whatever they're calling the organization Hajj Radwan founded, is like some sort of bacteria resistant to antibiotics: As soon as a survival mechanism is found, it's shared with everyone. He was an architect of political murder rather than a one-man show.

The fact is that we all were too slow out of the blocks. The Israelis should have killed Hajj Radwan before he destroyed the military intelligence headquarters in Tyre in November 1982. The United States should have killed him before he blew up our embassy in April 1983. Hariri should have recognized him for the threat he was and made the necessary accommodation.

Two years before Chuck and I started planning, Hajj Radwan had already done the bulk of damage he would do—the Marines, the two embassies, the hostages. Three years after our fumbled Hail Mary, Hajj Radwan released the hostages, thanks to diplomacy rather than force. He would make more attacks on the United States, including the one in Karbala, but they were petering out of their own accord. By 2008, Hajj Radwan was more or less retired.

MURDER EXALTED TO PRINCIPLE

In Daniel Defoe's *Robinson Crusoe*, the protagonist is stranded alone on an island, forced to learn how to survive. But life suddenly becomes a lot more complicated when Friday shows up. The two of them had to figure out how to create what amounts to a society. But think of the other equally plausible alternative: Crusoe and Friday fall out and have no choice but to compete with each other for survival—hunt each other down to destruction. Wouldn't their instincts have to develop a lot faster?

Like so many of my generation, I had my lethal instincts bred out of me from birth. Dr. Spock didn't condition us to put two bullets between someone's eyes. Trying to regenerate those instincts when I was in Beirut was doomed from the start. Purposeful murder, like sports or business, is something you have to do every day to get good at it.

In the Iraq War, during a botched raid on an enemy house, a Navy SEAL was seriously wounded in an ambush. It led the SEALs to switch from "dynamic entries" to "combat entries." What that involved was speeding up a raid, greatly reducing everyone's reaction time . . . and shooting anything that moves. There were a lot fewer SEAL casualties and more on the other side. But the drawback was that the raids were based on the same chatter and algorithms that cause drone missiles to miss. There wasn't a way to know whether they were killing the right enemy or not, let alone whether they were nipping a problem in the bud.

My guess is that what the wars in Iraq and Afghanistan will tell us is that even though our weaponry is of the highest lethality, our soldiers and spies are uncommonly courageous, and there's a whole generation of young Americans prepared to sacrifice themselves for their country, all of this doesn't add up to their comprehending the complexities of political murder.

Somewhere along the line we've deceived ourselves into believing that money wins war, that we have the great luxury of time, and that the show of force is enough to make our enemies submit. In stubbornly refusing to see our enemies for who and what they are, we've missed the fact that you can't kill what you can't see.

NOTE TO ASSASSINS: Assassins and psychopaths don't procrastinate. They treat violence as purely instrumental, only worth it when accomplished expeditiously.

> You can always count on a murderer for a fancy prose style.
>
> —VLADIMIR NABOKOV, *LOLITA*

Getting at the facts of an assassination is like taking matryoshka dolls apart—a lot of little lies within big lies. While I may have spent what amounts to thirty years writing this book and sent it to a lot of people for a reality check, from Hezbollah experts to ATF bomb techs, there are still large parts of the story I'm not sure I got right. There's always some new fact or story that comes along to surprise me. I apologize for errors of fact and interpretation I may have made. For instance, my working hypothesis is that Nasrallah knew about Hariri, but I don't know it for a fact. Even the facts I should have down I'm not quite sure about.

The day after Hezbollah TV aired its lie about my involvement in the attempt on Lebanon's only ayatollah, I called an old friend to ask him why he thought William Casey, the ex–CIA director, had made up the story about American involvement, as Bob Woodward recounted in his book *Veil*.

"Because it's true," he said.

I had no idea what he was talking about and told him so.

"I was there. I trained them . . . or at least I think I did. Here's the story."

In August 1984 a dozen bomb techs stood at the edge of an airfield and watched a twin-engine King Air set down on the base's single runway. They knew Bill Casey was on the plane, but they had no idea why he had decided to pay the base a visit. It wasn't the kind of place you casually drop in on.

The base is located on a remote inland waterway in a remote part of America. Protected by high fences, watchtowers, and thickets of old-growth trees, it's impossible for someone outside the fence to see the bomb ranges, trailers, and Quonset huts. But when the wind's right, you can hear the explosions.

Foreigners flown in for training have no idea where they are. To make sure of this, the windows of the plane are covered by thick blackout curtains. And once on base, no one is allowed out. No one is even allowed to make phone calls out.

One reason for the secrecy is that residing within the base's confines is more expertise in bombs than anywhere else. It's where the American government sends IEDs collected from around the world to be pulled apart and studied. After they're analyzed, they're rebuilt for testing.

When the King Air door opened, the base chief and two bomb techs were surprised to see a young woman in the door and a woman in her early sixties standing behind her. The two walked down the plane's stairs looking as if Jules Verne had just transported them to the center of the earth. A moment later, Casey shuffled into the plane's door—wearing a Burning Tree Country Club golfer's cap, T-shirt, and smudged painter's pants. Casey joined the two women at the bottom of the stairs and introduced them to the base chief and the two techs. The techs barely understood Casey through his notorious mumble that the two women were his wife and daughter.

The base chief offered to take everyone to breakfast, and Casey agreed, sort of.

"Yeah, they're hungry," he said, nodding toward his wife and daughter. "But I want to talk to this major you have here before I do anything."

Casey had given the commander of the Lebanese bomb techs an unintended field promotion. He was actually an army captain. He and his team had been at the base for the past several weeks, learning how to dismantle car bombs and other IEDs.

The chief and a bomb tech led Casey to an old Ford Bronco, its windows covered with wire mesh to protect against blast debris. They drove for about five minutes down a gravel road with pine trees on either side.

When the Lebanese captain saw the Bronco, he came out. When he recognized Casey, he stiffened and put on his green Lebanese Army beret. Casey shook his hand and got right to it.

"This guy Fadlallah's a goddamned problem."

The bomb tech was standing near enough to Casey to clearly hear what he said. He was sure he hadn't misunderstood, Casey's mumble having disappeared. Casey apparently wanted to be absolutely certain that the Lebanese captain knew he was talking about Ayatollah Muhammad Husayn Fadlallah.

"Isn't there something we can do about him?" Casey asked, more to himself than to the captain.

That afternoon the bomb techs training the Lebanese were given an addendum to the curriculum: a three-day segment on building "radio detonators"—devices that send out encoded radio signals to detonate bombs.

Nothing was put in writing, per Casey's orders. And it was only eight months later that the bomb techs wondered if this didn't have something to do with the Fadlallah attempt. Could it have been anything else?

Hajj Radwan obviously should have been the one to write this book. But since he didn't even keep a journal (as far as I know), it's left to someone like me to comb through the carnage he'd created to try to make sense of what he was up to.

The way I see it, Hajj Radwan had spent nearly three decades trying to bring a system to political murder. He went out of his way to avoid the obvious traps, such as blowing up trains and school buses. I would argue that it paid off by his own terms. By channeling violence, he obtained more than most assassins. When he managed to apply all of the rules, his success rate approached one hundred percent. If Hajj Radwan were around to give us a thumbnail sketch, here's what I think he would have said:

One: Assassination has to be pretty much a local affair, a settling of scores among people who really know one another. As with the Lao and Mafia assassinations, it works best when the assassin knows his victim by sight. He has no doubt about why the victim is a problem, what the stakes are, and how exactly his murder will improve things.

Hajj Radwan's assassinations worked best in Lebanon—if for no other reason than that it's a small country where there are only a couple of degrees of separation between people. And part of it goes back to the fact that Lebanese politics is a continually negotiated compromise—it's possible for one well-calculated murder to change one side's fortunes. In other words, Hajj Radwan could put a price on Lebanese blood.

The same considerations hold for Israeli assassinations. The Jews and the Arabs live in a confined space. Before Mossad puts a Palestinian on a "kill list," it will find out everything there is to know about him, from the elements of his crime to his underwear size. Mossad makes its mistakes, but it would never consider a shot in the dark—such as dropping a drone on an enemy you don't know by name or sight.

Two: Assassination is not that much different from the ancient rite of sacrifice, where a scapegoat is offered up to an enemy to resolve a conflict. It's what von Stauffenberg counted on when he made his attempt on Hitler, propitiate the Allies by murdering him and in the bargain save Germany. In Iraq, my implicit bargain with the generals was that if they got rid of Saddam, the Sunnis would remain the dominant force. Hajj Radwan's implicit offer to the Sunnis was that with Hariri out of the picture there'd be no war between the Shiites and Sunnis.

Three: When Machiavelli advises the prince to periodically cull out the bad apples, he's in effect classified assassination as a legitimate tool of governance. An in extremis, ad hoc form of justice. It's how Hajj Radwan justified assassinating the Lebanese president in 1989. Sacrifice the one to save the herd.

The one common element in all of this is that the assassin *must* have a deep, factual, bulletproof knowledge of the enemy, whether he lives

across the street or halfway around the world. It's the only way to anticipate a threat and deal with it in a timely and efficient manner. When
the Saudis offered up bin Laden to the Clinton administration, Washington wisely declined to take him. It was Saudi Arabia alone who understood the threat he represented and, accordingly, should have done
its own dirty work.

Without even a superficial understanding of the murky stew of clans
and tribes that govern the ragged edges of the world, the United States
isn't capable of efficient political murder. If we can't tell a Baluchi from
a Pashtun, how can we decide who deserves it and who doesn't? This is
one reason why the murders of Saddam, bin Laden, and Gaddafi produced nothing other than more bloodshed. As Wall Street would put it,
the United States mispriced violence.

It's not that I don't understand the attraction of drones, how they give
the White House a bump in the polls and Americans the illusion that
they're being kept safe, but the point is that the United States has confused ideas with people. Assassinating bin Ladin never stood a chance of
driving a stake into violent jihad, just as Rome did not kill Christianity
when it killed Christ. In other words, there's no point in killing the
Clausewitzes of the world but, rather, the general who's mastered his
tactics and is about ready to rout you on the battlefield.

And finally, there is this: If the central problem of humanity is justice, it can never be far from the assassin's mind that the act must always
be about cutting out the malignant cell to save the body. Anything short
of or beyond it, and he'll only make things worse.

CHRONOLOGY

March 15, 44 BC—Julius Caesar in Rome

May 14, 1610—Henri IV of France in Paris

July 13, 1793—Jean-Paul Marat in Paris

June 28, 1914—Archduke Franz Ferdinand in Sarajevo, Bosnia and Herzegovina

August 21, 1940—Leon Trotsky in Coyoacán, Mexico City

July 20, 1944—Attempt on Adolf Hitler by Colonel Claus von Stauffenberg at the Wolf's Lair, East Prussia

August 22, 1962—Attempt on French president Charles de Gaulle outside Paris

November 2, 1963—Ngo Dinh Diem in Saigon

November 22, 1963—John F. Kennedy in Dallas, Texas

June 6, 1968—Robert F. Kennedy in Los Angeles, California

November 28, 1971—Jordanian prime minister Wasfi al-Tal in Cairo

December 20, 1973—Spanish prime minister Luis Carrero Blanco in Madrid

August 23, 1974—Detective Inspector Peter Flanagan in Omagh, Northern Ireland

April 4, 1979—Ali Bhutto, father of Benazir Bhutto, executed in Rawalpindi, Pakistan

August 27, 1979—Lord Mountbatten in County Sligo, Ireland

May 5, 1981—Three Bonanno crime family members in a Brooklyn nightclub. Vito Rizzuto was believed to be one of the gunmen.

October 6, 1981—Egyptian president Anwar al-Sadat in Cairo

September 14, 1982—Lebanese president-elect Bachir Gemayel in Beirut

October 12, 1984—Attempt on Margaret Thatcher in Brighton, England

June 14, 1985—Hijacking of TWA 847

February 16, 1992—Hezbollah secretary-general Abbas al-Musawi in Nabatiyah Governorate, Lebanon

April 17, 1993—Turkish president Turgut Özal in Ankara (possible assassination)

September 25, 1997—Attempt on Hammas official Khaled Mashal in Amman

November 23, 2006—Alexander Litvinenko, former Russian secret service officer, in London

December 27, 2007—Benazir Bhutto in Rawalpindi, Pakistan

February 12, 2008—Hajj Radwan (Imad Mughniyah) in Damascus

ACKNOWLEDGMENTS

Let me start with the reader. I thank him for his indulgence in allowing me to alter the names of people whose identities are either unimportant or need to be protected. The Engineer's name was Yahya Ayyash, but I saw absolutely no purpose in cluttering up the text with foreign names. The same goes for my protagonist, Hajj Radwan. His real name is Imad Fayez Mughniyah. The same applies when I play around with some of the narrative. Again, it's in the name of protecting "sources and methods," as well as telling a more coherent story. The book was vetted by the CIA not for opinion or storytelling but to ensure it exposes no secrets.

The list of references I drew on is long. But there are a couple of sources I cannot fail to thank. First of all, the Lebanese police. Without their superb work I would have no idea Hajj Radwan was behind Hariri's murder. And while the tribunal conducted a thorough and fair investigation, I did not draw on evidence collected for the trial. Nicholas Blanford's *Killing Mr. Lebanon* is a wonderful source on Hariri's assassination, as his *Warriors of God* is on Hezbollah. Joby Warrick's *The Triple Agent* is the main source for my retelling the Khost tragedy. Michael Newton's *Age of Assassins* is the best book out there on modern assassination. A lot of his thinking bled into mine; I apologize for not citing him appropriately.

Special thanks go to my editor at Blue Rider, David Rosenthal, and my agent, Luke Janklow. If they hadn't encouraged me that there was something here—whatever this odd blend of memoir and political science is—this book would never have been written.